HEALING
CRIMINAL JUSTICE

A Journey to Restore
Community in Our Courts

Judge Jeffrey Tauber

JJJ Press
reentrycourtsolutions.com

JJJ Press
Richmond, California

HEALING CRIMINAL JUSTICE:
A Journey to Restore
Community in Our Courts

Copyright © 2019, Jeffrey Tauber

Cover photo by Adithya Sambamamurthy
Courtesy of The Center for Investigative Reporting
Used with permission

S

Book designed and published by
David Kudler and Stillpoint Digital Press (StillpointDigital.com)

978-1-938808-53-1

To the men and women of
the drug and problem-solving court field,
who are creating a new, more humane world
in which to live.

Both Sides Now.

Contents

HEALING
CRIMINAL JUSTICE

On NADCP's 25th Anniversary:

Over one million and a half persons have been participants in drug and problem-solving courts since the founding of NADCP in 1994.

Nearly a quarter-million drug and problem-solving court practitioners have attended educational programs at NADCP and NDCI trainings and conferences.

Three thousand-plus drug and other problem-solving courts have been established since NADCP's founding.

(Statistics provided by the National Association of Drug Court Professionals)

PREFACE

I COULD WRITE A BOOK[1]

I started out five years ago writing what I thought would be an archival history of the first twelve years (1990–2001) of the drug court movement and the National Association of Drug Court Professionals. It was to be a paean to the founders of the National Association of Drug Court Professionals (NADCP) on its 25th anniversary. I also hoped to foster a sense of pride and an appreciation for those who came before.

In writing that treatise I realized that there was more to do. I wanted to give NADCP's story context and make it valuable to those in the general public who are interested in how internal criminal justice reform works. And I wanted to tell it like it was, rather than put a shiny gloss on subjects that judges tend to shy away from.

I started out my judicial career as one of the nation's first drug court judges, with only the vaguest notion of why a drug court worked. I finished with the conviction that community is a critical component in a larger, more compelling narrative.

The central theme of this book, then, is the rediscovery of the healing power of community within the criminal justice system and our larger society. Drug court is clearly the "crown jewel" of the problem-solving court field. It is the place where many seek an answer to the opioid epidemic and drug abuse in general. However, drug courts are not a panacea but an important way station on the journey towards rediscovering the power of community.

This book also speaks to how leadership from within can change the trajectory of a major institution, even one as immovable as the criminal justice system. I hope to give those with the desire to make change from within a realistic view of what it may cost you to challenge the system. To do that

---

[1] Chapter titles are chosen from blues and jazz tune titles—a tribute to song writers and jazz artists.

I've been forced to examine my past and explore why I became a judicial activist and drug court advocate in the first place. I discovered that link in my upbringing, my travels abroad, and most of all, my love of music and my experiences playing tenor saxophone in the African-American blues clubs of Oakland, California.

I set out to change how the Oakland Criminal Court treated those with a drug abuse problem. At first it was a matter of self-defense: I didn't want to be responsible for the imprisonment of hundreds—potentially thousands—of drug users. I didn't have a larger perspective or vision. But that would come with time. I wish I could say that I saw drug court as a way to change an entire nation's attitudes and perceptions of a much-maligned population. But I began by having my own attitudes towards the drug user changed by my experiences in drug court.

Over the course of a decade I became convinced that the drug court model could change the way both the criminal justice system and the country itself see the drug abuser. I realized that the most important achievement we as reformers could accomplish would be to realign how we treat those who are not the most serious and violent of offenders but instead mere miscreants or run-of-the-mill criminals. That newfound humanity was often expressed in the way drug court judges treated those appearing before them: as human beings, worthy of respect. Not necessarily a revolutionary change but nonetheless one with enormous ramifications for the judicial system and society.

By the time I arrived in Washington, D.C., in 1996, I believed we had an opportunity to change the criminal justice system. I saw the drug court template working for offenders with other problems besides drug abuse. Over the past 25 years I have watched as that vision has become a reality, as problem-solving courts—courts modeled after drug courts and dealing with other disorders—have become a part of both county and state court institutions across the nation.

Finally, I came to view reentry courts as an important piece of the puzzle, offering an alternative to long terms of imprisonment. Reentry courts, as will be seen, offer a path forward, restricting entry to prison to all but serious and violent offenders, and are a means to support all offenders returning to the community after incarceration.

It's truly been a deep dive, and I hope there will be some wisdom garnered from the effort.

INTRODUCTION

The San Francisco Superior Court building stood in the shadow of the majestic City Hall building, with its golden dome and expansive hallways. Then the most recent addition to the Civic Center plaza, the Superior Court, made of marble and wood, is an imposing edifice in its own right. Its departments are dedicated to complex litigation and substantial financial claims and populated by high-end civil attorneys and their clients. Department 163, however, was not one of those.

Peter stood before me in Department 163. He was a participant in the San Francisco Parole Reentry Court (SFPRC), a new court-based rehabilitation program dedicated to the reintegration of serious criminal offenders into society.

The year was 2010. Reentry courts were a part of the larger problem-solving court field, which were, in turn, built upon the success of drug courts. Problem-solving courts had the potential to be a pathway forward for a nation overwhelmed by complex social justice problems rooted in alcohol, drug, and mental health issues. Drug courts were providing a template for a more humane and less punitive approach to treating the drug offender.

Drug courts, and their progeny, problem-solving courts, reimagined the traditional criminal courtroom as a forum for solving the community's most vexing problems. They focused on treatment and rehabilitation rather than punishment, relied heavily on incentives, applied limited sanctions, encouraged staff to reject traditional adversarial roles, worked collaboratively as a team, and espoused the idea of community as a source of strength, resources, and healing for participants. It was, in the end, an attempt to inject basic humanity into a stagnant criminal justice system.

Peter, African-American and in his early twenties, was slight of build and medium height, dressed in casual but clean attire. I'd been watching his progress from the bench for several months. Good looking, often with a mischievous smile that played across his face, he had a way of keeping court conversations light and playful, as if he was in on a joke. He also seemed to be among the most committed to the program, but this day brought who he was into focus.

With Christmas approaching I had asked everyone in the program to bring to the court holiday party some gift that reflected who they were—a somewhat puzzling request from a criminal court judge. (My guess is that none had ever attended a party of any kind in a courtroom.) I suggested that they read a passage from a book, sing a song, play an instrument, bring some food to share, or recite a poem.

Peter recited a poem. A parody of the classic "The Twelve Days of Christmas," he had written it specifically for the event and called it "The Twelve Days of Reentry." It gently poked fun at the program, staff, participants, and especially me. Though it stung a bit, it was funny and well written. I was impressed with Peter's wit and creativity.

Another participant, John, brought his five-year-old daughter Maria to court with him, as he often did. Maria wore a party dress for the occasion and offered to sing a song. Jane, our treatment counselor, picked up Maria and placed her on top of the counsel's table so she could be seen as well as heard.

She started out in a thin but steady voice but faltered at the end of the first chorus. The entire courtroom came to her aid, joining her in singing and finishing the song, a rousing rendition of "Jingle Bells."

It was a pivotal moment in the life of the nascent San Francisco Parole Reentry Court. The program had come close to being aborted on several occasions. Many were unsure what a reentry court was and why a retired judge from Oakland should be running it. Staff who'd recently been hired also had questions as to how a court could help reintegrate parolees back into the community. Some doubted my intentions, some my connection to reality.

Of course, that wasn't anything new to me. As an Oakland judge I had started the first drug court in California, which against serious odds had been extremely successful. In my first year as a drug court judge I placed over one thousand defendants in the Oakland Drug Court, achieving twice the success rate of the previous drug rehabilitation program. I would later go on to found successful California and national drug court associations.

Thirty parolees and their families and friends celebrating the holidays were packed into the smallest courtroom in the building, fitting for a retired judge "sitting on assignment." Sitting on assignment wasn't very different from being a substitute teacher. The office of the chief justice of the Supreme Court of California would send retired judges, as needed, to courts across the state to fill in for absent judges. The presiding judge of the county would keep the retired judge around until no longer required or favored, as the case may be. I had been sitting as a superior court judge in San Francisco for almost four years. I served at the pleasure of the county presiding judge and the chief justice and could be terminated by either at will (both of which would come to pass).

Then it was my turn to offer my gift to the parolees and other attendees. I wasn't looking forward to it, as judges don't normally pick up a tenor saxophone during a court session. In fact, it was my first performance in a courtroom. I stood at the bench in Department 163 of the San Francisco civil court building in my black robe, tenor saxophone in hand, and played "The Christmas Song," made famous by Nat King Cole. Though I had played the song countless times, I couldn't recall having been as nervous. I was being "judged" by an audience of parolees, their families and friends, and the court staff.

It was also what was called for, however; a reentry court required transparency. I couldn't expect participants to be open with me in court if I myself remained a distant authority figure.

My audience applauded politely. I followed with Elvis Presley's bluesy rock and roll classic "Heartbreak Hotel." I played it the way I'd learned to play in Oakland's blues dives: with grit and soul. This time their applause was like a wave breaking over the courtroom. It turns out that Elvis and I were a hit.

After the holiday entertainment we shared a feast in the handsome conference room next to our courtroom, with its glass ceiling and beautiful wooden conference table. It was a site we took advantage of because of its proximity to my courtroom, using it for counselling groups, teaching exercises, staff meetings, and now the San Francisco Parole Reentry Court holiday party. As far as I knew I had the only criminal trial courtroom in the building; all other criminal cases were being handled in the dark and cavernous halls of the criminal court building across town, on Bryant Street.

The Christmas luncheon was a sumptuous affair: a buffet of barbecued chicken, pork ribs, and brisket with sides of potato salad, coleslaw, vegetables, and breads, and desserts of carrot cake, pecan pie, and Christmas cookies—all of it the generous contribution of the Recovery Survival Network and its executive director, Lou Gordon. It was quite the scene: 30 parolees and their families loading their plates and rubbing shoulders with sheriff's deputies and court staff at the buffet table, everyone smiling and sharing good wishes for the holiday season. Seated around the great mahogany conference table were parolees next to parole officers, seated next to court staff, seated next to family members, seated next to sheriff's deputies, and so on.

It was an extraordinary Christmas feast, like none I have ever attended. People who were supposed to be antagonists, expected to distrust and dislike one another, were enjoying each others' company and sharing a wonderful Christmas meal. I think that the Christmas party was when the dam broke. With law enforcement, attorneys, court staff, and parolees, recognizing each others humanity. The doubts and scepticism of staff and participants about each other, and the reentry court program, and me, slowly melting away in the forming of a new community. It was the outcome I had hoped for.

One evening in July of 2018, I served as master of ceremony at "Yoshi's," an upscale jazz club in Oakland's Jack London Square. The Bay Area Blues Society Orchestra was performing for a fundraiser celebrating the completion of the Seventh Street Walk of Fame, a pathway of stars built into the sidewalk along Seventh Street in Oakland, where great music artists had played in the many blues and jazz clubs once found there. Ronnie Stewart, the band leader and president of the society, led an orchestra of twenty, performing before a full house of Oakland blues fans. Yoshi's itself was more than a music venue— it was the premiere jazz nightclub in the Bay Area. Its dark and intimate interiors, excellent acoustics, and storied history made it a special place for both nationally recognized artists and local musicians.

The evening was marked by a bravado performance by Oakland's greatest blues performers who have entertained the East Bay for the past 50 years. In my introductory remarks as MC, I briefly recalled how Oakland had been blessed with great bluesmen and how Oakland has supported the arts and especially the blues. I was amazed at the energy exchanged between the seniors on stage and those in the audience, which was mostly African-American, as was the band. To this day the blues remain at the heart of the Oakland community.

I was honored to be part of the evening. I had been a public defender, commissioner, and judge at the Oakland courthouse just a few blocks away.

Ronnie and I played together often over the years, first at Earl's, a small jazz club on Solano Avenue in the city of Albany (on the outskirts of Oakland). Ronnie was the guitarist for Maxine Howard, a local blues diva who, with her sharp wit and superb command of the stage, drove terror into the hearts of young blues musicians. More important was my connection, established over the years, with the musicians and many in the audience. Ronnie Stewart and I had been mentored as young musicians by local blues legend Haskell Sadler, better known as "Cool Poppa." A blues guitarist, singer, and composer, Cool Poppa was the first president of the Bay Area Blues Society. We were both members of its first board of directors.

Forty years ago Ronnie had a very different persona. An ex-Marine, he was slender, a sharp dresser, and a fast talker. He also played the guitar way too loud. Over the years that persona had changed. He was now the perennial president of the Bay Area Blues Society and the acknowledged leader of the blues community. He sported casual clothing, a thick torso, and a bald head. While he could display a mercurial temper, he knew practically everyone in the blues community and displayed in his caring for them a preacher's love for his flock.

At his request I would regularly participate as an MC in the annual Blues Awards celebration that would take place at large venues around Oakland. I was always impressed with the marvelous attire of many attendees, with the women in fabulous dresses and the men in tuxes. For years I wondered why the annual event would present twenty or more awards for every kind of musicianship, vocal excellence, and recording, but also for club management, studio sessions, financial sponsorship, radio, television, and press, not to mention special awards for dress, audience participation, and, I believe, longevity. As an MC I found it hard to find something interesting to say about so many awardees.

Ronnie never had that problem, however. He knew every awardee and would tell their story and explain their connection to the blues community in detail. And then it came to me. Many of these people had never received any community recognition and certainly not from a judge. It was the reason I was on stage as MC: many were finally receiving a kind of formal validation of their worth from a civic community leader.

It was a lesson I took to heart. When I started the San Francisco Parole Reentry Court, I would find a reason to reward individuals for their accomplishments, no matter how minor. Ronnie had been right all along.

I had a chance to talk to old friends at the Yoshi's event, some of whom I'd played the blues with for nearly 40 years. It reminded me of how much music, and especially the blues, have meant to me over the course of my career. Bobby Spencer, a great Oakland saxman now living in Los Angeles, stopped by to say hello. We reminisced and talked about how music changes who we are and how people respond to musicians and their passion for their music. He reminded me that it took a while before people believed I was a judge and that it changed how some people felt about judges in general, seeing them as musicians, human beings, and yes, members of their community.

And such is the case in the drug court and problem-solving court world in general: it's a place where judges show offenders that they believe in their potential, where judges allow that they are all part of the same community, and where one's humanity is acknowledged. In many ways that is at the heart of the drug court phenomenon: judges treating people well and expecting their best in return. The drug court taps into the most powerful force for behavioral change—the community—and the individual's need for acceptance within that community.

PART I
THE OAKLAND DRUG COURT

Founding Drug Court Judge Jeffrey Tauber appeared before the Alameda County Board of Supervisors (along with Judge Joan Cartwright and other supporters), arguing for the retention of the Oakland drug court program, in the face of looming budget deficits.

Meeting with President Bill Clinton at the White House in 1993, during the push to pass the "Violent Crime and Law Enforcement Act."

COMMUNITY: THE MOST POWERFUL CRIME DETERRENT

Community, or its absence, pervades everything we do. It controls our behavior through a socialization process that begins almost from birth. When it deteriorates, "niche communities" fill the void, which can prove as destructive as the gang culture of L.A., as uplifting as a church choir, or as life changing as a drug court.

Envision this scene: somewhere in a courtroom in America, a drug court graduation ceremony is being televised. The full complement of judges are sitting en banc, and the county sheriff, mayor, and city council members are shaking hands with former addicts who a year before had been selling drugs on city streets. A celebrity speaker stands at the dais, and sheriff deputies are rubbing elbows with the families of drug court participants. Graduates are sharing a non-alcoholic beverage and cake with police officers at a post-graduation party.

At least in part because of media exposure to drug court (and graduations in particular), the general public and the media have come to see the drug abuser as worthy of compassion and, when successful in treatment, even something of a heroic figure. In packed courthouses across the nation, mayors, police chiefs, governors, and chief justices stand shoulder to shoulder with former substance abusers and applaud the graduates of their community's drug court.

We can view such a scene as an example of the media's penchant for happy news. Or it might be something more.

In 1996 I was one of the robed judges sitting as a guest of Judge Bob Ziemian of the Roxbury Drug Court in Boston, Massachusetts. I couldn't help but feel the power in the human drama unfolding before me. It was more than a simple ceremony dramatizing the reform of a drug abuser. I had witnessed similar ceremonies in many courts across the United States, and in those instances had felt the same sense of awe, inspiration, and hope. This time I sensed something different. I felt I was observing a primitive ritual as old as the hills.

Today, I understand I was witnessing the power of community to effect change in the individual—and by extension help heal the community itself. Drug courts may be tapping into a powerful human need to be accepted by

one's community, as well as the community's need to make itself whole by rein-
tegrating the reformed outcast back into society. After that experience I began
to look for other signs of community behavior in drug courts and other prob-
lem-solving courts. As you read on you will realize, as I have, they aren't hard
to find.

CHAPTER 1

HOW LONG HAS THIS BEEN GOING ON?

We were alone in the judges' elevator at the Oakland Municipal Court: Presiding Judge Horace Wheatley and I.

The Oakland-Piedmont-Emeryville Municipal Court building was a place I knew well. I had spent the previous fifteen years there as Deputy Public Defender, private defense attorney, commissioner, and judge. Along with the cold, fortress-like county jail adjoining it, and the seven--story Oakland Police Department building across from it on Washington Avenue, its sterile design dominated downtown Oakland.

Judge Wheatley was African-American, about 5' 8" tall, and always impeccably dressed, sporting a bowtie and a goatee. He was something of a dandy—he drove a white Rolls Royce—and was known for keeping an axe handle on his bench, having once been punched out in court by an irate defendant.

"I want you to take over as judge of the drug court calendar in July," he said.

I wasn't surprised, but I wasn't necessarily pleased either. The drug court calendar was no judge favorite, but then again, neither was I. Having run against a sitting Oakland Municipal Court judge while serving as commissioner on the same court was not a judge-pleaser. Having sued all twelve Oakland judges individually and having won the election handily had pretty much sealed the deal. I would not be elected PJ (short for presiding judge) anytime soon.

Horace Wheatley and I didn't know each other well, though we sometimes chatted about the Oakland blues scene and our common connection to the music. I still considered myself a Jewish kid out of Brooklyn who'd moved to California in the early '70s. Since arriving in Oakland (touted by my friend

Ronnie Stewart as the "home of the West Coast blues") I had become a tenor sax player, spending much of my spare time listening to and playing the blues.

At one social event Horace and I attended, we found ourselves talking to one another about Oakland's disappearing blues clubs when, after a brief, uncomfortable silence, Horace abruptly and cheerfully announced, "Mingle," then walked away. Such was our relationship.

I told the presiding judge I would accept the assignment on one condition: I wanted the discretion needed to make changes in the drug court calendar. The PJ threw me a look of annoyance and said, "You do whatever you want to, but don't ask anybody to help you with your calendar." I told him he could count on it, and I kept my word.

At the time, 1990, Oakland's Drug Court was a program instituted by the Alameda County Municipal Court during the Reagan administration, a project of the Department of Justice. A number of counties across the nation had instituted Reagan-era fast-track drug courts. The idea was to process offenders quickly, moving them from arraignment to sentencing to prison. It was supposed to reduce the court workload, but it instead insured that our jails and prisons were overloaded with nonviolent drug users.[2]

I had spent most of 1989, my first year on the Oakland bench, clinging to its lowest rung, the DUI (driving under the influence) calendar, handling drunk driving cases all day, every day. This involved mostly taking pleas from defendants and sentencing them to the standard sentence of two days in jail, a heavy fine, community service, and DUI school. With the occasional jury trial to break up the monotony, the position would try most judges' souls. Though drug court was hardly a position judges sought out, it was a step up and a way out of DUI purgatory. Plus, I had some ideas I wanted to try out. Drug court might offer me the chance to do so.

The first thing I did after the "elevator meeting" with Horace was get a feel for how the existing drug court was run. I was well aware of the drug court's reputation for railroading drug offenders to prison, but the reality was even worse. Promulgated on the then-accepted dogma that "nothing worked" in the drug offenders' rehabilitation, the obvious solution was almost always

---

2 A contemporary news clip from the Oakland Tribune, as recalled: A young woman, sentenced to serve in the Alameda County Jail, tearfully waved goodbye to her mother. When her mother arrived home from court, however, she found her daughter already there. Concerned that her daughter had somehow escaped from the jail, she called the sheriff's department to inform them that her daughter was home and that they should come pick her up, only to be told that she had been released from jail because of overcrowding.

incarceration. That was to be my primary task for the next year or more: sentencing nearly a dozen drug offenders to prison, day in and day out.

The drug court assignment offered one saving grace: I would also manage the county's drug diversion program. Found in Section 1000 of the Health and Safety Code, the program had a remarkable history. Although drug laws were being enforced aggressively across the country, the California legislature saw fit to pass one of the most progressive drug laws of its day. It was surprisingly signed into law by then Governor Ronald Reagan in 1972. In actuality, H&S 1000 was written to rescue the sons and daughters of doctors, lawyers, and judges from the jaws of the criminal justice system.[3]

According to an extraordinarily candid October 1973 analysis of H&S Code 1000 by the California Bureau of Criminal Statistics (entitled "The Drug Diversion Program: An Initial report"), "the chief reason for founding the diversion program was to decriminalize 'simple possession of controlled substances' for first offenders, who are otherwise good citizens, so that their records will not be permanently marred by one act of indiscretion."

That analysis goes on to say that almost 60% of those diverted, known as "divertees," were in the 20–24-year-old age bracket, 83% of whom were white, while the most common charged offense was marijuana possession, at 75.3%.

I honed in on this penal code section as a way to humanize the drug court but not for those who had been arrested for marijuana possession—for the many drug users in Oakland facing serious felony drug possession charges. My idea was to slow down the process so that defendants would have a shot at succeeding in a rehabilitation program under the diversion statute and avoid both time in custody and a felony record. The more I read or talked to experts, the more convinced I became that we could do much better for Oakland than fast-tracking those with drug dependency to prison.

Part of the problem I faced stemmed from the classic criminal justice attitude towards drug offenders. It was axiomatic at the time that drug users would only clean up when they had reached the end of their rope, when they were literally in the gutter and desperate for any helping hand. That meant it was best to let them fail in court, much like they had in their lives. What that also meant was that the courts, law enforcement, probation, and even health

---

3 Under the accompanying section, PC 1000.4, the Diversion Statute allowed the court to place eligible misdemeanor and felony offenders in rehabilitation programs under the supervision of the Probation Department, with a dismissal of charges the reward for successfully completing the program. More to the point, it allowed successful participants to deny ever being arrested for the offense, even under oath to obtain "any employment, benefit, license, or certificate."

care professionals were off the hook. They could ignore a defendant's serious drug abuse and/or dependence until then.[4]

I came to believe that the traditional treatment position was inconsistent with the reality of the drug offender. I learned that there were many reasons for an individual to hit bottom, such as a spouse threatening divorce, family separation, job loss, failure at school, a friend's intervention, or the drug user being arrested on a felony drug charge and facing a term of incarceration.

The reality was that working with drug abusers was difficult and uncomfortable, often involving close contact with people who were neither pleasant or truthful or who shared little in common with the typical criminal justice or healthcare professional.

What many treatment and supervision professionals sought were people who didn't need treatment: the 30–40% of drug abusers who were neither drug dependent nor a high criminal risk, people who in most cases would be scared straight by the very court and supervision process itself. It was euphemistically called "skimming," or removing the cream off the top, for a reason.[5]

Before redesigning the Drug Court I needed to familiarize myself with what was considered state-of-the-art, court-based drug intervention, so I attended training conferences whenever I could. One, "Why 'Nothing Works' is Wrong!", introduced me to TASC (Treatment Alternatives to Street Crime) programs, whose mission was to build a bridge between the criminal courts and treatment.[6] I received information and encouragement from conference sessions, their presenters, and participants but little real guidance.

I looked to local experts such as Dr. Alex Stalcup, an unconventional but successful drug treatment practitioner who presented me with a framework for understanding the drug offender and how drug courts could work for them. He spoke of the need for immediate intervention, drug testing, and frequent contact with judges and other authority figures to maintain connections otherwise easily broken.

---

4 "Hitting bottom" is embedded in the Alcoholics Anonymous twelve-step process towards achieving sobriety. "Step number 1: the supplicant must admit he or she was powerless over their addiction." That was much the same as saying there's no point in treating drug abusers until they had survived long enough—an outcome that was in no way guaranteed—to become an older, wiser, more vulnerable self.

5 Today, one may cringe at our initial criteria for drug court: someone who is not violent or mentally ill or a high criminal risk, preferably with a college degree and a high degree of truthfulness and self-awareness. The unfortunate truth is that for too many courts in America, these are still the criteria.

6 TASC now stands for Treatment Accountability for Safer Communities.

I was now running the Oakland Drug Diversion Court, as well as handling as many as five preliminary hearings—felony probable cause hearings that often lasted an hour or longer—as well as 5–10 felony drug pleas a day, each of which took 15–30 minutes. With a busy daily calendar, it was difficult to think about making changes or reforming the system, but I had committed myself to doing so.

The existing drug diversion system was designed to fail for those who needed it the most: those with a serious drug abuse problem. Many Oakland Drug Court participants (read: poor, uneducated, jobless African-Americans) had serious problems with drugs and alcohol, as well as mental health issues. Something in the neighborhood of 30–40% of those referred for a diversion hearing never showed up on their next court date. An additional 10–20% who returned to court had not contacted the probation department as ordered or failed to appear for their appointment interview.[7]

None of this was surprising. What was surprising was that judges and other criminal justice professionals were upset and even offended when drug offenders, the most unreliable of criminal offenders, failed to follow somewhat complicated directions and time-consuming procedures. I focused on the "realities" of the drug abuser's life, recognizing that their lives were very different from those working within the criminal justice system. A series of principles began to arrange themselves in my head as I tried to figure out the elements of a successful drug court.

Element No. 1 was easy: The drug court was there to deal with the needs of the participant and not the bureaucrat. I began calling drug court reforms "reality based," because they reflected the real needs of the drug offender. Over the years I observed countless court insiders protecting their own interests over those appearing before them by setting court hours, processes, and procedures to accommodate the court and staff. That would change with drug court.

Element No. 2: Don't expect the drug offender to follow instructions and return to court when ordered to do so. We were dealing with people, drug

---

7 Defendants eligible for drug diversion were released from custody with a slip of paper with the probation department's telephone number on it. They were told to call the probation office in three days—not a day sooner or later—to make an appointment to see a probation officer in approximately one month. In the meantime the case was put off for 6–8 weeks for the interview to be completed and the probation report and recommendation written and delivered to the judge for review. The defendant then returned to court to either be inducted into the program or denied entrance and set for future criminal court proceedings.

dependent or not, who have spent their lives avoiding responsibility in general and, specifically, accountability to the courts.

Element No. 3 flowed from No. 2: If you've got the drug offender standing before you, don't make plans for future appointments, interviews, and hearings. Intervene immediately, do interviews on the same day as the arrest, and place them in a program with a specified probation officer the same day they appear in court.

Element No. 4: Make sure your staff is both experienced and committed to the program and its success, eschewing the modern bureaucratic love of interchangeable parts in favor of experienced staffers with long-term commitments to the drug court's goals.

Element No. 5: See the offenders often and develop a personal and direct relationship with them, making sure they understand that you want them to succeed in the program. For many drug court participants it would be the first time a judge (or any authority figure) showed genuine empathy and concern for them.

This last reality-based principle was to be the core principle of drug courts and later problem-solving courts. The judge, and by inference the court, needed to be personable and empathetic, demonstrating a sense of humanity that had been missing in too many courts.

I took meetings with the probation department, district attorney, public defender, and public health officials, but by and large they all stood on the sidelines and were willing to wait me out and, as I was told by probation insiders, watch me fail.

Finding personnel or other resources to run a drug court program was not going to be easy. Probation was the most obvious target. Though the Alameda County Probation Department had a statutory duty to supervise divertees under H&S 1000, it had a lamentable reputation for leadership and no discernable work ethic or any inclination towards innovation. The fact that they agreed to discuss their role in the drug court was itself a victory of sorts.

I proposed that the Probation Department process diversion eligibility overnight, rather than engage in the standard two-month-long process. The five-person team authoring the eligibility report would then be free to supervise, monitor, and maintain contact with the divertee more intensively than they did for any other probation population.[8]

---

8 To my mind, the probation department was unwittingly engaging in a game of "narrowing the net" or reducing the number of diversion participants and, consequently, their own workload. It was obvious to me that serious drug users would be lost in their

There was serious consternation about changing the status of probation staff from report writers to active diversion supervisors. I suggested to Probation that no Oakland judge was placing much credence on or necessarily reading reports generated from admittedly unreliable drug users. To my surprise, after initially refusing to consider the plan, probation agreed to my request.

Our equanimity only lasted a few days, however.

I was contacted by a union representative shortly after our tentative agreement and told that changing the role of report writers to supervision personnel was a change in job description and a violation of the union contract. It was strange to hear a probation representative argue that doing supervision, Probation's historic mission, was not part of their job description.

The probation rep showed up at my chambers with his union contract. I laid it out to him: this program could rejuvenate probation morale and give line staff—POs who worked directly with offenders—what they wanted since they had started their job: relevance. I was committed to this program, and Probation could be a partner in it.

It was a hard sell. Tall, thin, and nervous, the union rep listened and then, amazingly, agreed to a pilot period followed by a review after a reasonable period. He suspended his protest; he also never returned. (Of course, calling a program a pilot avoided many obvious hurdles.)

Most of my proposals went to the head of the Adult Probation Division, Robert Norris, a diminutive man of high intelligence but protective of his department and its prerogatives. We were never reduced to shouting matches, but our meetings grew more and more contentious. I insisted that Probation meet and drug-test participants on a weekly basis—at least for the program's first month—as Dr. Stalcup had urged. Mr. Norris countered with an offer for meetings and drug testing at the initial placement and after four weeks in the program.

We were stalemated, but I gambled that Probation would back down. I informed the department that we would implement the program in October of 1990 as a pilot project, taking individuals into the program on an ad hoc basis to test out our procedures. It was to morph into the Oakland F.I.R.S.T. Diversion Program on the first of January, 1991.[9]

---

drug addiction and fail to visit the probation department or appear in court if they didn't report to probation immediately. The ones who were able to follow directions and remain in the program were mostly the ones who would be scared straight and who least needed rehab and treatment.

9 F.I.R.S.T. stands for Fast, Intensive, Rehabilitation, Supervision, and Treatment. I don't know how I came up with the acronym, but it seemed to fit.

That got Probation's attention. Perhaps they realized that they might be left behind or that the press might get hold of the story, but they began to get serious about putting the program together.

I met with senior members of Probation on a weekly basis during the fall of 1990. However, I mostly got the same response to all requests: not enough staff or resources and, more to the point, "That's not how we do business in Oakland." In that there was some truth. The probability was high that no Oakland judge had previously bargained for standardized probation procedures for an entire program population.

I was, in a sense, invading their turf. I'm sure these were not concessions they made easily. Still, we compromised and agreed to probation supervision and drug testing, which was to occur at program placement and during the second and fourth weeks of the program. To my mind, this was grossly inadequate but the best I could get.

So much for the magisterial power of the judge.

Frank Tapia sat across a table from me eating pasta. We were at lunch at Ratto's, an Italian restaurant about two blocks from the Oakland Courthouse in an old, even historic, building that the criminal justice crowd frequented.

We were having lunch because I had made demands of the Probation Department, and the project had now been passed to a line probation officer. I was told that Frank had a background in psychology and, more specifically, Skinner behavior modification theory.[10] I was a bit disturbed to learn that Probation had selected a line officer to work on the project but thought I had little to lose by working with Frank. At least the conflicts were bound to lessen, I reasoned.

I was wrong.

After I described the general concepts of sanctions and incentives I wanted to build into the program, Frank grabbed a paper napkin off the table and over the next few minutes drew up the first draft of a contingency contract for the Oakland Drug Court. I knew almost immediately that Frank was just what the doctor ordered.

Frank was of Mexican-American background, about 5' 10" tall, and lean but athletic. He focused like a laser on any problem placed in front of him. He was a genuine self-made man, a fighter raised up from the streets of West Oakland. He could be bull-like but was genuinely passionate about one topic:

---

10 Based on the work of well-known psychologist B. F. Skinner, the operant conditioning theory suggests that behavior can be modified by consequences and through reinforcement.

Skinner behavioral modification. My knowledge of Skinner's concepts, however, was vague at best, dating back to a college psych course.

He was interested in the project and excited about my willingness to work with him. He saw it as a way to make the probation department and himself relevant and effective. From that point on I spent a good deal of time working through the program design with Frank and developing a structural framework—most importantly a contingency contract—for the Oakland Drug Court.[11] It turned out to be an extraordinary collaboration. Years later he told me that he had considered himself in retirement, for all practical purposes, until he had been assigned to the Drug Court project.

About that laser-like focus. When Frank had an idea he wanted to share, he thought nothing of calling me at home. I didn't mind; it was exciting and energizing to see his passion for his work. When you are struggling to create a new paradigm, and all about you are hostile bureaucrats who seek to thwart your goals, finding any ally is a godsend.

Of course, Frank had his downside. He didn't back down easily, even to a judge. He would contradict me in court, something judges, including your author, typically hate.

On one occasion Frank decide that it wasn't ok to put a divertee in custody for the weekend. He argued the point far beyond what anyone else would, even an attorney. He refused to shut up. I was tempted to hold him in contempt and place him in custody. But I resisted the temptation.

On the plus side, he would take on the head probation officer with some regularity, complaining about what he saw as errors in judgement by the department. It was my sense that the Oakland Drug Court set him free to be who he was, and he welcomed that freedom.

Not a whole lot of fraternizing took place between judges and probation officers at the time. Though Frank was as critical of me as anyone else, over the years we became close friends. He was awarded the first NADCP Pioneer Award at our inaugural annual training conference in Las Vegas in 1995, recognized for his extraordinary contributions to the development of the drug court model.

Jane Gross, a national correspondent for *The New York Times*, had gotten wind of Oakland's pioneering drug court. Her June 21, 1991, profile, published

---

11 A contingency contract is a form of intervention used to increase desirable behaviors or decrease undesirable ones. It specifies the target behavior, the conditions under which the behavior will likely occur, and both the benefits and consequences that result from meeting or failing to meet that target.

a year after I had taken over the drug court calendar, was the lead story on the front page of the newspaper of record's "National" section. It created excitement and consternation in Oakland.

The article itself describes the benefits of the F.I.R.S.T. program, extensively citing national experts. Professor Frank Zimring of UC Berkeley School of Law is quoted as saying, "The genius of the operation is the level of judicial involvement." [12]

Ms. Gross's article also contained certain errors.

First, my middle initial is S, not T. Second, the Oakland F.I.R.S.T. program wasn't the only drug court in the nation. Soon after the article ran I discovered that a second drug court was operating on the other side of the nation, in Miami, Florida. The Dade County Drug Court had started up in 1989, a full year before Oakland's treatment-based drug court. [13]

Still, the *Times* feature provided me with a certain celebrity that was helpful to the cause. A year and a half had passed since the "elevator meeting." During that time I, along with others, had constructed a program that worked *for* and *with* offenders. It didn't set them up for failure. Instead, it offered help, rather than demonizing them. It held them accountable while offering to partner with them in the creation of a new criminal justice reform, the drug court.

As opposed to Miami, where the entire criminal justice system and business community apparently came together to create their drug court program, I was initially alone in my quest. I had more adversaries than collaborators. The other judges, who initially felt threatened by my election, hoped I would hang myself on my reform. I read that my alter-ego in Miami, Assistant Presiding Judge Kaufman—to Miami's credit—was given a year to design and implement their drug court. I, on the other hand, spent my evenings and weekends toiling at the task. Such is the life of a judicial activist.

---

12 The full article can be found at: www.nytimes.com/1991/06/21/news/probation-and-therapy-help-some-drug-users.html.

13 In 1992 the Miami court was to grab most of the national attention as it became known that their program's assistant public defender, Hugh Rodham, was brother-in-law to the next president, William Jefferson Clinton. As well, Miami-Dade County State Attorney Janet Reno was to become the U.S. attorney general under the new president.

CHAPTER 2

CRY ME A RIVER

One day in late 2001 the incoming presiding judge, Carl Morris, left a message for me saying that he wanted to meet me before court at Club One, a health club in Oakland's City Center Plaza. Carl was a former probation officer and public defender who went on to become a judge in Oakland. I got to know Carl playing pick-up basketball at the Boy's Club on Market Street in Oakland. Carl was a fine athlete and considered the best basketball player at our lunchtime games. By comparison I was a scrub. He had a smooth, even languid, style, was an excellent shot, and rarely got ruffled during a game. It also was his style as a judge.

It was a scene out of *The Godfather*. I met Carl in the cedar sauna inside the health club. I don't recall why we met at that location, but I'm pretty sure it was Carl's choice. He had some bad news for me and had picked a location near a basketball court, a place, I suppose, where he felt most at home.

He told me that another judge would replace me as Drug Court judge the following year, in early 1992. The unwritten rule of the Oakland court was that a judge could claim the assignment of another judge who had served a year on an assignment, and Judge Joan Cartwright had requested mine.

I was surprised, as she had previously expressed little interest in the program. I was also devastated. Pouring one's heart into a court reform project is something few judges would ever consider. I spent countless non-court hours designing and building the Oakland drug court in meetings with judges, probation officers, court staff, and the drug court team; visiting treatment providers, methadone clinics, acupuncture providers, and rehabilitation centers; interviewing specialists from relevant fields; attending trainings and conferences; maintaining community, media, and political contacts; reading articles and texts on drug addiction; and, finally, writing about, evaluating, and teaching others.

I envisioned a different kind of criminal justice. I felt that all I had done, fought for, and achieved would now come to naught. But that vision, even if somewhat vague, was starting to take shape—and now a door had been shut in my face. It was a pattern I had experienced before and would again. And I had the arrogance to think that I could accomplish what others neither imagined or cared to imagine.

I tried to explain to Carl that the program was still in development and needed stable leadership if it were to succeed over the long term. At the same time I realized that I was treading on thin ice, suggesting that I had expertise or abilities in this particular area. Carl wasn't buying it though. To him nothing about the drug court seemed so special that another judge could not step in and take over without missing a beat.

I can't say I blamed Carl. He was following protocol and he preferred to avoid confrontation. The general attitude of judges at the time was that court assignments were fungible, an attitude that is still prevalent in courts, as well as other government agencies, to this day—a reluctance to single out anyone for special recognition or treatment. It allegedly was intended to prevent a judge from empire-building in a particular court assignment. But it also clearly dampened ambition and innovation within the court. Why create more efficient or effective procedures if the judge who takes over your assignment is likely to disassemble it? Aspiring to do anything better or differently from your peers was considered bad form, a crime I was often guilty of.

I left Club One wondering how it had come to this. The program had been famously successful, and the Oakland Drug Court had become a magnet for media attention. *The New York Times* had written about the program, along with local papers the *Oakland Tribune, San Francisco Chronicle*, and *San Francisco Daily Journal*. Local TV had done stories on it. The program had already received a commendation from the California Legislature and had earned the prestigious Ralph N. Kleps Award for Improvement in the Administration of the Courts from the California Judicial Council. It would shortly receive the 1992 nationwide Public Employee's Award for County Excellence.

Of course, that was the problem. Others wanted to bask in the glow of the drug court. The attitude among judges persisted that if one judge could make it work, any judge could.

At that time one was judged exclusively on what you did on the bench, not on what you might accomplish off it. The understanding that it would take more than just showing up was hard for many judges to understand. Yet, the drug court was a harbinger of a new kind of judging that relied on a judge's willingness to work with a different community of actors, both in court and in the larger society. To be an effective drug court judge would take more time and effort than most judges were used to, both behind the scenes and on the bench.

At the time I thought drug courts the equivalent to taking a step backward, going "back to the future," so to speak. Not everyone thought that was a great idea, calling it radical or, even worse, "social work." I suggested that drug courts were a return to a time when judges knew their "clients" and their families, doctors, and employers. If that was a myth, it was a myth with great appeal to me and many other pioneering judges, for it suggested the possibility of a court built on and with the community.

I was starting to put together a coherent drug court philosophy. After a year of early-morning writing, the first publication to describe the drug court model began to emerge, espousing the drug court's core principles, processes, and procedures. It was published by the California Judicial Education and Research Institute (CJER) in 1994, for 1,800 California judicial officers.[14]

In the introduction to *Drug Courts: A Judicial Manual*, I wrote:

> *Drug Courts mark a turning back of the judicial clock to a time when judges ran their own calendars and were responsible for their court's operations; defendants had to answer directly and immediately to the judge for their conduct, and the judge monitored the defendant's progress as the case moved slowly and purposefully through the judicial system.*
>
> *The courts have been forced to move away from that level of personal involvement because of an overwhelming workload, replacing it with an expedited case management model which relies on segmented case management, sentencing guidelines, negotiated pleas, and other strategies to speed up the process.*
>
> *The results have been predictable and disastrous. Court, probation, prosecution, and defense personnel accept responsibility for only a small segment of an offender's case; often dozens of judicial, probation, prosecution, and defense personnel see an offender over the course of a single case. No one has or is expected to take a larger view of the offender (or the system) because everyone has been given piecemeal authority.*
>
> *The drug-using offender quickly learns how to work within that framework and acts accordingly, manipulating and/or evading the court and program personnel. (Ironically, even when successful, the expedited management approach does little more than*

---

14 With many thousands more distributed across the nation, it was for several years the most widely distributed drug court publication in the U.S.

speed up the revolving door from our courts to our jails and prisons and then back again.)

Some have criticized Drug Courts as a radical and unwarranted departure for the courts. However there is nothing radical or even particularly new about how a Drug Court works. Court procedures are adapted to reflect the realities of the offender's substance abuse (see SS2-5). A cost-effective approach to the use of sanctions and incentives is applied (see SS11). Applying a direct, immediate, and personal approach to the defendant, a Drug Court handles all rehabilitation cases in a jurisdiction from start to finish (see SS2-19). Leadership and focus is provided by a single Drug Court judge and dedicated program staff (see SS20-24). Coordinated programs are created where all participants (not just the offender) are held accountable for their performance (see SS 30-34).

Many of the features developed by drug court were reforms that had been around for a very long time. What was special about drug court was that it brought so many effective rehabilitative reforms together in the same court.

More than any other innovation, drug court graduations reflected a critical new dynamic, bringing together members of the community to recognize and show appreciation for the success of the former drug user. The ceremonies provided an opportunity to celebrate the graduate's sobriety, present them with a graduation certificate—for many, the first recognition they ever received—and invite family and friends to share the achievement. They became a feel-good event that the media could focus on when woefully few such events were taking place in the criminal justice system. It made the judge, DA (district attorney), and other drug court professionals into local heroes, and gave them the opportunity to introduce the program and themselves to local, state, and national politicians and drum up community support for the program itself.

I presided over many drug court graduations, with relatives and friends of graduates celebrating the success of their newly sober relations. I called participants to the front of the courtroom, where the graduate was given an opportunity to talk about their program success and their newfound sobriety. In Oakland, with its large African-American population, graduations often tended to be more revival meeting than court session, with chants of "amen" and "hallelujah" aplenty.

Unfortunately, drug court was not seen as a legitimate court by many of Oakland's judges. I once watched judges standing in the hallway outside my courtroom laughing as a graduation ceremony was underway.

The courts have always operated with the judge as the final authority and arbiter. The extraordinary success of drug courts was due, in no small part, to the drug court judge's willingness to function as "the first among equals," rather than a distant authority figure.

My first experience with sharing judicial power occurred almost immediately after Frank Tapia famously drew up his contingency contract on a Ratto's napkin. He and his fellow probation staffers brought the draft version of the drug court contingency contract to me in chambers. I welcomed them and then read their contingency contract. I was conflicted: the contingency contract virtually ceded judicial decision-making to probation staff as if it were a contractual obligation.

It was a difficult meeting. The probation officers seemed anxious; I was as well. I mumbled something about it being a good beginning, but that it needed work. What they heard was me backing away from a commitment. I also understood that their enthusiasm for their work, as the drug court had no other hands-on staff, was key to the success of the program.

I asked Frank to stay behind after his colleagues had left my office. He was upset and told me that he had put his own reputation on the line in supporting the drug court. He had convinced his fellow probation officers that I was willing to share responsibility with them and make them partners in the drug court.

I told Frank that, as a judge, I couldn't promise to follow the contingency contract but that probation staff could judge for themselves whether I was abiding by our agreements.

This was one of those occasions that severely tried my commitment to the drug court model. I was constantly being reminded of how I was pushing boundaries. I was making demands on institutions that weren't built to accommodate innovation but to crush innovators.

I followed probation recommendations (based on the contingency contract) in almost all drug court cases before me. There were times I might have decided otherwise, but I had my agreement with probation in mind when I made those decisions. My commitment to Frank and his colleagues became a kind of check on my discretion, which, in a drug court, is probably as it should be. Everyone has to play by the same rules, even the judge.[15]

---

15 Of course, that didn't apply to my colleagues. I knew that when I took days off from Drug Court, any number of participants might have flunked out of the program by the time I'd returned. Judges who covered for me with some regularity would place defendants in custody for a single positive urine test, violating an agreed-upon drug court protocol that limited pre-defined sanctions, one that many Oakland judges refused to acknowledge or follow.

Nobody at the time, including me, seemed to understand the true importance of a contingency contract. The contingency contract did more than provide the offender with a blueprint for success in the program; it held them accountable for their own success or failure. Ultimately, it empowered the participant and, perhaps most importantly, the probation and treatment staff in their work. Where the probationer was responsible for meeting with the probation officer on a weekly basis, it also held the probation officer responsible for doing the same. It provided a check on all members of our drug court community.[16]

The clearest path to a community-based environment was getting the prosecuting and defense attorneys to take a step back from being antagonists. In Oakland that meant, quite literally, that attorneys would not speak for their clients but stand behind them or at counsel's table.

I followed a strict if unwritten rule in drug court sessions: no argument during a general session and no whispered conferences with attorneys at the bench. If requested to do so, I would pass a case to the end of the court session, when attorneys could argue a legal point to their hearts' content to an empty courtroom.

At first counsel bristled at the restriction, but they soon saw the benefits in a non-adversarial courtroom. Outcomes were generally better when counsel did not fight it out but worked collaboratively. To my mind, keeping all transactions in court open and transparent was key to maintaining the trust of participants. By avoiding breaks in the court's rhythm with extraneous legal matters, we were creating better outcomes, or in the jazz lexicon, *a better vibe.*[17]

From the beginning of my legal career, I understood that the biggest threat to reform wasn't failure by defendants or program participants but that of program and staff: an attorney's desire to win above all else, a rehab program's

---

16 In the CJER drug court manual I called it "Structural Accountability." Structures are put in place (in this case a contingency contract) that holds all parties accountable, as well as responsible to each other, for program success. Structural accountability also turned out to be a critical element in building a community-based court.

17 We pursued other means to reduce conflict between staff and participants and increase the motivation to cooperate. Al Chaquette, our first probation supervisor, suggested that line probation officers rotate through the program along with their participants. Drug users who previously claimed that their parole officers had not drug-tested them, failed to meet with them, failed to return phone calls, or otherwise failed in their official responsibilities would now face that probation officer in court—at which point participants' claims of probation officers' failures dropped precipitously. Of course, recalcitrant probation officers also needed to do their jobs or be called out by the judge for their failures to do so.

fear of treatment failures, a probation officer's fear of judicial interference, or a judge's reluctance to limit their own discretion. Any or all of these could poison court innovations.

After several months, probation officers' initial excitement for the program began to wane. Participants started flunking out of the program for failure to complete required tasks, such as meeting with their probation officers and treatment providers or failing to take drug tests. I was concerned.

Frank reviewed the statistics and found that some POs were flunking out participants who performed poorly and consequently were reducing their own workload. The most serious drug users, our targeted participants, were the ones flunking out. In response Frank designed a new program phase that held the parole officers' feet to the fire. If a participant failed to complete the required tasks over the first month of the program, the initial phase, they would be "recycled" through that same phase with the same probation officer.

The new procedure had the hoped-for effect of motivating the probation officer to get the participants to complete their core tasks so that their client could graduate to the next phase, at which point they would be shifted to another probation officer. Again, it was in essence a simple contingency contract set up specifically to benefit probation officers who did their jobs and sanction those who did not. And it worked: participants returned to their earlier success rates.[18]

Drug court had begun as the idea of a few judges and others in isolated communities. Those who pushed for it were often outsiders or rebels—judges who, for the most part, were not in leadership roles and were sometimes considered weak or marginal. But a spark had been lit in Oakland and it was to project considerable light across the nation.

The Alameda County Probation Department was to nominate Oakland's F.I.R.S.T. Drug Court Program for the 1992 Public Employees Award for County Excellence. In a letter dated March, 30, 1992, the Public Employees Roundtable (PERS), a coalition of 30 professional and managerial associations and an associate council of 58 government agencies, wrote to Bob Norris, the director of Adult Probation, who had been my adversary during months of negotiations regarding drug court.

---

18 Frank appeared to be unafraid to take on his own agency or anyone else along the way. He was even willing to defy his colleagues. He drew up an evaluation chart for the five probation counselors, including himself, working in the drug court. Among other things, the chart traced the client success rate of each probation officer. This was an extraordinary accomplishment when the probation department (to my knowledge) did not keep statistics of any sort on their probationers, let alone their probation officers.

This year we received more than 300 nominations from across the nation. There were many outstanding organizations, but yours stood out among the rest. You should take great pride in your accomplishments.

A group representing the Oakland F.I.R.S.T. Drug Court flew to Washington, D.C., where they were presented with the award at the Senate's Dirksen Building, attended PERS festivities on the National Mall and elsewhere, and were wined and dined at special PERS events.[19]

Probation, the agency that had initially fought against the drug court so fervently, was now claiming the drug court as its very own, a symbol of their hard work, vision, and innovation. The orphaned drug court that no one wanted was finding more than a few new "mothers of invention."

For a reform program to have any impact it would need to be evaluated. I decided to do an evaluation on my own, since it was clear no one else would. I collected data for a 1991 drug court evaluation and extended its findings for a period of three years. There was neither money for a formal evaluation nor much enthusiasm within the court or probation to do any evaluation. That reality came home when the program reached its six-month mark. I inquired as to what the probation department could offer as an evaluation control for the 1991 drug court population. Their response was that they kept little data on probationers and could not provide any on divertees prior to my 1991 drug court population. Initially shocked at the lack of any data from a major county criminal justice agency, I reconsidered, as any evaluation done on probationers would likely show a poor success rate.[20]

One Sunday several months later, in late October of 1991, I got a call from my cousin Donna, who lived across the bay in San Francisco. She asked if I was near the fire in the Oakland Hills. I told her that I didn't know anything about it but would check it out and get back to her. I turned on Oakland-based Channel 2 and learned that a fire was sweeping through the hills of the city. At the time I lived in a home perched over Lyons Canyon in the very Oakland Hills, with its canyon-facing side a glass wall looking over a creek and greenery. It was also considered a fire trap should a firestorm sweep through the canyon.

The Oakland Hills firestorm would ultimately kill 25 people, destroy over 3,000 homes, and cause $1.5 billion in property damage. At the time TV

---

19 Included in the group was my successor, the newly installed drug court judge, Joan Cartwright, probation supervisor Kathaleen Callahan, probation line officer Frank Tapia, public defender Elizabeth Campos, and myself.

20 I decided to follow the progress of the first 110 divertees placed in the drug court program, starting in January 1991. I followed the same number of divertees who had entered the program the previous year, from January of 1990, as a control group.

reports painted a terrifying picture of the fire sweeping through the canyons of East Oakland. When I stepped out of my home I saw my neighbors packing their cars. The fire would never reach my home, stopping over a mile away, but I learned an important lesson that day: I was so absorbed by my data and evaluation that I had no contact with the terror raging through my city nor the reality of the people living on my street. The women in my neighborhood were packing their cars with memorabilia and personal effects, while the men were taking business documents and tools. My car was packed with data and court files key to my drug court evaluation.

The "Three Year Evaluation of Oakland's F.I.R.S.T. Drug Diversion Program" concluded that, among other positive benefits, the program had achieved approximately twice the rate of successful program completions while accepting over one thousand participants, nearly twice the number in the previous year's program, and while reducing felony arrests by almost one half.[21, 22]

Over the next few years I watched as the checks and balances put into place between court and probation disappeared. The rotational probation officer reform was the first to go. Judicial control and institutional memory slipped away from the court and primarily reverted to a weak probation office. Drug court was becoming more and more like other calendars devoted to settling drug cases, with pleas of "guilty," and less and less about the offenders' rehabilitation.

The assistant presiding judge, Vern Nakahara, would claim the drug court next, cementing the idea that this was both an attractive judicial assignment and one that could serve as a stepping stone to higher office.[23]

I was slowly being disengaged from the Drug Court decision-making process. Having single-mindedly devoted several years to drug court reform, I

---

21 In 1995 the Government Accounting Office (Congress's investigative arm) reviewed six evaluations done on drug courts and found "two of the six were well designed." One was a RAND Corporation evaluation of the Phoenix, Arizona, drug court and the other the "Three Year Evaluation of Oakland's F.I.R.S.T. Drug Diversion Program."

22 A National Center for State Courts evaluation of Oakland's F.I.R.S.T. Drug Court Program at five years stated in its summary, "I believe you will find that the data you find summarized in the attached will confirm that the Drug Court continues to perform admirably. The conviction data is strikingly positive."

Both the "Three Year Evaluation of Oakland's F.I.R.S.T Drug Diversion Program" and the NCSC Evaluation can be found at: http://www.reentrycourtsolutions.com/pioneering-documents/a-f-i-r-s-t-at-ebp/.

23 Judge Nakahara would be elevated to the Superior Court the following year, 1995.

had difficulty stepping away yet found further attempts at reform in Alameda County frustrated by a general bureaucratic malaise. With my career increasingly becoming defined by what had been accomplished in Oakland, I began looking for challenges in other California counties interested in starting a drug court.

I was newly married, with a home in the Oakland Hills overlooking the San Francisco Bay. Having first dreaded the drug court assignment as a draconian demonstration of the power to punish, I had helped reshape a Reagan-era failure into a force for drug reform. At the same time I had few illusions as to how the Oakland Drug Court would fare in the future.

I had one consolation: not all was lost. A drug court on the other side of the continent just might keep the light of criminal justice reform burning.

LEAVING IT ALL ON THE FLOOR

The Bay Area Blues Society band on the USS Potomac.

It was 1975. After a year as a public defender I took a vacation. I found myself playing my harmonica on a small island off the coast of Nicaragua named San Andreas. I ended up highly intoxicated, playing Beethoven's "Choral Movement." Shocked at my newfound talent, I began to play harmonica everywhere and anywhere, finding that I could play melodies that had always eluded me.

Two years earlier I had realized how important making music was to me as I wandered the magnificent beaches of Bali, high on what are euphemistically termed "magic mushrooms." I promised myself that when I returned to the states, I would learn to play an instrument. Though I had always loved music (and the music of my generation), I never had much success at playing the music I heard in my head.

Now I started to sit in at music clubs. It was a new world. The band played as a cohesive unit. They took turns playing solos. There was an etiquette to sitting in. One was asked to join the band onstage or asked the band leader for the opportunity to sit in.

Generally, you were ushered off the bandstand after one or two songs, especially when they realized you couldn't play worth a damn. If they really didn't want you to play, or you hung around uninvited to play on a third song, they might double the tempo, change the key, or pull your microphone cord. Like appearing in court every day, sitting in required a certain toughness: you had to show up and "show them what you got." Not for the faint of heart.

The black blues clubs were the best. While white musicians played in tune, black musicians played soulfully. And the audience was appreciative. When I first visited blues bars I was nervous. Most of the time I was the only white guy in the club.

The first time I sat in with a black blues band was at a bar on San Pablo Avenue in Oakland. I found a seat at a table next to the bandstand. An older woman sitting at the table said hello, introducing herself as the wife of the drummer, Teddy Winston. She asked if I was a musician. When I told her I was, she asked if I was going to sit in. I told her that I hoped to. She yelled at her husband, "Teddy, get this boy to play some harmonica!"

I stumbled onto the stage and played as best could—I was applauded by seemingly everyone in the place. They were rooting for me. Nobody on the bandstand doubled the tempo, changed key, or pulled my microphone cord. They were generous with their music, their time, and their applause. People didn't seem to notice the color of my skin. What was important to them was whether I played from the heart, the way blues players do. Some call it leaving it all on the floor.

CHAPTER 3

STRANGER IN PARADISE

It was kind of like a circus: a small courtroom with space for perhaps a hundred people, everyone crowded in and talking at the same time, dominated by the booming voice of the judge.

Short, heavyset, jowly, and white haired, Stanley Goldstein had an unusual background for a judge. A former motorcycle cop, he spoke with what sounded to me like a heavy New York accent and usually could be heard over everyone else in the courtroom.

Assistant Presiding Judge Herbert Klein, the architect of Miami's drug court, is said to have picked Stanley because he saw in him traits that would make for an exceptional drug court judge: he was tough, streetwise, and irascible but also caring and funny at the same time.

Stanley would take the bench like a police magistrate in a screwball comedy. He exhorted the masses to pay attention and proceeded through a long calendar at a prodigious clip. Congratulating those who did well and castigating those with positive drug tests, he spoke to everyone with the same loud and brash voice, and the crowd loved it.

He had one joke I heard him tell more than once: "Many of you will see members of your family pass away as you move through this program. Some of you will fail to appear in court while grieving for your loved ones—sometimes the same loved one, more than once."

He let everyone know that he was in on their scams and was not to be taken for a fool, nor would he put up with "the crap" many had tried to put over on him. From Stanley I learned to talk straight and sometimes say the outrageous. As a matter of fact, the outrageous was what made the Miami Drug Court work. Most defendants who appear in court either nod off from drugs or sheer boredom. That wasn't going to happen on Stanley's watch. This was rehabilitation and confession as entertainment, showmanship and education clothed as court proceedings. You could tell he was having a good time, and that made all the difference.

I was interested in what made the drug court model tick, partly because I wanted to distill the essence of the drug court for general consumption, partly to establish "universal principles" we could all agree on, and partly to make my name in the field.

When I spoke to Stanley that first time in chambers, I was somewhat awed. He dominated the court in a way that I hadn't seen before. But I was also interested in his understanding of what was going on under the hood of Miami Drug Court.

Stanley had serious problems working with treatment and probation agencies in Miami. Apparently, the Miami-Dade County Probation Department wasn't interested in working with the Drug Court program, so the court created a special treatment agency. At the time Stanley was having a problem getting that same treatment agency to respond to his messages and phone calls.

What he was describing was in no way unusual. I'd had similar problems with probation and treatment agencies when working with the Oakland Drug Court. It was, in truth, an issue for many drug courts around the nation. It pointed to the fact that conflicting egos, biases, and interests posed a serious threat to drug court efficacy. In many places such conflicts are yet to be resolved. Of course, that kind of conflict is endemic to nearly any institution, governmental or otherwise.

In some ways the outsized personality of Stanley Goldstein had become a problem for the drug court field. The idea that one needed the charisma of a Stanley Goldstein to do this work was a deal-breaker for many who were considering starting a drug court.

By 1992 there had emerged a cadre of judges taking personal credit for whatever success drug courts had achieved. I wanted to get beyond drug court judges lecturing on how "they" made drug court work. Anyone who had worked in a functional drug court knew that it was the drug court team and the program's structure and ultimately its community base that were critical to the long-term success of the program. These teams and their effectiveness were not getting the attention on the conference circuit or in training sessions that they deserved.

It was up to those who understood the drug court to analyze, describe, and publish on the workings of the drug court model and the principles underlying them. I was more than willing to take on the task.

The first time I met Tim Murray was in November of 1991 at a Health and Human Services Conference at the Marriott Hotel in Washington, D.C. He was there with a contingent of Miami's drug court staff, including Bill Clinton's brother-in-law, Hugh Rodham, then assistant public defender in Miami's drug court.

Tim shook my hand, but it wasn't a particularly warm greeting and became less so over time. Competition for leadership of a new field such as drug courts was to be expected. Tim Murray was the Miami drug court coordinator and, candidly, the field's leader from 1989–1992. He accompanied Stanley to many, if not most of, the drug court conferences I attended.

Tim was tall and thin, with reddish-blond hair and supreme focus. To my knowledge Tim came out of the military. He was typically the smartest person in the room and the best speaker; he once told me that he never prepared notes or decided what to say until he was at the podium, and that was pretty much how I saw him. In contrast I would plot out my presentations and struggle to make them interesting. We were the personification of the classic tale of the turtle and the hare.

His program had been anointed as the premier drug court program, if not the premier criminal justice reform program, in the nation. Soon to be elected president, Bill Clinton had visited the Miami Drug Court on more than one occasion. Janet Reno, who had been Miami-Dade County district attorney when the Miami-Dade County Drug Court was initiated, was to be nominated attorney general and serve in the Clinton administration.

Nor could I blame Tim for his dismissive attitude. I was at best a small irritant: a municipal court judge from Oakland, a middling city situated on the other side of the continent, best known for being home to the Black Panthers, the Hell's Angels, and the Oakland Raiders.

The story, until then, was that Miami represented the one true path to drug court. Most court personnel would visit Miami, then the Mecca for drug courts. I felt I wasn't contradicting Miami's narrative that they had started the first major treatment oriented drug court in the nation—a year before Oakland—only that there was more than one path forward. And here I was, messing with their narrative.

Tim, reflecting Miami's overall dominance of the field, was somewhat inflexible about the need for others to follow in Miami's footsteps. My only advantage in that regard was that I felt no reason for others to follow the Oakland Drug Court, which was hardly the Rolls Royce of drug courts, with no budget and relying almost entirely on existing meager county resources.

There were clearly more courts in Oakland's situation than Miami's. My mantra was that there was more than one path to drug court nirvana.

The first drug court conference that drew a national audience was held in Miami in December of 1993. Over 300 participants attended, a good number of whom were from Florida, but the majority came from across the nation. The primary focus was the Miami model, and the presentations were well received. The event marked in a very real sense the zenith of the Miami drug court as the center of the drug court universe.

Kansas City District Attorney Claire McCaskill (a former U.S. Senator from Missouri) and I were standing at the rear of the conference hall. Her drug court program had been modeled after Oakland's, and Kansas City drug court judge Donald Mason and his clerk Pamela Taylor had been among the first to visit Oakland's drug court. As we listened to speakers extolling the virtues of the Miami drug court model, Claire expressed her exasperation at the judge-centric presentations.

I had met Claire soon after she had been elected district attorney for Kansas City. I had been asked to give a presentation in Kansas City to her staffers. I expected to talk with a group of perhaps twenty drug court and related practitioners, as was usually the case. I was surprised—perhaps stunned is a more apt word—to be ushered into an auditorium with something close to 200 in attendance. Such was my introduction to Claire and her special ability to focus on important issues and move the immovable.

Apparently, she had all key players on board the "drug court express" except for the county sheriff. After the speech and then my interviews with what felt like all the media outlets in the state, she shared with me her belief that the sheriff might not be a problem after all. And she was right. In the newspapers the next day, among other media outlets, the sheriff gave his full support for the program.

At the Miami conference Claire commented to me that she was getting complaints from her senior staff about how drug court interventions were reducing the number of trials. She found the complaints irritating, yet she expressed some satisfaction in receiving them, as they were an important confirmation of her drug court's success.

It reminded me of what a supervising DA in Oakland had suggested as I moved to open up drug court eligibility to serious drug users: he threatened to stop sending drug offenders to drug court if the DA's statistics couldn't justify their budget request to the county.

Both comments made me consider anew how economics were driving the prosecution of drug offenders. Like any good bureaucracy, the district attorney, police department, sheriff, and even the public defender and court depended on a continuous flow of bodies through the courts to maintain their operations and growth. Though some in the above institutions may not give it much thought, should drug offenses go away, substantial funding, jobs, and political power would as well.

Many years later, in 2010, I was in the uncomfortable position of telling truth to power. I was showing the San Francisco presiding judge statistics I had obtained from the sheriff, parole, and court services. They proved the San Francisco Parole Reentry Court would save the county jail, police services, and other county agencies over $1 million in the next year. Her response was that the savings would do nothing to help the courts survive the "Great Recession" budget cuts. Like any good bureaucrat her ultimate concern was her institution's bottom line.

I understood that the Miami conference would offer a crucial opportunity to make the case for an organized, rational approach to drug court education, one that recognized the importance of structure and community as critical to the success of the drug court model. I was just beginning, like everyone else, to understand this new initiative, but I believed I had enough experience with drug courts to put a conceptual face on this new phenomenon.

I wrote a paper for the Miami Conference that caused something of a stir. Perhaps the most significant part was found in its appendices, which argued for the establishment of an organization called the National Association of Drug Court Professionals (NADCP). According to the paper, NADCP was to provide national leadership to and serve the interests of the nascent field by promoting drug courts on a national level through education, training, organization, and lobbying.[24]

In the early 1990s Tim and I often found ourselves as presenters at the same conferences. Tim's presentation laid out the "Miami Drug Court Model." Its program's foundation included an independent treatment agency (also responsible for supervision and drug testing), treatment protocols that relied

---

24 The paper I wrote in 1993 for the Miami Conference was "A National Strategy for the Co-Funding of Unified Drug Court Systems: Proposal for Legislative Action." It was the first published paper that dealt with many significant drug court issues: including a plea for community-based courts, rather than judge-centric ones. The document can be found at: www.reentrycourtsolutions.com/pioneering-documents/national-strategy-for-the-co-funding-of-coordinated-drug-court-systems-1994/.

heavily on acupuncture, and a community-based coalition (an enviable source of funding).[25]

Oakland didn't have much in the way of resources, so we had to be flexible in our approach to the drug problem. We used what we had, and that meant the probation department handled a number of treatment functions, with a heavy emphasis on outpatient treatment programs (few residential beds being available). That lack of resources taught us important lessons about what was truly critical to an effective drug court.[26]

It was an exciting time. Oakland and Miami, without knowledge of each other's existence, had applied many of the same principles to their programs. It suggested to me that informed and aware practitioners concerned with reducing criminality, drug usage, and incarceration would logically reach similar conclusions and create similar programs. Now those universal principles could be applied to other drug courts and court-based rehabilitation programs across the nation.

It was an outcome I had been working and writing towards: the understanding that one didn't have to follow in the footsteps of another drug court to be successful. The general acceptance over time of "Reality-Based or Universal Principles" ultimately led to their going viral as the "Ten Key Components" in 1997.[27]

Conflicts between Tim and myself were as predictable as bulls butting heads but also had serious implications for the field. The limitations of the "Miami Drug Court Model" made drug courts less likely to become institutionalized across the nation. Many courts lacked the resources, funding, or political will to establish acupuncture protocols, and few courts could claim

---

25 To a substantial extent my personal history of drug court at the time was heavily focused on California, since that was where I lived, worked, and did much of my drug court advocacy. In my early writings about the Oakland Drug Court I noted drug court principles that to me appeared to reflect the universality of drug offender behavior. It was a narrative that relied largely on my experience with the Oakland Drug Court. In my CJER drug court manual I describe those principles as "Reality-Based Design Features."

26 In Oakland we cobbled together a protocol that slowed down the court process, allowing treatment to take hold. We relied to a large extent on the expertise of program co-designer and probation officer Frank Tapia, the rehabilitation expertise of drug treatment physician Dr. Alex Stalcup, and the political acumen of Judge Peggy Hora, my colleague, confidant, and strategist who co-chaired the seminal Countywide Criminal Justice Substance Abuse Subcommittee.

27 "Defining Drug Court: The Ten Key Components" was an NADCP project completed for the Department of Justice in 1997. It served as the bible in planning and implementing drug courts and has become the most widely distributed drug court literature of all time.

to have judges with the extraordinary judicial presence of Stanley Goldstein. Interested jurisdictions needed to understand that whoever their drug court judge was, their program would have substantially greater success if they created program structures that followed "reality-based" or universal principles of drug courts.

Tim was to become director for the Drug Courts Program within the Office of Justice Programs. In that capacity he provided financial assistance to NADCP, for which I am grateful. After a short stint in that capacity he left the drug court office and became assistant director of the Bureau of Justice Assistance. He continued, mostly in that capacity, during the Clinton administration.

Though we remained competitors through the '90s, we remained cordial, never allowing an open conflict to erupt. Twenty years later we were to share a cab ride and conversation and, finally, a sense of camaraderie and equanimity.

CHAPTER 4

HOW HIGH THE MOON

While Miami was establishing itself as the birthplace of drug courts, across the continent California was becoming a hotbed of drug court activism.[28]

It was spring of 1992. I sat in a conference hearing room, waiting to be called as a speaker. Though I had been a public defender, defense attorney, commissioner, and now a judge, I was anxious as I waited for my opportunity to speak to an audience, any audience. I had started public school with a slight stutter that I only overcame after a year of working with a speech therapist at Public School 188 in Coney Island. I later overcame my fear of public speaking as an adult by focusing on my purpose as a speaker, which, thankfully, was mostly talking about other people and subjects I cared about.

I sought funding for the Oakland Drug Court. Alameda County was not a rich county, and the chances that we could pry funds for drug court from the county government were slim to none. It was a particularly difficult problem, because no one at the state or local level wanted to accept fiscal responsibility for a drug court program. When I went to the California Department of Alcohol and Drug Programs (CDAP), they became apoplectic at the idea that a criminal court wanted to use public health funds for criminal justice programing. Law enforcement was even more resistant to the idea that its money would be used to rehab addicts, which they believed to be a public health responsibility.

Approximately $500 million would be distributed by the U.S. Department of Justice to states and territories through Edward Byrne Memorial Justice Assistance Grants. That year some $49 million was available in California for

---

28 According to the 1997 Congressional GOA Report, Florida led in the number of drug courts with its twelve to California's six operating through 1994. That lead was to be reversed and then some over a two-year period, with 41 California drug courts established to Florida's 22.

various criminal justice purposes, including district attorneys, local police, sheriff's departments, the department of corrections, and even the courts and public defender offices. Byrne Grants appeared to be the pot of gold at the end of the rainbow—and just as elusive.

In the summer of 1990, before I began my Drug Court assignment, I attended a meeting of the Oakland Interagency Council on Drugs at the Lakeside Park Garden Center, a sort of show-and-tell for the drug-involved at which a couple dozen agencies and non-profits told each other what a terrific job they were doing in the fight against drugs.

Doug McKeever, an Analyst for the governor's Office of Criminal Justice Planning (OCJP), spoke of the use of federal funds provided by the Byrne grant in Alameda County. I followed up with letters and phone calls to Doug and his colleagues at OCJP, asking for more information and notice of OCJP grant meetings.

That's how I ended up at an OCJP hearing just a few blocks from the Oakland Municipal Court. I had signed up to speak before the OCJP board. They were in Oakland for their yearly fact-finding mission, ostensibly to decide how Byrne grants would be distributed across the state. One of the four hearing locations that year was at the Parc Oakland Hotel (now the Oakland Marriott). If it had been held elsewhere I probably wouldn't have been able to attend.

Office of Criminal Justice Planning Director Ray Johnson called my name, and I stepped up to the podium. He asked me for my comments. I explained that I was a municipal court judge from Oakland presiding over a drug court. I described the need for funding to sustain the drug court in its rehabilitative work.

I received looks of puzzlement from the committee members. Director Johnson appeared nervous at my comments. It appeared that anyone pitching a rehabilitation program was in the wrong place. But he courteously thanked me for my comments and moved on to the next speaker, a law enforcement representative. I was, in fact, the only non-law enforcement speaker, though not many of those were in attendance either.

It was apparent from attending just one such hearing that they were mostly form without substance. Nothing much seemed to be happening. The reality was that almost all Byrne grants were funneled directly to law enforcement agencies. It was my belief at the time that federal grant funds were divided up among county law enforcement agencies in more informal settings. Though drug rehabilitation was a specific federal and state option for Byrne grants, law enforcement saw this money as their personal property and were not necessarily eager to share it to rehabilitate "addicts."

I knew that a drug court's access to funding was critical to its survival in Oakland and elsewhere in the state. I solicited letters of support from then local State Senator Bill Lockyer and Assemblyman Tom Bates, endorsing state funding for drug courts, and I was back at the Byrne hearings the next year and the year after that. Each time I invited along practitioners to speak on behalf of drug court funding.

My efforts to open up Byrne grant funding finally bore fruit in 1995. Director Johnson invited me to join a special Edward Byrne Memorial Justice Assistance Grant Program Funding Commission tasked with reforming Byrne grant funding in California. I joked that it was part of Director Johnson's strategy to keep me away from the podium.

It had the opposite effect.

Although public notice was required, few outside of law enforcement insiders knew when or where the hearings were to be held, so attendance was minimal. As a member of the funding committee I now had several months' notice of hearing dates across the state. I sent my own notices to members of the newly formed California Association of Drug Court Professionals, as well as to drug court advocates with whom I had contact.

That year a flood of speakers argued for drug court funding. I sat on the board and attended the 1995 hearings, listening as three out of every four speakers advocated for drug court funding. Amazingly, the floodgates for funding were now open, with $500,000 made available for California drug courts in 1996–1997 and $1 million for each year from 1998–2000. Over 100 California counties were to receive Byrne grant funding over the next five years.

I didn't know California Chief Justice Ron George. From afar he appeared stiff and formal. His primary go-to guy, California Administrative Office of the Courts (AOC) Director Bill Vickery, was something else entirely. Of medium build, 5' 10" tall, and prematurely gray, Bill was a whirlwind of activity and enthusiasm. As a new Oakland judge, I had heard Bill talk about his ideas.

Bill hailed from Utah and had the missionary zeal of its founders. Moving in several directions at the same time and making friends and enemies alike, he espoused new ideas about how the courts needed to work within an open society. He saw the courts as a positive influence. He characterized those who came before the court as customers, not supplicants trembling before the majesty of the courts. The statistics he provided supported his position. Those who stood before the court were overwhelmingly there for civil matters or minor criminal offenses. No more than 10% of criminal cases involved serious property theft or physical violence.

On that basis Bill argued that we had a duty to treat those before the court as citizens deserving of the best service we could provide. It was a simple but compelling argument. He advocated for friendly customer interfaces, including kiosks at malls and other innovative approaches. He wanted people to have easy access to the court and to do so with confidence, rather than fear. His attitude was contagious.

When I began to flesh out the parameters of the drug court model, I incorporated many of Bill's ideas. I saw the drug offender, and particularly the drug user, as a population to be served. Drug court hours and services would be designed to serve the drug user and their special needs and not the court, its staff, or associate agencies.

I was introduced to Bill by Pat Morris, a San Bernardino judge who was to play a pivotal role in the development of drug courts in California and around the nation. Bill Vickrey became an immediate and enthusiastic supporter of drug courts. His support was critical to the extraordinary expansion of the drug court model in California. As described later, his support for drug courts and the nascent problem-solving court field was the driving force behind their unanimous endorsement by the nation's state chief justices and eventual institutionalization across the nation.

I also had contact with Andy Mecca in 1992, the new director of the California Department of Alcohol and Drug Programs (CDAP). His initial opinion was that drug courts needed to get their funding from criminal justice agencies. Andy lived in Marin County, about half an hour from my courthouse. On several occasions I met him at a cafe on the Tiburon waterfront, where we cordially came to an understanding. He didn't have any money for drug courts, but he was open to changing his mind in the future.

And so it was that California's Administrative Office of the Courts (AOC) and the California Department of Alcohol and Drug Programs (CDAP) reached an accord whereby drug courts were funded through a partnership agreement codified in the Drug Court Partnership Act of 1998. At least in California, drug courts would no longer be orphans of the state.

California was an example of exceptional state leadership on behalf of drug court reform. That leadership extended from the very top of the judiciary, from Chief Justice Ron George to his Director of the Administrative

Office of the Courts, Bill Vickrey, to Director of OCJP Ray Johnson and Director of CDAP Andy Mecca.[29]

The extraordinary expansion of drug courts in California was partly a response to the media's interest in and even fascination with the good news stories coming out of the Oakland drug court. With Rod Duncan, a media-savvy friend and former presiding judge, making the initial introductions, the Oakland Drug Court became the courtroom success story heard round California.

I was lucky to have Rod Duncan in my corner. He was very smart and had a strong sense of right and wrong, a quirky sense of humor, and a reformer's perspective. He had come up as an investigative reporter and still had many contacts in the print media. He had also been a key aide to State Senator Nick Petris and had the instincts of a first-rate politician.

He advised me to get to know the local media and assisted me in making contacts both in the Bay Area and nationally. A number of articles were to come out in early 1991 about the new drug court program in Oakland, and Rod Duncan was the one pulling the strings that got them published in the local *Oakland Tribune* and the more prestigious *San Francisco Chronicle* and *San Francisco Daily Journal* (the lawyer's newspaper) across the Bay.

At first it was unclear as to whether the Oakland Drug Court would survive, let alone expand into other jurisdictions, but there were signs that what we were doing was making a difference and attracting attention both locally and across the nation.

Courts and judges across the state came knocking. I was in demand, invited to speak at dozens of judicial and other criminal justice conferences and trainings during the early 1990s. The Oakland Drug Court had become something of a magnet for prospective drug court judges and their criminal justice colleagues from across California. I would often follow up their visits to Oakland with my own to their jurisdictions to consult and help train drug court teams.

What put us over the top was the full-page article in *The New York Times*, written by an associate of Rod Duncan, Jane Gross. When the article came out its impact reached far beyond the Oakland court. The skeptics on the bench who had agreed to allow me to start my pilot project were surprised

---

29 While I was in Washington, D.C., from 1996 to 2002, I stayed in touch. In 1996 I wrote a letter from D.C. to Bill Vickrey, recommending that the AOC establish a drug court committee within the AOC to manage Edward Byrne grants. Soon after, the AOC reached an agreement with the governor's criminal justice agency to accept responsibility for the distribution of Byrne grant funds throughout California. To my knowledge it was the first such agreement between the two entities.

and shocked by the recognition that the Oakland Drug Court had garnered. It provided a cushion for the program and my stewardship of it, at least for a time.

With a dozen or more California jurisdictions interested in starting a drug court, the D.C.–based State Justice Institute, an NGO under the direction of David Tevlin, agreed to fund a statewide California drug court conference in 1992. More than 100 participants attended the event at the Claremont Hotel in Oakland, to my knowledge the first statewide drug court conference in the nation. It was presided over by judges Peggy Hora, Mary Morgan, and myself.[30]

With the success of the State Justice Institute conference behind us, I suggested to fellow California drug court practitioners that we come together to form a California drug court association. I knew of four existing drug courts in California counties and several other counties ready to take the plunge. So in 1994, at a judges' conference in San Francisco, judges Steve Marcus of L.A., Tomar Mason of San Francisco, Frank Hoover of Bakersfield, and I formed the California Association of Drug Court Professionals, the first statewide drug court organization in the nation. I was elected president, Judge Tomar Mason vice president, and Judge Steven Marcus secretary.[31]

I believed that a statewide organization, no matter how limited, would be of great assistance in the development of the state's drug courts. It would also help keep drug court funding focused on state and local government,[32] as well as on federal agencies.

---

30 Among other luminaries, Miami-Dade County Drug Court judge Stanley Goldstein gave a presentation. Mimi Silbert, director of Delancey Street, one of the most successful rehabilitation programs in the nation, gave a brilliant after-dinner speech on the potential for rehabilitation. The conference helped increase the level of interest in drug courts in California. (It also included a small contingent of interested Arizona representatives, including judges Ron Reinstein and Susan Bolton, who were to start drug courts in Arizona based on the Oakland model.)

31 Among the early advocates and California drug court pioneers unable to attend the Founders Meeting were judges Steven Manley of San Jose, Harlan Grossman of Richmond, Frank Hoover of Bakersfield, Peggy Hora of Hayward, Pat Morris of San Bernardino, head public defender David Judge, and head court administrator Ed Brekke, of L.A. County.

32 The successes of the California Association of Drug Court Professionals and the California Administrative Office of the Courts in promoting drug courts were substantially responsible for my push at the 1997 NADCP Conference in L.A. to establish the Congress of State Drug Court Associations.

CADCP did not do anything extraordinary until Judge Steven Manley of Santa Clara County became its president in the year 2000. Steven Manley had been a legal aid lawyer before my brief tenure as a Santa Clara County public defender. When I presented on drug courts at various California judges' training conferences, I got to know Steven and his strong interest in drug courts.

Over the past twenty years Steven has had as large an impact on drug and problem-solving courts as anyone. When I first visited his drug court in 1996, he had recently started his program. He had a relatively small courtroom with perhaps a few dozen participants.

Fast forward 25 years. I have visited his courtroom at least a half dozen times in the intervening years, during which time he has created an unmatched institutional presence. A team of judges run the reentry, mental health and veterans courts, as well as adult, juvenile, and family drug courts.

Judge Manley has become the gold standard for working a problem-solving court calendar. He is tough, cantankerous, funny, empathetic, efficient, and eternally optimistic about the prospects for successful program completion. In essence he is the new, improved "Stanley Goldstein" of modern problem-solving courts. He typically deals with over 100 defendants a day. Santa Clara County itself has dedicated an entire court building to drug and other problem-solving courts, called "collaborative courts" in California. He has been president of the California Drug Court Association[33] for almost twenty years. I attended the annual CADCP conference in Sacramento in 2018 and was impressed by how engaged everyone was, how much the movement in California had grown, and what an extraordinary job Judge Manley has done as leader of the California movement.

But his greatest achievements have been before the California legislature. He appears to spend as much time in Sacramento as he does in San Jose. He is a trusted and highly regarded expert in the field of collaborative courts, at least partly responsible for the expansion of problem-solving courts in California and definitely responsible for the resources needed to sustain them.

He has been equally generous with his time and expertise as a member of the NADCP Board of Directors. He is a mainstay of the organization's congressional outreach, which has kept drug courts and NADCP at the heart of the court and prison reform field. I tip my hat to the extraordinary Judge Stephen Manley.

If there is a thorn in this rose, it is the question of how we create a new generation of Steven Manleys. The pioneers of drug court tend to have a special

---

33 The name of the association has since been changed to the California Association of Collaborative Courts.

affinity for their creation, something difficult to pass down to the next generation. We will be watching carefully as Judge Manley attempts to transfer his unique capabilities to a new generation of problem-solving court judges.

I'm not sure how the connection was made, but in early 1991 I was put in contact with Peter Greenwood, a senior criminal justice consultant for the RAND Corporation, an important thinktank out of Los Angeles. He was advising the Maricopa County Court in Phoenix, Arizona, as they started a court-based drug rehabilitation program. He visited the Oakland Drug Court, where he spent several days overserving the court in operation and talking to personnel and officials.

At least 6' 8" tall, Peter is an imposing figure, with a friendly demeanor and engaging smile. His eyes lit up when he observed the Drug Court in action. He was eager to get Maricopa County court judges and others to visit Oakland to see what we were doing. That same year Maricopa County judges and staff visited the Oakland Drug Court before starting their own drug court the following year, based on the Oakland model.

Peter and I became friends and spent time over the years visiting blues clubs in Oakland and hanging out at his home in Malibu. On more than one occasion he wrote glowing letters extolling the virtues and cost-effectiveness of the Oakland Drug Court, which I was able to present to the Alameda County Board of Supervisors.

His was an important new alliance for me, as the Board of Supervisors was always looking to reduce county expenditures. When budgets were tight, rehabilitation personnel, including probation officers, were the first to go. I would spend a significant amount of time getting to know the members of the Board of Supervisors.

On one occasion in 1993 the drug court program was targeted for elimination by the Board of Supervisors. I researched how many Alameda County jail beds were available for housing San Francisco's inmates as a result of Oakland drug users spending less time in custody. I was able to demonstrate that the Drug Court was emptying cells in the county and earning the county $1 million over a three-year period. The local papers ran with the story and the board continued its drug court funding.

Peter invited me to my first RAND conference, on the future of criminal justice rehabilitation, in April of 1991. At the end of the conference weekend, held on RAND's campus in Santa Monica, a show-and-tell exercise was planned. We were requested to individually critique a single article by an academic who had written for publication. I was given an article written by

Berkeley professor Frank Zimring, a brilliant academician, on a subject I no longer remember. What I do remember was my irritation that the article was written in a language I barely understood and which in any case would never reach the practitioners who might benefit from it.

I was somewhat put off by the self-congratulatory feel of that session and, being an instigator of sorts, I wanted to shake things up a bit. I told them what I thought. There was an audible gasp from the 50 or so conferees. Apparently, the critique part of the conference was not that at all. Still, I felt I had made my point. Years later when designing the *National Drug Court Institute Review*, I recalled the RAND conference and made sure that our review was written for practitioners and not academics. Though I thought I had burnt that bridge, I was invited back to RAND on other occasions.

In a strange way being forced out of the Oakland Drug Court helped create a whirlwind of activity statewide. I was happy sitting on the Oakland Drug Court, working directly with drug offenders—those considered by many as the least among us. I felt that I was where I was meant to be. When I was ousted I turned to spreading the drug court model across the state through lectures, presentations, trainings, and writings. I was 46, with a surfeit of energy and motivation and a martyr's passion for redemption.

I cannot claim credit for the immense progress that was accomplished by the drug court movement in California in the 1990s. But as it is sometimes said, someone had to get the ball rolling. I initiated, recommended, designed, or helped implement many of the drug court projects and programs that California pioneered in the 1990s, from cohosting the first statewide drug court conference in the nation (1992), to writing the first judicial manual on drug courts in the nation (1994), to founding the first statewide drug court association in the nation (1994), to successfully advocating for the first Edward Byrne federal grant funding for drug courts (1996), to hosting the 2000 NADCP National Drug Court Conference in San Francisco, with a record 3,000 in attendance (numbers not to be matched for almost ten years). I had found my passion and would embrace it.[34]

---

34 The result of judicial activism within the state was the implementation and planning of approximately 140-plus drug courts, which in the year 2000 comprised nearly 20% of all existing drug courts in the nation.

INTERLUDE 2

JAMMIN'

Playing the blues with Ronnie Stewart at the Chris Club in Vallejo.

I was getting to know the East Bay blues scene in the mid-1970s. One particular band played every Friday, Saturday, and Sunday night at the Berkeley Square Bar and Grill on University Avenue: the Lee Harris Band, an all-black blues and swing band featuring Lee Harris on piano, English Pepper on bass, Teddy Winston on drums, and Kenny Herrera on tenor saxophone.

Any player could sit in. Not only that, they didn't usher you off the stage after one song. They were friendly, providing advice, suffering my lack of finesse and skill, and encouraging me to stick with my music.

I started showing up often to play with the band, drinking gin and 7UP with them during breaks and sharing the music. At some point I was invited to be a member of the band. Over the next four years I learned how to play in a blues band and how to build a solo: first by stating a blues riff, exploring it, returning to the riff, and then closing it out, leaving the audience wanting more. Kind of like closing argument in a jury trial. Of course, not everyone approached their solo in the same way. Dr. Wild Willie Moore, a fine tenor saxman who often sat in with the band, would sometimes begin his solo on stage, then meander out the front door, only to walk back in a few minutes and pick up on the closing riff of his solo.

The sax player with the Lee Harris Band, Kenny Herrera, became a friend and mentor. He told me to get rid of the harmonica and get a saxophone, "a real instrument." He promised to teach me how to play. And though he never did teach me much, I made the switch, and it opened up my musical horizons.

What I was trying to do was hard. I was over 30 and learning to play music. I was putting in long hours as a lawyer in court, then returning home to practice my horn, working to develop a decent tone and sense of rhythm while learning scales, arpeggios, chord patterns, and songs.

There was only one temporary setback: about four weeks after buying my first sax (an alto) and practicing my horn in my room in our communal home, my housemates had had enough. All five came to my room to give me the word, "You can stay, but that thing has to go."

So I took my horn and found a new home in a converted garage on a creek in Oakland, playing my music without criticism or rebuke from my neighbors, mostly frogs, crickets, cats, and the occasional skunk.

CHAPTER 5

FEVER

We sat around a dining room table: myself, my wife Maryanne, and her friend James from her union organizing days. Through James my wife had connections with Bill Clinton (i.e., an FFOB, "a friend of a friend of Bill"). James was a writer with literary connections.

He could wax eloquent on the state of the nation and the impact of social change rooted in the '60s. In casual conversation over dinner he asked me about my work with drug courts. Then, almost out of the blue, he asked the question that would turn my life upside down.

"Do you have any ideas for criminal justice reform you'd like me to get to Bill?"

Naturally, I had plenty of ideas that I would love to share with Bill Clinton.

After spending the last two years planning and implementing the Oakland Drug Court—with over one thousand drug users entering our program in its first full year—I had become a true believer, and I wasn't shy about sharing my beliefs.

My new White House contact promised to get my policy recommendations to Bill Clinton himself. With that kind of assurance I immediately set to work on my policy statements. That, however, turned out to be *five* policy papers and involved several months of writing.[35]

---

35 I submitted the policy recommendations as a series on drug- and crime-related court issues: "Five Policy Statements on National Criminal Justice Drug Control Issues." They were: "A National Strategy for the Coordination of Local Criminal Justice Systems"; "A Strategy for the Cost-Effective Incarceration of the Drug-Using Offender: The Success of Smart Punishment"; "The Principles of Court-Ordered Drug Rehabilitation: A Reality-Based Approach to the Drug-Using Offender"; "A National Drug Court Strategy: Redefining the Role of the Court in the Drug Age"; and "The Importance of Structural Accountability: The Creation of Structures that Promote Program Effectiveness." The

The policy papers were submitted to the White House, though I never heard back from the Clinton administration directly. That wasn't necessarily a bad thing. I had been asked by an administration insider (or so he described himself) to produce policy papers on drugs and crime, and I had done so.

The papers had another important benefit: they established me as someone who had connections to the White House (which were dubious at best) and as someone who had actually conceptualized policies on a national level. I distributed those policy papers at conferences and presentations. They were an important calling card, giving my words substance and even a kind of gravitas at a critical juncture in my career, a time when I was particularly susceptible to the siren song of Washington, D.C.

With that casual suggestion in 1992 that I write policy papers for the Clinton administration, my attention had shifted from local and state drug court issues to focusing on a mission to develop a national policy for drug courts. I had been bitten, and the fever would soon follow.

It was March 10, 1993, and I had just presented a statement to the President's Commission on Model State Drug Laws, then sitting in Philadelphia, Pennsylvania. I was planning my return to Oakland when I spoke to my wife from the Philadelphia International Airport. I asked her if she had heard back from the White House regarding my policy papers. She told me she hadn't, then asked, "What about just showing up at the White House with your policy papers?"

Pennsylvania was bitterly cold, with snow flurries and promises of a snowstorm on the way, so it was questionable whether anyone would be working at the White House. The idea sounded crazy, even to me, but I called a number I had been given for the Criminal Justice Section of the Domestic Policy Council. In that pre-cell-phone era I expected to be routed through office personnel or to reach an answering machine or service. Instead, someone picked up on the first ring.

"Jose Cerda," he said.

He sounded nasally, as though he had a cold. He comprised the criminal justice section of the White House Domestic Policy Council, and his portfolio included, well, virtually everything, including gun control, community policing, domestic violence, and drug policy. Shocked that I actually got a live person on the other end of the phone (I later learned that Jose didn't have an answering machine installed until 1995) I explained who I was and why I

---

policy papers can be found at: www.reentrycourtsolutions.com/pioneering-documents/five-policy-papers-1994/.

was calling. Jose seemed unimpressed by my titles or resume but nonetheless invited me to D.C.

I hung up the phone and booked a flight.

I checked into the Tabard Inn, recommended by my wife's friend, which turned out to be my home away from home during the early years of the Clinton administration. The following morning I walked to the Old Executive Office Building, next door to the White House, for our meeting. After a screening that lasted an anxious fifteen minutes, I was given my badge and wandered down the wide green corridors of this august building completed in 1888. It didn't take long to stumble upon Jose's office on the second floor and then Jose himself, behind an enormous oak desk buried beneath an avalanche of papers and pending legislation.

Jose gave me a warm welcome. Of average height, with dark hair and a slight build, he wore glasses, and his mind was quick and always roaming, which at times made him seem distracted. He did seem genuinely fascinated by the drug court concept. I was fascinated that a twenty-something had been put in charge of criminal justice at the White House. We talked for more than an hour. I left Jose with the policy papers, monographs, and manuals I'd written, feeling as though I had made a friend at the White House.

Jose and I remained close throughout the Clinton administration. He would turn to me for advice and assistance, as I would him. I enjoyed the time we spent together socially. He introduced me to fine D.C. restaurants (including my first $50 shot of brandy). Over the next eight years he remained an ardent supporter of drug courts, which helped to establish both the credibility of the drug court field and my credentials within it.

Some months after our first meeting Jose called me to ask, "Would you be willing to enlist drug court judges in support of the Omnibus Crime Bill?"

The Violent Crime Control and Law Enforcement Act was slowly winding its way through a reluctant Congress. Coming in at 356 pages, the Omnibus Crime Bill, as it came to be known, represented the most extensive rewriting of criminal justice law in American history. He told me that it contained a drug court section with $1 billion attached to it.

Without hesitation I replied, "YES."

This was to be our first major opportunity as drug court practitioners to prove ourselves politically effective. I appointed or perhaps anointed myself leader of something I called the National Coalition of Drug Court Judges.

It was, of course, mostly smoke and mirrors. We were at best a loosely organized group of drug court judges and others who wanted to find resources to fund their programs. It seemed like I was the only one willing to Pput in the time or energy to make it happen. In truth I had no real experience in lobbying, and my understanding of the congressional legislative process was regrettably limited.

Comically, I worried how we could spend $1 billion on the drug court field with its fifteen nascent drug courts across the nation, even if we were to demonstrate exponential growth. I was to quickly learn that only those projects receiving appropriations were funded, no matter what was in the authorizing legislation (in other words, drug courts were ultimately authorized at $29 million for 1995–1996 but received an appropriation of approximately $6.5 million its first funding year).

Still, I recognized this as an important opportunity to expand drug courts and their resources and influence nationally. I asked Jose to send me a copy of the bill and began making phone calls to judges, DAs, and other drug-court practitioners. Some weeks later I flew to Washington. I had requested a copy of the bill several times but had not yet seen a draft.[36]

When I visited Jose in the White House he admitted that he had not actually read the drug court section or the full bill. He pointed me in the direction of the lead counsel for the Senate Judiciary Committee, chaired at that time by Delaware's senior senator, Joe Biden, to get a current draft of the bill.

Counsel for the Senate Judiciary Committee, Steven was a questionable sort with slicked-back hair, the kind of Ivy League careerist one meets in D.C. When I visited with him I got the feeling he was sizing me up. He kept busy, talking on the phone and with colleagues in his office, suggesting that he did not deem me worthy. He did manage to provide me with a current copy of the bill. I read the drug court section and wondered why I was in D.C.

Title V, Part 5 of the 1994 Crime Act was entitled "Drug Court." There was, as advertised, a billion-dollar authorization. Unfortunately, the "Drug Court" section (for years 1995–2000) covered various criminal justice reforms, prison construction, and other non-drug-court topics. However, there was no mention of drug courts anywhere except in the section's title.

I wondered if I was being used to gin up support for the crime bill among drug court judges through the attachment of the title "Drug Courts" to one section. I shared my feelings with Jose. I had spent weeks contacting drug court judges nationally with the promise of drug court funding and had traveled to D.C. only to discover there was no such proposed legislation. Jose apologized

---

36 I consulted with those with lobbying experience in D.C.: District Attorney Claire McCaskill of Kansas City, MO; Nelson Cooney, Vice President at CADCA; Jay Carver (then director of D.C. Pretrial Services); and Jose himself.

and asked if I would work with him, the Senate Judiciary Committee, and the Justice Department to make the drug court section more substantive and devoted to drug courts.

I spent the next two days meeting with and communicating by phone and fax with lawyers from the Department of Justice. Its lead counsel was heading up a team tasked with writing the substantive "Drug Court" section in the 1994 act.[37]

In its final form the "Drug Court" section was a major victory for drug courts, describing the purposes and parameters of the drug court model and funding to the tune of $29 million for fiscal year 1995–1996. My only concern was Senator Biden's insistence that "violent" offenders be excluded from the drug court provision. He explained to me that drug courts were a major change to existing law and needed to be introduced gradually. I expressed my belief that those with violence in their past often needed the services of a drug court the most, and that by excluding them we were sending the wrong message to drug courts: that they should take it slow and focus on less serious offenders. I didn't convince him, and to this day the exclusion remains.

I watched on C-SPAN as the bill was called to a vote and then passed, then celebrated along with other drug court practitioners across the country. I also received a call from Jose. He said that he wanted me to be on the platform, sitting with dignitaries, when the president signed the Omnibus Crime Bill.

I was elated, knowing that I had made a difference, even if a small one, on the national stage. I asked him if the drug court judges themselves could also be recognized for their hard work. He agreed to set aside twelve seats in the audience for drug court judges and other practitioners. The president signed the bill on September 13, 1994, at a special ceremony in the White House Garden. I sat behind Vice President Al Gore and next to Congressman Joe Kennedy (with whom I traded stories about our summer vacations, mine pretty forgettable, his Hyannis Port).[38]

I was enormously pleased when Jose told me that I was to be honored with a gift of a presidential pen used by President Clinton to sign the Omnibus

37 I provided her with my Clinton "policy papers," a study of Oakland's Drug Court, and a draft of my 1994 CJER drug court manual, pretty much everything that had been written substantively on drug courts up to that point.
38 The judges who were able to attend the ceremony were (I believe), Richard Gebelein (Wilmington), Bob Fogan (Fort Lauderdale), Michael Getty (Chicago), Harl Haas (Portland), Eugene Hamilton (DC), Jack Lehman (Las Vegas), John Parnham (Pensacola), Bill Schma (Kalamazoo), John Schwartz (Rochester), Jamie Weitzman (Baltimore), and District Attorney Claire McCaskill (Kansas City).

Crime Bill. The pen and a framed copy of the "Violent Crime Control and Law Enforcement Act of 1994" is prominently displayed in my home. (For landmark legislation, the president often signs an act using as many as twenty pens to be presented to those who assisted in the bill's passage.)

After the fact it's possible to revisit one's past and view it in a very different light. I was passionate about funding a new criminal justice reform paradigm, the drug court. The bill contained important reform-related sections, such as Violence Against Women and Community Policing, among others. Clearly, I was less concerned with the remainder of the Omnibus Crime Bill than with getting those provisions funding drug courts included in the bill.

That there were problematic sections of the bill, and even serious negative consequences in its passage, did not occur to me or the others who worked for the passage of drug court funding. Looking back, I would change sections of the bill if I could. But I can't say I would eliminate a bill that gave life to drug courts and, most importantly, their progeny, problem-solving courts.

Some attack established reforms as not going far enough or even being reactionary. In hindsight it's easy enough to condemn reformers who came before, ignoring what was feasible at the time, what good was accomplished, and what sacrifices had to be made. It's somewhat painful to be attacked as a reactionary. That, however, is the price one sometimes pays as a judicial reformer.

At the time I was pleased that our coalition had done so well in its first attempt at lobbying Congress. It was a display of drug court power and credibility, which impressed everyone, including myself. I realized that reliance on local practitioners (especially judges and DAs) and their promotion as regional stars should be at the very core of who we were. Few training dollars and relatively little expertise for drug courts were available around the nation, but an expanding group of effective drug courts (many with politically connected judges) were developing a sense of camaraderie and a philosophy of mutual assistance.

I had learned, through our drug court coalition's efforts on behalf of the 1994 Omnibus Crime Bill, that judges could have enormous influence on local, state, and federal governments and were not reluctant to use it. Many of us were repressed politicians at heart, more than happy to travel to Washington, D.C., to lobby our congresspersons and/or senators or visit with them in their home states (preferably, during a visit to drug court).

I began to envision how drug courts and their practitioners from different regions of the country could play an outsized role in showcasing the drug court model and educating new drug court practitioners through a nation-wide educational and mentoring network. We had created a cohesive and collaborative nucleus of judges and other criminal justice leaders in 1993, and they would stand together to create NADCP the following year.[39]

---

39 Among our coalition leaders in 1993–1994 were judges Joel Bennett (Austin), Sue Bolton (Phoenix), Bob Fogan (Fort Lauderdale), Richard Gebelein (Wilmington), Michael Getty (Chicago), Stanley Goldstein (Miami), Harl Haas (Portland), Eugene Hamilton (DC), Jack Lehman (Las Vegas), Steven Manley (San Jose), Steven Marcus (Los Angeles), Bill Meyer (Denver), John Parnham (Pensacola), Bill Schma (Kalamazoo), John Schwartz (Rochester), Ronald Taylor (St. Joseph), Henry Weber (Louisville), Jamie Weitzman (Baltimore), and Bob Ziemian (Boston). Also District Attorneys Claire McCaskill (Kansas City) and Bill Ritter (Denver), Public Defender Michael Judge (Los Angeles County), Pretrial Services Director Jay Carver (DC), and Program Coordinator Tim Murray (Miami)… and many others, unfortunately lost to memory.

PART II
COMING UP

On the Stump.

An Oakland Horn Section.

AN EPIPHANY IN MOROCCO

It was 1973. I had passed the California Bar and took off for a round-the-world trip (though I had no itinerary). The trip was to last almost a year and a half. Europe was too cold in February, so I took the ferry from Spain to Morocco and spent a month acclimating to a world still steeped in the middle ages.

The trip through the Atlas Mountains to Marrakech was a frigid nighttime bus ride along winding mountain roads and through heavy snowfall. The bus was like most Moroccan buses: driven by a certified madman. No Moroccan bus driver could forgo the thrill of passing other vehicles on hills or blind curves. It appeared to be a matter of honor or something close to it.

Normally, I accepted a bus driver's eccentricities calmly or at least suppressed my panic, but seeing my ashen, cringing fellow passengers scream at the bus driver did little to assuage my fears. That we made it through is a matter of fate and not probability.

Carpets, dresses, smoking paraphernalia, and more were to be found in the myriad shops along the narrow streets of the Medina. You could stop at shops where men sewed garments by hand or used spinning stone wheels to sharpen knives. So many of the things sold on the market seemed to be made nearby, and you could visit the workshops and, over a glass of tea, haggle with the proprietors about prices.

One night I sat in an outdoor café in Marrakech and watched the traffic under a full moon. I noticed a young boy I had observed earlier in the day begging for alms; he had no legs and sat on a crude platform with wheels. It was a pitiful sight. That night, however, he was playing tag with his friends, laughing and scampering about the marketplace on his wheeled chariot.

It occurred to me that this was a lesson about community worth remembering. Too often what we take as unacceptable, pitiful, and needing to be hidden from sight can be an acceptable part of a vibrant community elsewhere. Even tragic circumstances can be endured and surmounted if a community accepts you as one of their own.

CHAPTER 6

LONG AGO AND FAR AWAY

Aristotle said that the act of living in balance and moderation brings the highest pleasure. Unfortunately, it's a concept that didn't work too well when I was growing up in Brooklyn. What I remember is people screaming and beating on each other. It didn't seem to matter what ethnic group you belonged to; communication still occurred at high decibels and frequency.

I would prefer to skip my early years and talk about how drug court reform came into being, but there's a relevance to my upbringing that provides a key to understanding this judicial activist: I felt persecuted and victimized by my peers. It's not necessarily the most admirable of motivations but an important preset for me.

My family was working class, living in what could be described as a Jewish enclave in south Brooklyn: Coney Island. My parents were provincial and inward looking. When my paternal grandfather abandoned his family, leaving them without any means of support, my father had to quit school in the fourth grade and find work. My mother had aspired to a better life, but when the Great Depression hit Brooklyn she had to quit Hunter College after her first year. She spent the next decade as a waitress in Brooklyn. Neither of them had any aspirations beyond raising a family and survival.

Family lore had it that my maternal grandfather, David Neufeld, had come to the U.S. from Poland in the 1880s as a boy. He lived on the streets of the Lower East Side and ate the stale bread that bakeries put out for the poor. Somehow that led to his employment as a baker and then a leadership role in the bakers' union.

He was a deeply religious man. His temple—a small structure of orange brick—stood two buildings away from my grandfather's house. He would venture out several times a day to pray and kibitz with the other old men. When I was born he was in his seventies and was by then president of the temple. A lover of chicken soup and schmaltz (a kind of butter made with chicken fat and salt), he smoked fat cigars all day and drank schnapps with his cronies after services. He lived to be 98.

He was the paternal head of our extended family and a man of God. I learned from him, almost by osmosis, how one lives a good life. He was tolerant of others and showed empathy for the poor (something rare in that era). When life seemed unbearable I would walk the five miles to his small wooden house next to the temple. He would welcome me with chicken soup and talk to me until I calmed down and was ready to return home.

I didn't win the "Most Likely to Build a Drug Court Movement" award in public school. In fact, I received a string of "U"s (for "Unsatisfactory") on my report cards under "Works and Plays Well With Others." A bit of a nerd, I tried to fit in with little success. What made it worse was that I was tall, skinny, and awkward. I was picked last for team sports and picked on first by bullies as they built the schoolyard hierarchy.

In school I was often in trouble for talking during class and for demanding attention from the teacher; I was often late, rarely turning in my homework on time. I came out of public school wounded, and I carried that wound forward.

Maybe the natural progression for a reformer is to start out as a trouble-maker. Some would undoubtedly suggest I remain one.

Where I found solace and escape was music. My sister Eileen, two years older than me, taught me children's songs, which I would sing anywhere and everywhere: on the streets, in the alleyway behind our home, and occasionally solo in school auditoriums. I wanted to be a singer when I grew up. My parents tried to encourage my love for music through piano and guitar lessons, but I wasn't interested. From the radio I learned pop songs sung by Tony Bennett, Dean Martin, and especially Eddie Fisher, (who happened to be the one Jewish pop singer among the pantheon of great Italian-American singers).

At my grandfather's temple I would listen to the drone of prayers and songs offered up on the High Holy Days, but I struggled to understand the meaning and music. For a kid living in the Jewish ghetto that was Coney Island, I didn't have a whole lot of exposure to roots music. What was available was overwhelmed by "How Much is that Doggie in the Window," "Sh-boom," and other equally forgettable pop songs.

The Nat King Cole Show on TV in the early '50s was a revelation: a black man was singing and playing the piano with style, grace, and humor. I first heard the blues in the mid-'50s, mostly white covers of black music. One blues hit, "Shake, Rattle, and Roll," was marketed as rock and roll and sung by the great black bluesman Big Joe Turner. It had joyful exuberance, riotous lyrics, and a great sax solo by Sam "The Man" Taylor.

By the time black singers and their music had made an impact on the pop world in the late '50s, my fantasies about being the next Eddie Fisher had disappeared. My voice changed with puberty, and by the '60s I was an enthralled listener but rarely a singer. I let the magic of Ray Charles, Fats Domino, and Chuck Berry do the singing for me. But the music changed something in me (as Don McLean had sung), opening me up in ways hard to define.

An unspoken bond had emerged between the great black singers and musicians of the '50s and my generation, which shattered racial stereotypes when it seemed nothing else could. Rather than listen to the racial slurs and dogma that had existed in my neighborhood, I was exposed to something that could be described as poetic and soulful.

Much later I became aware of the connection between great Jewish composers and the black jazz musicians who transformed their music into living art. George Gershwin, more than anyone else, speaks to me of a willingness to reach out to African-Americans through music, which he incorporated into his sublime melodies. And I am transfixed by the genius of jazz saxophonist Rahsaan Roland Kirk turning Richard Roger's ballad "If I Loved You" into a powerful spiritual offering.

My formative years were the '60s. I subscribed to the theory held generally by my contemporaries that we went to law school to change the world—by changing the system from within. The truth is that neither I nor anyone I knew had any idea how to make that a reality, nor any clue what such reform would look like.

I graduated from Boston University Law School but can't claim to have been an exceptional student. I did have an interest in the environment, which in 1969 struck a chord both in me and the general public. I decided that the law school needed to advocate for environmental change. Unfortunately, the Environmental Law Club I started with other students did little of substance besides place its members in student internships.

During my second year of law school I was placed as an intern with the Massachusetts Attorney General's Office, in what must have been the public health section. Most of the attorneys had little interest or energy for their work. I recall them mostly hanging out. Except for coffee breaks upon coffee breaks, snacks upon snacks, and lunches upon long lunches, I didn't see them accomplish anything. I didn't fit in. They saw no value in a law student who had an interest in environmental issues.

It was my first exposure to bureaucratic inertia. The section director was a smallish man with a moustache and (I think) a toupee. He was suspicious of my interest in environmental law and deeply skeptical of any movement in that direction within his division. I was under his supervision and remember little of what I did in that part-time position, except for my summer internship.

As a summer intern I was asked to supervise a group of ten to twelve college and graduate students, mostly from the families of well-connected politicians and lawyers, and engage them in environmental work. I was excited to lead my own crew of investigators. As we had no clear understanding of what the real problems were, I had them prepare briefs on major environmental issues in the state of Massachusetts.

None of the briefs were of much import, but at the end of the summer I handed in a final report to my section head. Nothing happened. My mentor at the agency, a more sophisticated student intern and politico, encouraged me to send the paper directly to the attorney general for his personal review; I did. I was fired the next day, no doubt for disloyalty and failure to work through channels.

It was my first experience with the pitfalls of truth-telling, honest criticism, and manipulation by a colleague. I learned a lesson I would unfortunately relearn on a regular basis throughout my career, seemingly without cognition or memory: don't go over your boss's head and don't challenge authority.

That Boston summer was extremely hot and my summer internship difficult. After work at the attorney general's office, my habit was to return to my off-campus apartment, watch TV, and smoke marijuana with my roommates while listening to the rock music that had become a fixture in our lives. The age of psychedelia was pervasive. With it came new music in a kaleidoscope of colors. We listened to the Doors, the Grateful Dead, Creedence, the Rolling Stones, the Temptations, the Four Tops, Marvin Gaye, and, of course, the Beatles.

One night, listening to Led Zeppelin at high decibels, a police officer walked into our apartment. The door had been left ajar. He looked around, saw and smelled marijuana, told us to turn the music down, and left.

We were shocked. At the time I believed that the officer's sensible, knowing, and flexible approach to an illegal yet widespread cultural phenomenon—marijuana—had saved our legal careers.

After law school I was granted a job interview with the Environmental Protection Agency (EPA) in Washington, D.C. Given my limited finances I decided to take the overnight bus from Boston. Because of my long legs I expected to be cramped and uncomfortable and decided to take a sleeping aid for my trip. I had no experience consuming marijuana and no knowledge of how long the high would last. I was willing to give it a try and cooked up an ounce of marijuana in a pan of chocolate brownie mix.

Just before I got on the bus I ate one, then a second, and finally a third cookie, just to be certain I'd get a good night's sleep. I found myself in another space entirely as I approached the EPA offices in D.C. the next day. The problem with the interview was that I never seemed to connect with my interviewer. He would ask me a question, and I would answer a different one; when I asked him a question, he would invariably answer a different question. And that's how the interview went for what felt like the longest job interview ever. I was despondent about how poorly the interview had gone, so you can imagine my surprise the next week at finding a letter inviting me to work at the EPA. It made me wonder about the decision-making process within the federal government.

I had also applied for my dream summer job with Ralph Nader's Center for Study of Responsive Law in D.C. (then known popularly as "Nader's Raiders"). I didn't think I had much of a chance at getting a job there.[40]

Incredibly, I was offered the job and accepted. Shortly after I was also offered a position with the Natural Resources Defense Council (NRDC), an environmental law firm that had recently been formed in New York City. Because my fiancé at the time lived in New York, I decided that it might be best if I split my time that summer between Nader's Raiders and NRDC. I went to Nader, explained my dilemma, and offered to continue working on his project, with NRDC agreeing to pay the tab. He was amenable, as he wasn't entirely sure what I was doing in D.C. in the first place.

Nader tasked me with an investigation of the Nixon administration's Refuse Act implementation. The 1899 Refuse Act gave the Army Corps of Engineers the responsibility for controlled dumping into navigable water. It also allowed private citizens to sue polluters and earn large monetary awards. The Nixon administration, apoplectic about the idea of citizens suing polluters, ordered the Corps to develop regulations for issuance of permits to

---

40 Recently, I googled the Center for Study of Responsive Law and learned that just 200 Raiders had been selected from among 30,000 applicants the year before I joined. Ralph Nader had been my idol. I had read all of the investigative books coming out of the Center. He famously proclaimed, "Almost every significant breakthrough has come from the spark, the drive, the initiative of one person."

discharge into those waters. To bring citizens into that regulation process, I was asked to write a manual that would assist citizens in intervening at Army Corps administrative hearings.

I went to Washington, as usual, without a clue as to how to proceed. I began by contacting Nixon administration officials and asking questions. The problem was that I hardly ever understood the answers. I thought I wasn't making progress because I wasn't smart enough.

David Zwick, my supervisor with the Center, gave me the best advice I would ever receive concerning bureaucracy, suggesting that I might be having difficulty because the people I was talking to didn't have much understanding of what they were talking about. I began to listen more carefully to those I interviewed and to pick up on their general lack of expertise and competence, or both. There were exceptions, however. I interviewed EPA Director William Ruckelshaus (later to become the attorney general who presided over Richard Nixon's demise). In general though, those I interviewed tended to be as ignorant of the issues as I was.[41]

I worked on the Refuse Act citizen's manual for almost a year. It was published and distributed. Unfortunately or fortunately, as the case may be, the Clean Water Act was passed and the Refuse Act, though not repealed, was tossed into the dustbin of history. So a year's work was negated in the inevitable rush towards progress.

While working on the Refuse Act project I learned that I wasn't cut out for long-term, low-yield research and writing. I watched a colleague at the NRDC work on the Storm King Project, an environmental challenge to the plan conceived by New York City electricity giant Con Ed, which intended to shear the top off Storm King mountain and pump water up its side so they could release it during peak electricity demand. He had been working on that project for a number of years and would for many more before the case would be resolved.

I, however, couldn't see myself working on a long-term environmental project or any long-term project, for that matter. I was a child of my generation. I decided to move to California.

---

41 I should insert an addendum to that observation. There was to be a debate between Nader and Caspar Weinberger, (then a mid-level official within the Nixon administration) on the Nixon administration's implementation of the 1898 Refuse act. I was able to lay out the intricacies and problems associated with the Nixonian approach to water pollution law in a fairly complicated briefing. Nader absorbed it within a few minutes and went on to articulate our position in a masterful way, far better than I could do myself. Fast-forward ten years to a Hayward luncheon honoring Nader. I sat next to him and spoke to him briefly of my work at the Center. He didn't seem to recall my work or me.

I had visited California during the summer of '68 and believed it to be the land of milk and honey, a place where beautiful women cavort on white sand beaches and people opened up their homes to strangers. Of course, by the time I arrived to stay, in 1972, the halcyon days of hippiedom had come and gone (retreating north to Mendocino County, it seemed). I found a rental in the Berkeley Hills and began my bar exam preparation course.

A week later I came down with an inexplicable illness that puzzles me to this day. I couldn't get out of bed. I literally had to crawl to the bathroom. The hippie youth whom I lived with gave me plenty of space but little assistance. I came out of my stupor just as strangely as I had entered it: after a week or so I woke up and felt fine. I tried to rejoin the prep course but had little heart for it. I was way behind the other students.

So I did what I often did in times of stress: I played basketball. As I said, my skills were nothing special, but I loved the game. I played basketball at the UC Berkeley gym and went to the beach often. Not having a car limited my excursions, but I'd catch a ride to Muir Beach several times a week. I body-surfed and barbecued chicken over an open fire.

My girlfriend encouraged me to take the bar exam as a rehearsal for next year's. Before taking it I met a man who probably did more for me than any practice exam could have. He had been a bar grader or such and told me that graders typically had less than a minute to grade a bar question. He explained the secret to the test was to underline key concepts of law in your essay.

So I took the exam, expecting to fail. I was in Venice Beach, west of L.A., visiting a friend. I had just ridden my Honda 400 motorcycle to the southland when the results came out. I had passed. I must have done an exceptional job of underlining. Not having expected to pass, my success presented certain challenges. I wasn't sure what to do next.

CHAPTER 7

ON THE ROAD AGAIN

After graduation from law school I began my initiation into the world of comparative sociology. In common parlance, I went looking for the action.

One of the more irritating criticisms of the drug court concept is the accusation that the drug court judge is trying to be a social worker or sociologist in a black robe. Personally, it's a description I've never been uncomfortable with. I think judges need to be aware of the world around them, the vagaries of criminal law, the extraordinarily varied penalties that different societies have placed on malfeasance over the millennia, and even how different cultures view the same transgressions.

Now I would become a risktaker, at least in part because I had been so devoid of that characteristic as a youth. I challenged myself to take on arduous and dangerous tasks, such as hitching across deserts, trekking through the Himalayas, and setting out on difficult ocean swims. In retrospect I had been looking for ways to assert myself.

The next step for a risktaker was the one I had dreamed about for many years: I would become a vagabond, travelling the globe. I started by visiting a bookstore in Berkeley. There I bought a book that changed my life: *Vagabonding in Europe and North Africa* by Ed Buryn. That was what I wanted to be—a vagabond. The author's cover photo depicted a hardened man with a sunburn, moustache, and a cowboy hat disembarking from a bus somewhere in the desert. I read the book several times. I was smitten with the idea of being a traveler rather than a tourist (though the difference sometimes escapes me). I spent the next few months planning my journey, though I had no real goals or parameters for my trip.

In January 1973 I flew from John F. Kennedy International Airport to Brussels via Iceland. Brussels was cold. No, it was freezing. I travelled to Paris. I stayed in a cold-water flat on the Left Bank. I had to climb several flights of stairs to reach my bed, but I had discovered the books of Henry Miller as a neophyte hippie in Berkeley, so I knew what to expect. I was living the Bohemian life, though mostly I was miserably chilled and wet. My visit to Paris was short. I took to the road.

Putting my thumb out I crossed France. I took a train across the Pyrenees in my search for warmth. One of my fondest memories is sitting in a booth on a train with my leather hat and a pouch full of red wine. I was offered a cigarette by a Spanish soldier and offered up my wine. And a good time was had by all. I discovered that cigarettes were part of a traveler's universal language. Offering a cigarette or asking for one, or a match, was an excellent way to begin a conversation.

My only goal was to travel south. I assumed that when I got to the Mediterranean Coast of Spain I would find warmth, white sand beaches, and beautiful women. I found beaches in places like Torremolinos and Malaga, but the coast was almost as cold as Paris and pretty much closed down for the season. I had reached a fork in the road. I could turn east to Italy and Greece or keep moving south with the prospect of finding my ideal climate in Africa. I had a destination of sorts: a friend from law school, Andy Adede, had returned to his home country of Kenya after we graduated from law school in 1971, and I wanted to visit him on the east coast of Africa, some five thousand miles away. He wasn't expecting me.

I crossed the Mediterranean by ferry and landed in Casablanca. Morocco was, as expected, cold, but I was hearing stories of hot times on beaches along Morocco's Atlantic coast. But it would have to wait. First I was to visit one of the few remaining cities that still existed in the middle ages, Fez.

I had never heard about Fez before coming to Africa, but it was a great place to start an African adventure. Couscous replaced rice as the preferred grain, along with mint tea that contained as much dirt and sugar as it did mint leaves and water, but it was hot and cheap and everyone was drinking it. What kept me alive was the yogurt. It came straight from the goat and had a thick, creamy, sweet skin on top. Delicious.

I was taken aback by Fez. I found it exciting: so much was happening all around me as I walked through its streets. I stayed at a small hotel on a dollar a day. Its old city, called the Medina, truly felt like a medieval Arab city, with donkeys and narrow passages, hawkers, and small shops where everyone tried to grab your attention and get you to buy something.

From Fez I travelled south to Agadir. Along the way I found the beaches I had dreamed of, which proved to be everything promised and less. Thousands of youth from around the world were camped out on the beach: hot weather, no clothes, no sanitation, with food and water at a premium and nowhere to go to escape the sun. I had gone from the freezing horror of France to the over-the-top heat and discomfort of a Moroccan beach.

But I had a plan, and it didn't include staying in Morocco for the spring. I set out for Algeria. Having spent a month in Morocco I was now a semi-experienced traveler. I knew how to ask for sleeping quarters in French, how to order from what was cooking in the kitchen, how to traverse the medina without picking up an army of small children begging for money. I knew how to write home to request money from my bank account, making sure to have the letter cancelled in front of me, lest the stamp be torn off and the letter cast aside. And yet I was still several thousand miles from my supposed goal in east Africa.

The crossing into western Algeria is a vague memory, but its rolling green hills are still clear in my mind. We approached what appeared to be an idyllic village in the middle of nowhere. I responded according to the vagabond's creed and asked to debark the van to explore the village and environs, entrusting my survival to providence.

Actually, I was well equipped to survive in the Algerian hills. I had a North Face traveler's backpack that contained everything and anything I might need if stuck in an arctic blizzard or a desert dust storm. I was somewhat used to setting up camp by the side of the road and waking up the next day refreshed and ready to move on.

I approached one of the men in the village and attempted to communicate with him in my limited French, but no one in the village apparently spoke the language. I was able to communicate my request for a place to sleep, and that night I learned a few basic things about travelling in traditional communities: they tend to be enormously generous, inquisitive, and curious about you, where you've come from, and where you're going. This small village turned out to be something of an extended family, the women having their own quarters apart from the men. I don't think I encountered a single female during my brief stay.

I was placed in a large, somewhat opulent bedroom, probably the headman's quarters. He approached after a solo meal of couscous and meat (vagabonding means not asking where the meat comes from). We couldn't converse, but I unfolded my map and showed the headman where I lived, where I had travelled, and where I was going. He used the map to show me where I was and various routes through the region.

The following day I left the village feeling that I had been treated with great hospitality. An idea was coalescing in my brain, one that had begun to take form when I was crossing the Mediterranean and wondering where to go next. I would now cross the Algerian desert, otherwise known as the Sahara, reach the coast of West Africa, and travel across Central Africa, entering Kenya from the west to find my friend Andy.

While applying for a visa, I met a French couple at the Nigerian Embassy in Algiers. They were planning to cross the Sahara Desert to West Africa with their Volkswagen bus and invited me to join their adventure (you can always use another strong back when pushing your van out of a sand dune). We travelled together for several weeks, crossing the Sahara Desert as far as Tamanrasset in the south of Algeria. From time to time we got stuck in the sand and had to use the steel rails brought along for the purpose of extricating ourselves from such situations.

From Tamanrasset I caught a Land Rover south and then a truck covered with more people than fill most New York subway trains. I then traveled farther south through Niger and then Nigeria, where I spent almost a week on a fossilized steam train on the way to the coast (an old man kept pace for several hours as he walked alongside the train).

While in the Sahara and West Africa I lost my sense of time. I had no schedule, no one to meet, and a questionable goal at best. I felt no hurry to get anywhere and would often walk miles through the desert, singing to myself songs from the Paul Simon or Cat Stevens song books. I had no watch (I don't recall how I lost it); I read the time using a crude sundial consisting of a stick and the sun. I even stopped trying to keep up with the news, giving up on the *International Herald Tribune, Time* and *Newsweek*. My new mantra was, "None of the news, all of the time."

In Lagos, Nigeria, I had a spiritual moment of sorts. I reached the beach late at night and put my pouch containing my valuables under my head and my pack next to me. I woke to find the pack gone. I was wearing shorts, a sleeveless T-shirt, and floppies, and I had a towel. I sat on the beach looking out at the ocean for a long time. I have had few feelings of elation in my life as I felt that morning. I no longer had my North Face sleeping bag, which was good to −30° Fahrenheit, or heavy leather motorcycle jacket (plus 25 more pounds of unused gear in the pack). Of course, that elation was somewhat dampened when I realized that I couldn't brush my teeth, wash my face, or handle a dozen simple activities without basic possessions.

Dutch travelers in a nearby Volkswagen bus took pity on me. They were going to be guests of the Venezuelan Embassy for lunch and invited me to join them. How strange to be seated next to the Venezuelan Ambassador to

Nigeria while dressed in shorts, a T-shirt, and floppies while being served by waiters in white gloves—just one more incongruous experience in Africa. I travelled with my Dutch saviors for several days, getting my bearings and accumulating necessary travelling accessories.

The most frequent question I encountered in Africa was, "Are you CIA?" The second most frequent question was, "Why do you leave your village to travel so far?" It was a painful question when asked then and still is today. Why do we leave our community so easily?

West Africa was where I first began to feel a difference. People were rooted in family, village, and tribe. It was an impression reinforced as I traveled the world. Modern Western societies break down community and produce isolated individuals. People no longer feel accountable to or responsible for one another. Drug abuse, violence, and mental health breakdowns are just some of the consequences of that isolation. The horrible mass shootings that terrorize our society are only a small symptom of that separation sickness.

During my travels in Africa I met a number of foreign travelers of African ancestry. At the time I sensed their frustration at being treated as tourists and being called a *mzungu* (literally translated as "someone who roams around" or a "wanderer"), the same word used for European tourists. Cultural differences and customs seemed to have greater meaning in the traditional African world than racial or ancestral heritage.

I was taken by one driver to his village to meet his chief. The whole village assembled under an enormous tree in the middle of the village and sang and danced for this traveler, an experience as indelibly imprinted on my brain as any in this life.

Travelling in far-off lands, away from family and friends and dependent on the kindness of strangers, was a new experience. I found the strangers to be warm and generous and forgiving of my trespasses. I was to spend a month in West Africa (Nigeria, Dahomey, Togo, and Ghana). For days I met no one who spoke English or even French. I devoured any book—*War and Peace* took me less than a week to read—I could get my hands on. Strangely, ten years later in Oakland I would be playing West African music in a Ghanaian band with some of the finest African musicians in world.

I spent a year and a half travelling across three continents, visiting more than 40 nations. Perhaps the most important experience I was to have was trekking in the Himalayas along the Jomsom trail to the Tibetan border.

There I met Barry in a travelers' café in Kathmandu that was playing Neil Young and Bob Dylan on a beat-up stereo. We hit it off pretty well. We were both planning to trek into the Himalayas and realized that venturing into the mountains alone was not wise.

And then that crazy coincidence that defines a life: Barry turned out to be a criminal attorney and a public defender from my adopted home in Alameda County, California. His ambition was to trek both the Jomsom trail to the Tibetan border and the longer, more treacherous trail that would take him to the Mount Everest Base Camp.

Barry loved being a criminal defense attorney, and over the next month I soaked up his enthusiasm for his work and the people he represented. Listening to him I learned more about criminal law than I ever could in a classroom. For the first time I saw myself following a new path. It seemed like an answer to a quest I had begun long ago.

Having acquired the necessary trekking permits in Kathmandu, we began our journey. We travelled by bus to Pokhara and then by foot to a place called Jomsom, on the Tibetan-Chinese border, and back. It was a wild ride. Starting at Pokhara at 5,000 feet, we hiked up to 7,000 feet, back down to 4,000, up to 8,000, then down to approximately 5,000, and so forth. The Tibetan village of Jomsom itself was at approximately 9,000 feet. We hiked between two of the highest mountains in the world, Dhaulagiri and Annapurna.

It was fall and the rainy season was over. In the valleys you could scan the horizon and see dozens of waterfalls. Barry often found marijuana growing by the side of the road and took a minute to rest and roll a cigarette. It took us about two weeks to get to Jomsom—perhaps because of those brief interruptions—mostly climbing stairs carved into the mountains hundreds of years before. The climate constantly changed with the elevation, from plateau to tropical forest to high county to the freezing mountainside.

The Nepalese are hardy people. They were friendly and willing to take us in for the night. Nepalese authorities limited the number of trekkers in the mountains, even in the '70s, so there was little competition for accommodations. We did see many a Nepalese walker, often shoeless or wearing floppies, carrying a basket strapped around her forehead. One time two men passed us while carrying what appeared to be a refrigerator up the mountain. There were no automobiles, motorcycles, or even carts with wheels anywhere.

At night we would find shelter in a Nepalese home (mostly large, circular huts). At the higher elevations everyone, including the dogs, would huddle together in a mass of humanity (and otherwise) in a corner of the dwelling to preserve heat. I carried a lightweight sleeping bag I had bought as a replacement for my pilfered North Face model. It wasn't made for sub-zero weather but was fine for sleeping indoors, even in a drafty hut.

Throughout our journey we seemed to find ourselves in life-threatening situations. A good deal of the time we walked along narrow ledges hundreds of feet above rocky streams. Crossing these streams could be a terrifying experience. To this day I retain the mental images of the bridges (which is a very generous term to describe them) we crossed. The very first bridge we traversed was at least 50 feet above a rocky stream. It consisted of a twenty-foot-long log perhaps two feet in diameter and, except for a single strand of wire about three feet high that ran alongside it, that was all. We walked across the log with our packs on our backs, using the wire to keep our balance. There is no way I would cross that log today, nor would one likely find such a primitive bridge along that trail.

A lot of our conversation rambled, primarily due to my trekking companion's aforementioned fondness for trailside weed. But the constant conversation about defense lawyering stuck with me for months after we parted company in Kathmandu. Murder trials with shady defense counsel and shadier district attorneys, judges who would shut you down and ignore your motions or decide cases on a whim but rarely on the law, the subtleties of working a case and appealing to juries—I was fired up and, by the time I returned home, ready to fight for the common man.

INTERLUDE 3

THE OAKLAND BLUES COMMUNITY

MCing Bay Area Blues Society award ceremony with Ronnie Stewart.

When I began to play music I found that not only were my ears opening up to new sounds, my heart and mind were also opening up to the music and the culture of the blues. The African-American community that I had known in passing was becoming a second home for me as a musician.

I found the connection to the blues and black musicians a link to a different way of living and thinking about the world. These musicians lived gig to gig; music truly was their life, and they were willing to share that life with me if I was willing to put in the time to learn. It was an offer I couldn't refuse.

Drummer Teddy Winston and his wife wanted me to meet a great harmonica player, A. C. Robinson, who had played with his brother, guitarist L. C. Robinson, for years in Bay Area blues clubs. A. C. had given up playing the blues to play his harmonica and sing at a Pentecostal church in Oakland. I would visit A. C. in church. As he played his harmonica up front, a throng of people joined in the reverie, some dancing in the aisles, others speaking in tongues. They were truly leaving it all on the floor.

When the Bay Area Blues Society was formed in the '8os, Cool Poppa was elected its president. I assisted in its incorporation and was an initial member of the board of directors, along with Ronnie Stewart, now the Blues Society's president. Over the years I've played regularly with the Bay Area Blues Society Caravan of All-Stars. I've also been frequently drafted as an MC for what once was an annual Blues Awards ceremony.

Playing tenor saxophone in the blues bars of the East Bay led to a musical side-career of sorts, with gigs at local blues clubs and the occasional performance at blues festivals in the Bay Area. I reached the pinnacle of my blues career when I was asked to play in blues legend Johnny Heartsman's horn section at both the Monterey Jazz and Monterey Blues Festivals in the late '8os. Though we played the second stage, known as the garden or blues stage, it was a thrill to play where so many blues greats had performed.

CHAPTER 8

I FOUGHT THE LAW
AND THE LAW WON

My legal career began on a somewhat strange note. I had returned from travelling in May of 1974, eighteen months after leaving on my around-the-world journey, and was staying in Berkeley with a good friend, Susan, while looking for a permanent place to live. At the Coop, a long-ago attempt at a community grocery market, I found an advert for a room in the North Oakland neighborhood of Rockridge, close to the Berkeley city limits.

I showed up and met the clan: five young (25–30 years old), semi-hip people, like myself, who had come together to live communally. I had my own room, kept my own possessions, and shared all bills, groceries, and the cleaning and cooking. We dined together almost every night; some of us were good cooks. I mostly did the dishes but was pressured into learning how to put together a few basic dishes like split-pea soup and stir-fried vegetables, which I prepared only upon request.

Saturday night was the best night of the week. We typically sat down to a big meal with friends, sometimes ten to fifteen at a long, wooden dinner table. We generally had quite a feast, with tequila, beer, and pot to go along with the meal. Afterwards, we would play records we all knew and loved, with the Rolling Stones' "You Can't Always Get What You Want" and Jimmy Cliff's soundtrack from the film "The Harder They Come" as favorites. We danced around the living room and the downstairs areas with a happy abandon, tired out, and crashed. A typical Saturday night.

After a few weeks of getting acquainted with my surroundings I decided to look for work. I needed the money, but more importantly I had graduated from law school in 1971 and it was now 1974. I was definitely falling behind my fellow graduates. I got the notion from someone that I should send out letters of introduction to the heads of law offices or government agencies in the Bay Area.

I sent out a dozen requests for employment to public defender's offices and received one response, from Santa Clara County. I was excited. I didn't know exactly where San Jose or Santa Clara County was, but I was ready to make my way south for the interview.

I had bought a yellow Volkswagen bug, which was good, solid transport if you didn't need to go over 65 miles an hour and were happy playing harmonica with one hand and downshifting with the other. I had taken up the harmonica and was having a bit of success playing simple tunes. As there was no radio in my VW Bug, I started making some of my own. Luckily, there was no ordinance against playing harmonica and driving at the same time.

I appeared at the public defender's office well groomed. I had gotten a haircut but still had rather long hair and a full beard. The interviewer, Assistant Public Defender Howard Siegel, took a liking to me. We talked for a long time.

Luckily, he was more interested in my trip around the world than he was in my lawyering skills, which were limited. I may have dropped Ralph Nader's name in there once or twice and my experiences at NRDC, but he didn't seem much impressed. So I pretty much stuck to my world travels.

Howard asked me if I could start the following week, and I of course said I would. Surprised by my good fortune I shook his hand and became a deputy public defender.

I was nervous about being a defense attorney. I had never been particularly quick on my feet. When I'd spoken in class I would sometimes forget what I was saying before I finished saying it. More than that I didn't have a personal history of hard work or study. School didn't always come easy, but a modicum of effort usually pulled me through. This was going to be different.

I arrived for my first day with little idea as to what a defense attorney did. I did take a brief course in defense trial work with an excellent—but recently disbarred—Michigan attorney who worked in the Bay Area as a consultant and sometime defense lawyer instructor. It was an eye-opener. There were twelve young lawyers or so in the class, and each of us was to prepare a segment of a trial and play the role of attorney. The trial performance was recorded and critiqued by the other new lawyers.

I was to examine a defense witness. I didn't think I did a bad job until I watched myself on tape. I was mortified. I smiled—no, grinned—through the entire direct examination, mirroring my anxiety. An important lesson learned: recording a performance, be it as a lawyer or musician, could be helpful in defining reality.

My first case as public defender involved alcohol. The charge was "driving under the influence." The defendant had driven while intoxicated into a gas station, knocked over the gas pump, and slumped over his steering wheel. I sat in the Boalt Hall library at Berkeley that weekend trying to prepare for what was undoubtedly the worst drunk driving case I was ever to encounter as attorney or judge. Luckily for me the defendant failed to appear for court, allowing me to escape calamity.

Interestingly, it isn't the difficult trial case that causes defense counsel the most anxiety; it's the case where one really has nothing to say on behalf of one's client. Caught red-handed in the store, on camera, plus an admission and the property in the bag, and yet your client insists on having their trial.

Standing before a judge on even minor matters could clog my mind and jumble my syntax. I got into the habit of writing it down so I wouldn't mess it up: "My name is Jeffrey Tauber, attorney for defendant [to be filled in], and we wish to enter a plea of 'not guilty.'"

For me the most stressful part of the job was going back into chambers and talking informally with the judge. They were omnipotent forces who controlled my client's fate and myself. Making jokes and telling stories like some of my contemporaries did in chambers was beyond my capacity.

This was the mid-1970s, and female lawyers were not yet common in court. In one judge's chambers in particular, the judge and attorneys would regularly comment on female jurors. I knew that it wasn't the way a judge was supposed to act. Though I had no clue I would one day be a judge, it made me aware of how a judge's conduct, on or off the bench, could impact the quality of justice.

Santa Clara County in the mid-'70s was mostly white and middle class, with a preponderance of engineering and white-collar professionals. Minority populations didn't seem to garner a lot of empathy. Some of the judges were obviously biased, showing disdain and even open prejudice towards people of color.

I found myself representing black and brown men much of the time, though their percentage in the general population was relatively small. I was a bit more defiant than some, a little more willing to go to trial than settle cases, constantly peppering the DA with objections and the court with motions and generally making myself a pain in the ass.

After trying a dozen or more cases with success, I was ready for a new challenge. A small clique of San Jose police officers, known for their abusive behavior during traffic stops, were literally adding insult to injury by beating up on drivers; if my recollection serves me, Latinos in particular. The public defender's office had taken a number of these cases to trial without much success. In most instances the jury would side with the police officers and convict the injured defendants on the traffic charge, as well as on resisting arrest and battery on a police officer charges; the jail time was significant.

It was something of an embarrassment to the public defender's office. Deputy public defenders had, for the most part, taken to pleading the defendants out to the charged traffic offenses and a lesser misdemeanor (disturbing the peace, for example) to avoid more serious convictions. Finally, defendants would have to give up their rights to proceed in a civil case in exchange for having the DA drop the resisting arrest and battery charges.

It was a set-up for sadistic officers who liked to beat up on defendants. I was fairly new to the office when I learned that police officers were getting away with assaults. I was naïve enough to be shocked.

Being assigned to the DUI detail meant pretty much all my clients were alleged drunk drivers—defendants who didn't particularly elicit sympathy. I began to seek out police brutality cases to take to trial, rather than accept the district attorney's standard offer. My fellow public defenders were happy to offload their least favorite cases, so I took every DUI-brutality case that came my way to trial. I reveled in the confrontation with the police officers. My tactic was to literally get in their face and accuse them of brutality. I would often get a rise out of them, which revealed an aggressiveness unexpected by the law-abiding jurors of San Jose.

I had a run of six cases of resisting arrest and battery on a police officer. Each jury returned "not guilty" verdicts on the resisting arrest and battery charges.

I was making a name for myself. The public defender's office asked me to give a training session on how to successfully take on police brutality charges in DUI cases. A senior public defender approached me afterwards and told me that he admired my aggressiveness at trial. I was surprised by his words. And it was true to an extent: I had become a combatant in court. Though I started the job being somewhat timid, I had somehow morphed, through my defense of clients in police brutality cases, into a semi-tough defense attorney. Hard to believe, but it was very real and comforting for someone who had been a victim of abuse growing up.

I found that I empathized with most defendants. The saying "There but for the grace of God go I" became my mantra. I would try to talk to defendants about more than their cases—their lives. Most were without resources and plagued by substance abuse issues, failed marriages, and broken families, with little education and few job prospects. They often found themselves in a criminal justice labyrinth that returned them to the courthouse time and again. Sometimes, I would almost jokingly suggest to defendants with long criminal histories that they were such lousy criminals, they should look for another line of work.

I didn't lose many cases as a Santa Clara public defender, but there was one in particular that was hard to stomach: my last police brutality case. Though it's been a very long time I still recall confronting Judge Edward Nelson, a heavyset giant of a man, about his keeping the jury deliberating after 10 PM, something unheard of then and now. His response was, "Tauber, that's not your call. I'll keep this damn jury out as long as I want."

The jury returned verdicts of "guilty."

It was a hard loss for which I felt personally responsible. I hadn't handled the evidence issues well and promised myself that it wouldn't happen again. I took to reading the evidence code and training manuals and going to every training session on evidentiary issues I could find. I worked harder at becoming a competent trial attorney than at anything else I had ever done.

I sometimes talked to defendants about their alcohol issues. Some were so seriously dependent that there was little anyone could do. One well-educated and well-dressed older gentleman being charged with public drunkenness had been convicted many times for this minor offense. I encouraged him to seek treatment. At first he didn't respond. Then, with a tired, knowing expression, he asked me, "What for?" It was if he had said to me, this was his life and he would make up his own mind as to how he would live it or leave it. I asked no more questions of him.

I became a fixture at the Santa Clara County Probation Department, especially in my last year when I was handling felony cases. I knew the names of the individual probation officers who handled my clients' cases and visited them at their desks to share information and documents that would hopefully mitigate the harm caused by my clients. They seemed pleased by my willingness to personally reach out to them on behalf of my clients.

Once, I was stopped and asked by one of the old hands if I was a new probation officer, given the amount of time I was spending at the Probation Department. It was my impression that creating a collaborative approach to their sentencing made a substantial difference in my clients' sentences. It was an experience that helped shape my collaborative approach to a court-proba-tion partnership in the Oakland drug court.

My tenure as a Santa Clara County public defender came to an end when I was hired by the Alameda County Public Defender's Office. I badly wanted the job. The long work hours plus the commute between Oakland and San Jose was taking a toll on me.

However, I didn't last long in the Alameda County Public Defender's Office. In Oakland I felt like an interchangeable cog in the criminal court's wheel of justice. As many as a dozen public defenders might work on a single case before it wound up with a trial attorney. At least in Santa Clara County I was given a new case right after the initial court appearance—the arraign-ment—and would keep it in most cases through sentencing. I got to know my clients, empathized with them, made the motions that needed to be made, and accepted responsibility for their case and in some ways for them personally.

I ended up following the herd and passing on cases that were too diffi-cult or time consuming or when I didn't like the defendant. It was easier to pass a case on than accept responsibility for a defendant. I didn't like what Oakland's system—known as horizontal representation—did or didn't do for our clients, and I was unhappy with what it did to me. I had become a part of a system. Clients passed through my hands on their way to trial or a plea and sentencing without my being held responsible to or accountable for them.[42]

I lasted six months as an Alameda County Deputy Public Defender. I was asked by a friend, Luke Ellis, to join him in starting a fledgling law office. I jumped at the chance to get off the public defender conveyor belt. But the Alameda County Public Defender's Office had provided me with a valuable lesson that helped shaped my philosophy when I later planned my drug court program.

My experience as a private defense attorney was a bit difficult. My part-ner at the time, Luke Ellis, had little trial experience but was a charmer and an extremely capable attorney. He became the second defense chair to Tony

---

42 The Santa Clara Public Defender's Office called their system vertical representation at the time, and I was to learn that most large public defender's offices had traded the more personal responsibility and accountability of vertical representation for something called horizontal representation. Under horizontal representation you typically saw the file and the defendant briefly as it moved through the court process and would only be given direct responsibility for the case until trial. Instead of going to trial with all the necessary motions filed and argued, I would find often notes intended for the next public defender, reminding them of a motion that needed to be filed.

Serra, an extraordinary man and the attorney representing Huey Newton in an infamous murder trial held in the Alameda County Superior Court.

As a law firm our major problem was that private criminal defense work didn't pay particularly well (and we were lousy businessmen). I represented Huey on several motions and got to know him better than I was comfortable with. Huey would occasionally stop by the Berkeley Square Bar and Grill where I played the blues on weekends. He was usually high; he seemed to be a dangerous and unstable person. He also didn't pay his attorneys' fees.

When I was a defense attorney, people often would ask how I could represent someone who had committed horrible crimes. My response was simply that it was their right to have a jury trial, be represented by competent counsel, and be treated equally under the law, which meant that sometimes you would have to defend someone who was seemingly indefensible. That is how our legal system works.

I did learn from my experience as Luke's law partner that having a positive relationship with your clients could be a very good thing. One evening Luke showed up at the office after work wearing a bloody shirt and pants. He told me how he had gotten a defendant out of custody and later met up with that defendant and the defendant's girlfriend outside the bail bond office. The client pulled a gun and shot his girlfriend and himself dead. Luke didn't have a scratch on him. Sometimes it pays to get along.

Through my years as a defense attorney I was building my own construct of what an effective sentencing structure might look like. My isolation in growing up made me feel the need for a communal approach to my job (not unlike the sentencing circles employed in many cultures around the world). My need to take risks and stand out, in trying something new and different, was emerging. My experience as an attorney with direct responsibility for and accountability to my clients made me a strong proponent of committed, personal representation. My experience travelling around the world showed me how differently other cultures view antisocial behaviors, many in a much more benevolent and pragmatic way. And my experience playing blues music in the African-American community brought with it a connection to many of my clients. Finally, I had come to the realization that when there was something worth fighting for, I was a fighter.

CHAPTER 9

THE SAN FRANCISCO BAY BLUES

My tenure as a criminal lawyer lasted twelve years. What surprised me most was my tenacity in defending my clients. I felt a moral and emotional commitment to do everything I could on their behalf. Some judges were moved by my sincerity, but for others my constant objections and impassioned pleas evoked irritation.

When I started handling more serious offenses, this messianic complex was nearly my undoing. I threw myself into my work as I had never done before. I was handling serious felonies and found myself exhausted and emotionally depleted. If I was in trial in a murder case I would spend all my waking hours (and, as far as I know, sleeping hours) analyzing and developing trial strategy. I dreamed of a non-lawyering gig and I continued playing tenor sax in hopes of a music career, while friends who were terrific musicians couldn't find gigs to support themselves.

I would soon become a court commissioner—a subordinate or baby judge—because of a murder trial that hadn't gone well. Brian Smith, an eighteen-year-old from a white, middle-class family in Fremont, got tangled up in a fistfight, during which a friend pulled a knife and killed a boy. No one claimed Brian had a weapon or was even aware that his friend possessed or used a knife in the fight.[43]

On the night before final argument I left my law office sometime after 2:00 AM to drive co-counsel John Harrigan home. Upon returning to the office I found a man carrying my electric typewriter down the stairway. In a daze I confronted him, demanding that he put the typewriter down and leave

---

43 An example of the antiquated felony-murder rule, still partially valid in California: a defendant who commits a felony may be held responsible for a murder committed by an accomplice during that felony.

before I called the police. He did, and I called the police and went back to my office to continue working.

About an hour later I was surprised by a knock on the office door. An Oakland police officer had been going from office to office, looking for the burglary victim. I had completely forgotten about the attempted burglary, my confrontation with the burglar, and my call to the police. It was the kind of total immersion in a case I often experienced.

I lost the case, my one defeat in ten murder cases over a three-year period. I was devastated. I was beginning to suffer from tremors. At the time pumping gas seemed like a better career choice.

It just so happened that two commissioner positions had opened up in Alameda County. I didn't give them much thought until the day before the deadline to submit an application. My feeling was that I stood little chance, as I was considered something of a maverick around the court. My friend Leslie, a lawyer herself, pushed me to apply for one of the commissioner positions. On a lark I submitted a resume at the application deadline, figuring I couldn't do much worse than some of Oakland's sitting judges.[44]

Roderic Duncan, then presiding judge of the Oakland Municipal Court, was a bit of a maverick himself. He saw the municipal court as something of a scourge to the poor and lower classes of Oakland. As opposed to most, it took Rod years before the other municipal judges elected him to be presiding judge.

I didn't know Judge Duncan well, but I liked his presence on the bench: little formality, a twinkle in his eye, and real graciousness to lawyers and defendants alike. I had appeared before him on many occasions representing local blues musicians, and he appeared to appreciate my willingness to work pro bono. Also, on at least one occasion he had come to see me play the sax at one of Oakland's blues clubs.[45]

I decided to do some politicking. I found Judge Duncan in his court chambers. He greeted me warmly. I told him that I was going to apply for one of the commissioner positions. He didn't commit to supporting me but told me that he thought I would make a good commissioner and would talk to the other judges about my bid.

---

44 In California a court commissioner is an attorney hired by a county to serve as a subordinate judicial officer, mainly handling minor matters such as small claims, traffic, and misdemeanor cases.

45 During one of my court appearances before Judge Duncan, he explained to a blues player I was representing pro bono that I was "a wonderful musician." Thinking about what he had just said, he added, "Also, he's a good lawyer."

I met with a number of the judges on the court, and most were friendly and cordial; all I could expect. Meanwhile, the presiding judge did what he could to move my candidacy. As it turns out, that was enough. I was selected for one of two open positions along with Phyllis Hamilton, who would later be appointed to the federal bench.

One thing I did discuss with the presiding judge after my selection as court commissioner was his concern that the people of Oakland were not getting a fair deal from the traffic court. The presiding judge wanted me to make changes that would straighten it out and didn't mind if I turned it on its head to get it done.

At first I just sat on the bench and observed the process. It didn't take long to figure out that the court was preventing many low-income citizens and people of color from gaining access to the traffic court. People often came to court to have their traffic record cleared so they could get a valid driver's license, often a prerequisite to employment. Mostly, these were people who had failed to appear for a court date on an infraction, as noted on their citation, and had a misdemeanor Failure to Appear (FTA) charge levied against them. That FTA needed to be resolved before DMV would issue a license. These citizens found that they couldn't even get their case before the court without either putting up the full amount of bail, which was typically thousands of dollars, or by going through a contorted legal process designed to discourage them from even trying.[46]

The process could take three months or longer. Thousands of Oakland residents were bewildered by the court's process and gave up any hope of getting a valid driver's license. Bluntly, it was a racket that kept Oakland traffic offenders from getting into court to clear traffic tickets. Instead, it was a system that served the interests of the court, the clerks, and everyone else interested in keeping the numbers before the court down.

I talked it over with the presiding judge; he wasn't surprised. He encouraged me to tackle the problem head-on, which he understood was the way I usually handled situations.

---

46 Appearing at the clerk's office, they would wait in line to be given a court date, return on that date, wait to be called in court, stand in front of the commissioner, and be told to send a letter to the court explaining why they had failed to appear. Once the letter had been received by the court, the explanation read and accepted by the commissioner, they would be scheduled (by mail) for a court hearing. At the court hearing the offender would plead guilty to the offenses, be given proof that the case had been resolved (necessary for the Department of Motor Vehicles to grant a license), and be ordered to pay an extraordinary fine and fee, often over $2,000.

I went to my two fellow commissioners and shared my observations, neither of whom showed much concern, as that was the way traffic cases were handled in Oakland, which was fine with them. In fact, the one longtime commissioner had been around a dozen years and had either helped design the system or stood by as it was implemented.

Their responses were difficult for me to fathom. As long as that process, unjust as it might be, treated everyone the same, it was okay with them. They had achieved a position of some status and privilege as a part of the court's professional class and saw nothing wrong with perpetuating that system.

I devised a plan and took it to the presiding judge. I would collect data on Oakland's traffic cases and its handling of FTAs, review how other counties handled the same problems, and present an alternative to the full court.

My first task was to get the traffic data from the head traffic clerk, Paul Takata. He was dumbfounded at the idea of making changes to the traffic calendar. At first he refused to provide the data I requested on the basis that collecting the data was too cumbersome. This was the beginning of a knock-down, drag-out fight between Paul and myself over changing the court's traffic system.

It became crystal clear that the clerks, as well as the other commissioners, resented my attempts to make misdemeanor Failure to Appear (FTA) charges easier to resolve for defendants. They saw it as being more work for them. Paul candidly told me that the present system was the only thing preventing the court from being drowned in FTA cases.

I stuck to my plan. I would take my case over his head and that of the other commissioners to the judges themselves. I kept my own data on the FTAs being resolved. I called courts across the state and asked questions about how they handled FTAs. I visited courts close by and watched how they handled their traffic calendars: the Contra Costa, San Francisco, and other Alameda county courts. I collected data on other courts whenever it was made available to me.

In the end I had enough data and information on other courts to support the hypothesis that Oakland traffic offenders were faced with more obstacles and complexity than any other court I had investigated. My proposal was for those who appeared at the clerk's office in the morning to be seen by the commissioner that afternoon, with no future dates, no letters to the judge, no future pleas; it was all to happen on the same day.

Paul and the traffic clerks were incensed, as were my fellow commissioners. I had been on the bench less than six months and was proposing major changes to how those coming before the court would be treated. I wrote up my proposal, integrating as much data from other courts as I could find to support my position.

I submitted it to the judges of the court. With the guiding hand of Presiding Judge Rod Duncan, the other judges approved the plan. After all, none of them actually sat in traffic court except on the rare occasion when a commissioner was out ill. The spigot had been opened, and the pernicious traffic offenders with their FTAs flowed into court.

Within a few months the verdict was in: afternoon calendars were filled with FTAs but, incredibly, by limiting the number each day, the clerk's office was easily able to handle the increase. Lines at the traffic window were drastically reduced, and clerks were no longer confronted by angry, frustrated, belligerent, sometimes hysterical Oakland residents. The high levels of anxiety and tension that traffic clerks were used to were disappearing with the introduction of same-day service.[47]

My experience as a commissioner (especially in traffic court) was teaching me some very basic lessons about how bureaucracies work. I learned from the traffic clerks that the ultimate solution to any dilemma was to satisfy the bureaucrat in us all, making it work for them so we would all benefit from reform.[48]

I was beginning to feel the tug of ambition. I wanted to reach the next level. It was difficult to think that my career path might be closed off at the commissioner level, handling the work judges didn't want to do. I saw myself in a higher, more prestigious position.

I was used to the pressure of the job, but I didn't like it. I sought the independence to decide cases free of the expectations inherent to traffic court—not that there weren't pressures on a judge, but the people elected you, whereas court commissioners served at the pleasure of the judges.

As a commissioner I understood that if a police officer said you went through a stop sign, unless there was reason to disbelieve the officer, you went through the stop sign. If you decided the close calls in the cops' favor, you did what was expected of a traffic commissioner and you had no problems. Of

---

47 I presented a paper and accompanying data on the Oakland traffic court changes at a California commissioner's conference, and it was distributed by the California Commissioner's Association and I believe by the Administrative Office of the Courts across the state.

48 I recently sat in traffic court as a retired judge in several Northern California courts and learned that most California counties use a similar same-day setup for all traffic matters. If you're in by 9:00 AM or whatever the cutoff, you get on calendar that same afternoon.

course, if you found the defendant not guilty in too many cases, the police department and DA could become your enemy… and you might find yourself looking for another job.

The courts were, as they are today, determined to subsidize their operations by taking as much money from traffic offenders as possible. Commissioners were encouraged by the judges to impose the maximum fine. I tended to undercut the other commissioners substantially, which caused further irritation with my colleagues. I rarely set fines above $1,000 as I saw the traffic court for what it was: a means to squeeze those at the bottom to pay for institutional expenses. Today, so many fees, penalties, and operating expenses are attached to fines that, as likely as not, offenders walk away with double and sometimes triple the amount of the maximum fine in appended costs.[49]

Of course, defendants other than traffic offenders, sometimes called "frequent fliers," appeared before the court for relatively minor offenses. Some criminal histories ran ten pages or more, with dozens of arrests and convictions for traffic misdemeanors, domestic disturbances, assaults, petty thefts, and drug possession charges. This was the focus of our work as commissioners, cleaning up after the "losers" found in the lower reaches of our community. It was our task to consolidate multiple cases, put the "lowlife" in jail for relatively short periods, and release them into the community.

Ultimately, my experiences in the Oakland Court helped me understand the place of the judicial officer and court commissioner in our community. Shortly after taking the bench as a court commissioner I watched as Freddie Roulette, a fine lap steel guitar player, approached the bench on a traffic case. Freddie was someone with whom I played at blues bars. He looked straight through me as if I weren't there. What he saw was authority and power, and that could only mean one thing: trouble. Other blues musicians appearing before me in my career stared straight ahead as well, showing no sense of recognition (I, apparently was completely camouflaged in a black robe). I had ceased to be human in their eyes.

I was isolated from both my fellow commissioners and my friends in the blues community. Being on the bench is, in any case, an isolating condition. Those I knew as friends when I was an attorney would call me by my first name when we weren't in the courthouse, while everyone else associated with

---

49 A few years later I found my proclivity to undercut other commissioners' fines of particular interest to my colleagues on the Oakland bench. In 1989 I was running for municipal court judge and in a lawsuit with the court, its judges, and the county. I was asked a number of questions during a deposition as to what amounts I would fine defendants for traffic offenses and whether I consistently undercut the other court commissioners in setting fines and fees.

the courts—and many others—used the honorific "Judge" before my name. For someone who had lived as an outsider for much of my life, it was disquieting. But it came with the territory.

INTERLUDE 4

COOL POPPA AND
THE DAY ON THE DIRT

Playing the blues with my buddy Kenny Herrera, who introduced me to playing the saxophone.

Cool Poppa, a veteran blues guitarist, composer, and singer, took me under his wing. Pop hired me to play gigs when I didn't have the "chops" on sax to warrant it. We played mostly clubs—which some called dives—on the wrong side of the wrong side of town. I followed him into some seedy joints to play a gig, and he walked me to my car on the other side of the gig. He also reflected the tone of the Oakland blues community at the time, a tolerance of others and a willingness to share.

My favorite blues club was the Deluxe Inn, where on Friday and Saturday the music wouldn't really get going until midnight and go till dawn. It boasted great fried fish and chicken and a counter where breakfast was served in the middle of the night. On most nights Sonny Rhodes, a wonderful lap steel guitar player, played the blues all night long with his eyes closed. Sonny's band offered plenty of room for sitting in, as it typically played for six to eight hours. It would get so crowded after 1:00 AM, when the other clubs closed down, you could hardly find room to dance unless it was a slow blues (in which case the amorous dancers would be packed together.)

There were terrific blues clubs back then, such as the Deluxe Inn, Eli's, Ruthie's Inn, the Three Sisters, the Shalimar, and many others. Today, there's one regular blues venue left in Oakland: Everett and Jones, a wonderful barbecue joint in Jack London Square. The Bay Area Blues Society band, led by Ronnie Stewart, plays there on Saturday nights.

For a number of years in the '80s my law firm sponsored a big July Fourth blues party on a dirt plot in front of my home. We called it Day on the Dirt, a riff on Bill Graham's Day on the Green extravaganzas at Oakland Stadium. Dozens of blues, rock, and jazz musicians showed up, as did an audience of more than 100, with amazing fried chicken cooked up overnight by Cool Poppa's sister and beer and wine for all. A mixed tribe of Oakland lawyers and blues, jazz, and rock musicians and their friends and families came together for a holiday extravaganza.

Over time I listened to many a blues players' stories about traffic tickets, abusive police officers, drug and alcohol cases, and domestic violence charges. On occasion I was able to help out, appearing in court pro bono when blues musicians or their family members found themselves in trouble with the law. I talked to the DA and judge and usually resolved the problem; an attempt at returning a generosity of spirit.

CHAPTER 10

AT LAST

In the late 1980s and early 1990s Rod Duncan and I ran most Sunday mornings along East Bay trails. Rod was fifteen years older, a rangy and athletic 6' 6". He ran with his dog and stopped to talk to everyone and anyone we came across on our runs. He was always an intelligent and concerned mentor. I leaned on him heavily for advice and then solace as I negotiated treacherous political terrain. Surrounded by Eucalyptus trees on a run on the fire trail above the Berkeley campus, he talked about how the courts were often callous and indifferent towards the poor and disadvantaged.

Being something of an outsider himself, Rod was someone ready to suggest the outrageous, and I was foolish enough to take his ideas seriously. It was in 1987, during a seven-mile run along Bay Shore Island, that he broached the idea that I consider a run against a seated Oakland judge, Lou May. May was a Reagan appointment, a conservative judge, and generally thought of as marginally competent. Rod commented that May was coming up on his 70th birthday, and his judgeship would be up for election.

I was 40 years old, with the naïve optimism of someone approaching middle-age, believing that I had more to give to the courts than resolving neighbor-on-neighbor small-claims grievances. But there was a problem. Governor Deukmejian was a conservative and I a liberal. There was no chance that he would appoint me to a judge's position. It made Rod's suggestion tempting. I went to the clerk's office and asked to see the listing of judges with their election dates. Lou May was up for election in June of 1988.[50]

---

50 At the time a judge's pension was reduced by 30% if he or she remained beyond their 70th birthday. Lou May would need to retire within nine months of his new term or suffer the consequences. The governor would then fill his newly vacated seat with another white, middle-aged, middle-class prosecutor, as was his wont when vacancies opened up on the bench.

I was reluctant to talk to anyone about the possibility of a run against a seated judge. I wasn't sure it was a fight I could or should take on. The decision, however, was made for me: my campaign for Oakland's municipal court was launched when Rod made an off-the-record comment to an *Oakland Tribune* columnist. I hadn't planted the story; I hadn't even asked Rod to do it. But it was out there all the same. A few sentences appeared in the *Oakland Tribune* about a commissioner who was eying a retiring judge's position, and with that I was in it up to my ears.

I went to talk to one of the more senior judges with strong political ties to labor unions. He was open to my challenge to May. Just as quickly, however, the roof fell in. I was visited by the assistant presiding judge, Joanne Parelli.

She was a short, lean woman of extraordinary intelligence (later to be appointed a justice of the California Appellate Bench). When I was a defense attorney I had known her as one of the top prosecutors in the Alameda County District Attorney's Office. Since being appointed to the Oakland bench she had become the assistant presiding judge to Presiding Judge Judy Ford.

She asked point-blank, "Are you going to run for Lou May's position?"

I told her that I was exploring the idea but hadn't made up my mind.

She clearly wasn't satisfied with my answer and pressed me for a decision.

I refused to give her a direct answer, stating that I would decide before the filing deadline for candidates (I believe it was February 10, 1988).

She made it clear that the judges would not stand for insubordination, and that I would be fired from my position if I were to file as a candidate for the position.

I felt enormous pressure from her to declare that I would not run against Lou May. I also understood the danger of making any definitive statements.

An exploration of my options had exploded into a major conflagration. Judges who at first supported me as an up-and-coming judicial officer running against a poorly-thought-of conservative judge rethought their positions. They realized that my challenge could be seen as a challenge to their judgeships and a bad precedent if other commissioners were to run against sitting judges in the future.

I wasn't sure what I should do, as I had gone too far to back down. If I did relent I would likely be dismissed as a commissioner in the not-so-distant future on trumped-up charges. In any case I would never be seen in the same way: a local commissioner who took on a sitting judge, something that had never been done before.

The Alameda County judges joined in a solid front against me. I wasn't sure how to go about running for office, what steps to take, whom I needed on my side, and how to raise money—the many issues facing someone challenging a sitting judge. Of course, there was ultimately a critical legal issue to be resolved: did I have a constitutional right as a contract employee to challenge one of my bosses, a judge, for elective office?

Everything came to a head early one morning in December of 1987, when the presiding judge, Judy Ford, called me in my office and instructed me to come to her chambers immediately. PJ Judy Ford and Assistant PJ Joanne Pirelli were waiting for me. Judge Ford informed me that the Oakland Municipal Court judges had voted to relieve me of my position as commissioner for incompetence and failure to faithfully execute the duties of my office, plus the inevitable "inability to work harmoniously with the rest of the court." She demanded my keys to the building. Judge Parelli, seemingly a witness to an execution, stood next to the presiding judge and said nothing. I was escorted back to my chambers by a deputy sheriff. The bailiff took my keys to the court building and waited as I gathered up my belongings, and I left the building. I now had no option left except the one before me: run for judge.[51]

I ran on a platform of reform. I soon learned that there was community support for a reform candidacy. I was supported by the Alameda County Labor Council, the local Democratic Party, local newspapers, and the media in general. I ran as an outsider with an agenda to change the system. One piece of campaign material sent to Oakland residents exhorted all to vote for Jeff Tauber to "Stop the Revolving Prison Door."

I had strong support from the African-American community and its ministers. I met Elihu Harris, a powerful politician who at the time was an assemblyman from Oakland, at a restaurant in Oakland's Chinatown. He was, and is, the fastest-talking and quickest-thinking politician I've ever known. I was concerned that racial politics might become a part of the campaign and knew that an African-American lawyer, Jeffrey Carter, was considering declaring for the judgeship. Elihu came right to the point: he had talked to his contacts in the courts and I was his man. When I brought up other potential challengers, he said the only thing that mattered to him was character.

His State Assembly office in Oakland became my home away from home, a strategy center, and a source for staff and community resources. Nearly every Sunday he had an intern take me to several African-American churches

---

51 The disaster was somewhat ameliorated by the fact that the Alameda County Bar Association had recently polled its members, and the review of Oakland's judges revealed that I was rated highest for "excellence" among the sixteen municipal court judges and commissioners, while Judge May was near the bottom.

to speak for a few minutes before being endorsed by the pastor. I spent nearly six months in a grueling campaign, walking neighborhoods, holding fund-raisers, giving speeches, and more. Both the blues and Afrobeat communities supported my candidacy, staging several benefits for my campaign featuring local bands such as Mapenzi, O. J. Ekemote, and Kotoja (as well as a concert by Andy Narell, a world-renowned steel drum player).

I retained a fine civil attorney, Jeffrey Ross, who sued the county and the seated Oakland judges for $25,000 each for firing me without cause and violating my constitutional rights to run for public office and to equal protection under the law. Federal District Court Judge Eugene Lynch ruled in my favor, granting me a temporary injunction that allowed me to remain a commissioner on the ballot with my agreement to step away from my position while I ran for office.

On June 8, 1987, I was elected municipal court judge of the Oakland-Piedmont-Emeryville judicial district with 68% of the vote. I resolved my case against the county with a $95,000 settlement, which paid for my attorneys, my election campaign, and part of my approaching tour of the South Pacific.[52]

Winning the election was a monumental moment for me. I had taken on the entire Alameda County court system and won. Literally, all Alameda County judges (including my friend Rod Duncan) had signed an advertisement endorsing my opponent, Judge Lou May. It apparently was the thing to do if you wanted to be a part of the club. It was a club that I wouldn't be invited to join.

My term was to begin in January of 1989, six months after my election. I had six months with no job and no responsibilities. And I had a boyhood dream of traveling by tramp steamer through the South Pacific.

I had another reason to make the trip. I wanted to see what courts and jails looked like in other parts of the world. Peggy Hora, an Alameda County municipal judge from the city of Hayward, offered to write me a letter of introduction I could use as I traveled across the South Seas. The letter turned

---

52 In a strange turn of events during the run-up to the election, the judges hired Jeffrey Carter, the attorney who had contemplated running for judge, to my position as commissioner. Jeffrey gave an extraordinary interview on Channel 2 News, saying he had been given the job on the condition he not run for Lou May's judgeship. This exercise of raw political power, taking Jeffrey out of contention in the race for judge, was to have a significant impact on my lawsuit.

out to be a gold pass to the criminal justice and law enforcement world of the South Pacific.[53]

Watching the courts at work in distant lands is what the English call a "busman's holiday." I had an opportunity during my trip to soak up information about how basic criminal justice systems operated (or failed to). In Fiji, on the basis of Judge Hora's letter of introduction, I was granted an interview with the chief justice and the opportunity to visit the main jail. I was treated with respect and deference and as a special honor was invited to the guards' housing unit, where we all got high in a traditional kava ceremony.[54] It was then, on my South Seas journey, that I began to seriously contemplate the comparative experience of drug use around the world.

I visited several courts in Fiji, Tonga, Western Samoa (today known as Samoa), and American Samoa. All had foreign magistrates, to the best of my recollection—New Zealanders who presided over their courts (except for American Samoa). I thought that using foreign judges or even judges from a neighboring village was a problem in places where communities are so insular and conflicts so localized.

I had read about a custom among Polynesians that involved a wrongdoer making amends, called *ifoa*, to the victim and the victim's family by bringing food and gifts as a form of informal restitution. It was understood that the offender's family would also take whatever measures necessary to control the offender's conduct in the future. I was told that a family would literally camp out on the neighbor's steps until they accepted the proposed restitution. It's a wonderful concept and one that makes sense when the transgressor is known and the damage is relatively minor.

I was in a Samoan court when a magistrate from New Zealand was asked to accept *ifoa* in the case before him. He rejected the offer out of hand, and I cannot say I completely disagreed with him. The defendant had intentionally thrown a rock at a girl and blinded her in one eye. Something more than

---

53 Peggy Hora had been an early supporter as I aspired to be a judge. She gave me valuable advice and advocated for me behind the scenes as I campaigned. We discussed on many occasions what reforms were feasible if and when I joined the court. She expanded the countywide committee on DUI issues to "DUI and other drugs" when I joined the court and suggested that I join her as co-chair of the committee. That committee later turned out to be a crucial advocate for the Oakland Drug Court when I had little support within my court to start a treatment drug court. Later, she was to form and preside over a Hayward treatment drug court, which became a model and mentor court for jurisdictions interested in collaborative law enforcement participation.

54 Kava, a drink derived from the root of the kava plant, has a pleasant, numbing effect. It is found in sleep-inducing herbal teas and such and in a more concentrated form will definitely get you high. Kava bars have opened in San Francisco and other large cities.

restitution was clearly called for. But the idea of bringing peace to the community by making restitution, and even more importantly by relying on the family itself to control the miscreant, had an authentic ring to it.

In Samoa, while visiting a prison seemingly built into the side of a mountain, I experienced one of those rare comedic moments in criminal law. Although the weather was unbearably hot and humid, huge cauldrons reminiscent of those used to cook tourists on TV were being stirred. Prisoners were housed in cells that resembled caves. I asked the prison commander about the inhumane conditions, and his reply was that the prison basically closed down on the weekend and everyone went home, only to return the following Monday to continue their prison terms.

I found that to be a wonderful insight into another culture's approach to incarceration. Over the years I enjoyed telling that story as an example of how varied punishment can be in different cultures. That is, until I read a story in the newspapers about how Samoa had been cited by FreedomWorks, a prison reform non-profit, as a nation violating prisoners' basic human rights. To this day I wonder whether the criticism was truly warranted or whether this was a case of imposing Western standards on another culture's concept of an otherwise acceptable sanction.

Fiji, as well as the other island nations I visited, consisted of many hundreds of islands, although those that were habitable were relatively few. (The main island of Fiji, Viti Levu, has 600,000 people.) I was more or less committed to travelling across the South Pacific region to visit Fiji, Western Samoa, and Tonga. Of course, I only stepped foot on perhaps twenty of those islands, as transportation presented a substantial hurdle.

I had a strange premonition that I would perish in a plane crash while flying between islands. It was a powerful yet irrational fear that I would never take the bench as a judge if I were to fly. So I took ferries instead, unsteady, leaky, overcrowded, overloaded boats that sometimes went down at sea. On one occasion I was stunned by the beauteous prayers being spoken and psalms being sung by Tongans as they left their main island of Tongatapu for the daylong journey to Vava'u—until I learned that the previous ferry had gone down with all souls aboard.

I thus developed a special travel strategy, partly out of a temporary fear of flying, partly out of my desire to reduce costs, and partly because of my romantic image of tramp steamers plying the South Pacific. I found a German freighter that travelled between the South Sea Islands and took travelers aboard in exchange for a small contribution of $15 a day, which benefited the sailors' health fund. I stayed in the boat's infirmary, probably the most antiseptic travel accommodations I had ever enjoyed. I took the tramp steamer between Fiji and Somoa, and Somoa and Tonga. The journey between island groups took two to three days, offering plenty of time to read, relax, and think about my new career as a judge.

In January of 1989 I was to become a fully constituted municipal court judge, with a promise to beat the system and reform the courts but no real plan or ideas for how to do so.

PART III
NADCP BEGINNINGS

Applause for Attorney General Janet Reno after her plenary speech to the seminal 1996 NADCP Conference in DC (clockwise): Assistant Attorney General Laurie Robinson; Marc Pearce, NADCP Vice-President; Judge Frank Hoover, drug court judge from Bakersfield, CA; Presiding Judge Eugene Hamilton of the DC Superior Court; Chief Public Defender Michael Judge of Los Angeles County; myself shaking hands with the Attorney General.

Drug Czar General Barry McCaffrey, Director of the Office of National Drug Control Policy (ONDCP) is presented with an award by NADCP President Jeffrey Tauber, for his singular contribution to the creation of the National Drug Court Institute (NDCI).

COMMUNITY-BASED SANCTION IN AMERICA

Colonial America, made up of many small, insular, and stable communities, relied heavily on community-based or "alternative" sanctions to enforce a strict social, economic, and religious code of behavior. While it's true that some of those sanctions may now be considered unacceptable (i.e., corporal punishment), other forms of alternative sanctions are very much a part of the modern criminal justice system. The use of warnings, servitude, and restoring the victim may be known by different names today (admonitions, restitution, community service) but share similar functions.

Incarceration, on the other hand, was rarely used as a sanction, and while a conventional sanction today (and some would say traditional), it was a radical departure from the "community-based sanctions" in place some 200 years ago. It is generally agreed that incarceration only began to achieve acceptance when societal and community-based sanctions began to lose their effectiveness.

According to Professor Lawrence Friedman, widely considered the dean of American legal history, "This was a constant in colonial history; criminal justice as social drama." As he wrote in his book Crime and Punishment in American History, *a trial was "an occasion for repentance and reintegration: a ritual for reclaiming lost sheep and restoring them to the flock. [...] It was a public, open affirmation of the rules and their enforcement; a kind of divine social theater."*

The parallels to the drug court could not be clearer. Living in a time when society has substantially broken down, when people are leading isolated lives and the efficacy of societal pressure has been much reduced, the drug court provides a communal structure for the drug user, providing support, rehabilitation, resources, and a sense of community where none had existed before.

Within that community "alternative" or community-based sanctions have a newfound importance. Sitting in the jury box for a day is the equivalent of wearing a dunce cap; the admonition from the judge in front of the drug court community is a shaming that all understand. On the other hand, the rehabilitated drug user is welcomed back into society at a very public graduation ceremony presided over by community leaders.

According to Dan Kahan in his article "What do alternative punishments mean?" one commentator wrote, "It is ironic and yet oddly appropriate that although 18th century America turned to imprisonment because alternative punishments had lost their ability to shame, late 20th century America is turning to alternative punishments because imprisonment has lost its ability to deter and rehabilitate."

CHAPTER 11

BLUE SKIES

By 1994 I had a leadership position among a small coalition of activist drug court practitioners and judges. Now I had to decide whether or not to take the leap and attempt to build a major league criminal justice reform organization from the ground up.

I met Carolyn Cooper and Joe Trotter of American University's Justice Programs Office sometime in early 1994. At the suggestion of Judge Tomar Mason of the San Francisco Superior Court, I joined them for dinner at a restaurant in San Francisco. They were friendly, solicitous, and curious about my understanding of the drug court concept.

I didn't know Tomar well but understood that she was struggling, along with the San Francisco County Clerk, Gordon Park-Li, to win her colleagues' approval for a San Francisco drug court. Unfortunately, it was and still is common for judicial innovators to face resistance from more conservative colleagues. Over dinner we discussed the field generally. I brought up the topic of starting a national drug court organization. They were excited about the possibility and open to discussing the idea further. American University's Justice Programs Office turned out to be an excellent partner in the field's startup.

Over dinner someone suggested that a drug-testing company in Santa Clara County called Syva (then independent, now part of the Siemens Corporation) might be willing to make $50,000 available to fund a national drug court organizational meeting.

I was leery of accepting money, directly or indirectly, for the purpose of establishing a drug court association. Most of us in the field, especially the judges, had ethical concerns about holding money or controlling its use. That would go double for drug-testing companies that might operate or wish to operate in our communities. I also felt that this might be the field's last opportunity to determine its own future.

Around that same time Caroline introduced me to Robin Kimbrough, a staff member at the American Bar Association who was very active on behalf of drug courts. She was a regular at conferences and trainings where drug courts were a focus. She had also visited the Miami and Oakland drug courts.

After her visit to the Oakland Drug Court we met for lunch at a restaurant in Jack London Square. We discussed the Syva offer. Robin brought to my attention a non-profit organization based in Alexandria, Virginia, the Community Anti-Drug Coalitions of America (CADCA). I learned that CADCA was a national anti-drug organization doing important work building community alliances across the U.S. It was funded by the Robert Wood Johnson Foundation (RWJ), the largest philanthropical organization in the U.S. focusing solely on health. Robin told me that CADCA might be willing to accept the moneys and handle logistics and expenses for a drug court organizational meeting.

With Robin acting as our intermediary and CADCA agreeing to accept full responsibility for the $50,000 Syva gift, I had the chance to move an organizational agenda forward. I began contacting the twenty or so existing drug courts, along with several who were actively developing a drug court.

Because of my leadership role the previous year with the informal National Coalition of Drug Court Judges, I was in a strong position to set the meeting's agenda, as well as get drug court leaders from around the nation to the table. Approximately 25 representatives from twenty jurisdictions, mostly judges, met in the United Way Building in Alexandria, Virginia, from May 9–10, 1994. Our purpose: to form a national drug court organization.

We met in the United Way's opulent boardroom, seated at an enormous conference table. We were scheduled to leave Alexandria the next afternoon, May 10, whether we were successful in creating a national organization or not. For the second and last day I had scheduled an up or down vote to force resolution on the organization's charter, mission, principles, and officers.[55]

---

55 Those present, based on documents and recollection: Judge Frank Hoover, Bakersfield, CA; Judge Jamey Weitzman, Baltimore County, MD; Judge Ronald Taylor, Berrien County, MI; Judge Jack Lehman, Clark County, NE; Judge Michael Getty, Cook County, IL; Judge Robert Fogan, Broward County, FL; Timothy Murray, Dade County, FL; Judge William Meyer, Denver County, CO; Judge John Parnham, Pensacola, FL; District Attorney Claire McCaskill, Jackson County, MO; Judge Henry Weber, Jefferson County, KY; Judge William Schma, Kalamazoo, MI; Judge Rick Martinez, King County, WA; Judge Steven Marcus, Los Angeles County, CA; Judge Sue Bolton, Maricopa County, AR; Judge Harl Hass, Multnomah County, OR; Judge Richard Gebelein, New Castle County, DE; Judge Joel Bennett, Travis County, TX; Pretrial

We got off to a slow start, with little accomplished that first day save for the mission statement and general principles. I asked for volunteers to continue to work into the night on a draft of the new organization's bylaws. We holed up in a small room at the Holiday Inn.[56]

As leader of our small group I struggled to finalize the simple bylaws, a task normally completed quite quickly. In the end Judge Bill Meyer's presence at the evening's session was the catalyst that broke the stalemate. His determination, as well as intellect and mediation skills, were key to producing a final product.

As difficult as it was to finalize our organizational structure, it was generally understood that if we didn't get it done at that meeting, we likely never would. In the end that realization was a powerful motivator. The name National Association of Drug Court Practitioners (NADCP) and the charter, as well as all officers, were approved unanimously at the second morning session. The organization was to represent and be led by individuals reflecting the entire community of practitioners involved in or interested in the drug court field.

I was elected NADCP's president; I was brimming with ideas and energy to move the organization forward. Realistically, my election may have had less to do with my popularity than my work ethic. The truth be known, there was no competition for the job. District Attorney Claire McCaskill (Kansas City, Missouri) was elected vice president. She was to be an exemplary co-leader, active in the organization and, as we contemplated the future, a wonderful strategist.[57]

Services Director John Carver III, Washington, D.C.; Chief Judge Eugene Hamilton, Washington, D.C.; Public Defender Michael Judge, Los Angeles, CA; Head Clerk Ed Brekke, Los Angeles County, CA; Judge John Schwartz, Rochester County, NY; Judge Bruce Beaudin, Washington, D.C.; Judge Bob Ziemian, Boston, MA; Drug Court Coordinator Tammy Woodhams, Kalamazoo, MI; Judge Jeffrey Tauber, Alameda County, CA.

56 I believe those who volunteered to work late to resolve organizational issues included Denver judge Bill Meyer, Rochester judge John Schwartz, D.C. federal judge Bruce Beaudin, Boston judge Bob Ziemian, Kalamazoo judge Bill Schma, and drug court coordinator Tammy Woodhams.

57 Elected as member-officers of the board of directors at the Founders Meeting: Judge Jeffrey Tauber of Alameda County, CA, elected president; Claire McCaskill, then district attorney of Kansas City, MO, elected vice president; Eugene Hamilton, presiding judge of the Federal Court in Washington, D.C., elected treasurer; Jamie Weitzman of the Baltimore Drug Court, elected secretary. Elected as board members at large: Judge Joel Bennett of the Austin Drug Court; Head Public Defender Michael Judge of the

NADCP was born on May 10, 1994. Community Anti-Drug Coalitions of America (CADCA) issued a press release announcing this momentous occasion on our new NADCP stationery, proclaiming, *DRUG COURT JUDGES AND TREATMENT PROFESSIONALS LAUNCH NEW NATIONAL ASSOCIATION.*

For me NADCP's proclamation was just one of many rites of passage crowding in on one another. I stayed on in Alexandria to meet with CADCA staff to discuss future plans. CADCA Vice President Nelson Cooney offered to formally represent NADCP in Washington, D.C., and to seek funding for our new organization. I was pleased with Nelson and CADCA's help up to that point and accepted their offer of future assistance on behalf of the NADCP board.

Nelson had commissioned a commercial artist to come up with a logo for the new organization. She showed me several options. One jumped off the page: a brilliantly conceived merger of a caduceus, the Greek symbol for the healing profession, and the gavel, a symbol for the courts. It embodied the mission of the organization better than anything I have seen since and helped establish our identity.

Republicans took back the House and Senate in the 1994 elections, the worst possible time for the drug court field. The '94 Omnibus Crime Act had authorized $1 billion for drug courts over a five-year period. Come 1995 the new Congress, under Newt Gingrich's direction, might not fund drug courts at all.

It was my task to mobilize drug court leaders (judges and DAs in particular) to lobby Congress for an appropriation. The general expectation was that there would be no Republican support for new initiatives coming out of the Clinton administration. I was counting on existing relationships between our drug court leaders and congressional members and new connections forged during our lobbying efforts for the Omnibus Crime Bill to change that.[58]

County of Los Angeles; Jack Lehman of the Las Vegas Drug Court; and Tim Murray of the Miami Drug Court.

58 Occasionally, I got lucky and actually met with an important congressional leader. One such occasion was a meeting set up by Judge Patrick Morris of San Bernardino, California, with his congressman, Jerry Lewis, powerful chair of the House Appropriations

I was able to shuttle drug court leaders—mostly judges and DAs—to visit their congressional leaders on a rotating basis. I would provide them with an informational package to leave with their legislators, including talking points, testimonials, press releases, etc. The challenge was to match important Republican members on critical committees, (such as Criminal Justice and Appropriations) with drug court judges (and others) from their jurisdictions. Too many had made herculean efforts to initiate drug court funding in 1995–1996 to list them all.[59]

Drug courts were funded to the tune of $7 million by Congress, which was barely enough to start up a drug court office at the Department of Justice, not to mention fund staff, initiate needed drug court projects (i.e., training, education, and development of standards), and provide grants to new drug courts. Still, NADCP had flexed its muscles and had once again shown its ability to influence Congress.

Curiously, our constant contact with Republicans afforded us an unexpected reward: the Edward Byrne Memorial Justice Assistance Grant. The grant was being reviewed and revised by the new Republican majority. A question remained as to whether the Republicans would continue funding it.

The answer came from Republican North Carolina Congressman Fred Heineman, who sponsored what I fondly remember as the "Heineman Amendment," extending to drug courts the honor of being one of eight valid purposes for a renewed $500 million dollar appropriation. It was a shock to all of us. At the behest of a conservative former chief of police from Raleigh, North Carolina, Congress created a specific drug court funding source for several years (until eligibility was modified once again).[60]

Committee. Pat had spoken to his friend the congressman, and he was all in. I didn't have to show him any press releases, fact sheets, or testimonials. Unfortunately, that was the exception to the rule. In the early days I spoke to some members of Congress but mostly to twenty-somethings just out of college acting as buffers for their bosses.

59 I reluctantly single out just a few (whom I can recall): Judge Richard Gebelein of Wilmington (a former attorney general for the state of Delaware and associate of then senator Joe Biden); Judge Jamie Weitzman of Baltimore, MD; Judge Steven Manley of San Jose, CA, Judge John Schwartz of Rochester, NY; Judge Harl Haas of Portland, OR; Judge Henry Weber of Louisville, KY; Judge Sue Bolton of Phoenix, AZ; Judge Ronald Taylor of St. Joseph, MI; and Judge Joel Bennett of Austin, TX.

60 Unexpected but important new statutory language required that funding be approved by local community authorities. Its effect was to encourage drug court judges and other practitioners to reach out to mayors, city council members, sheriffs, and police chiefs to build critical support for the institutionalization of drug courts in their communities.

In 1995 NADCP submitted a grant application for drug court education and training funds (which our practitioners had lobbied hard for). Instead, it was awarded to a D.C. insider with strong connections to the DOJ, Barry Mahoney's Justice Management Institute.

It became pretty obvious, even to me: NADCP would not be receiving any significant grants or project responsibilities just because we had officers and a logo—i.e., the facade of an organization—nor because we had successfully lobbied for the funding itself. To compete in the major leagues we needed to prove our capacity to initiate and implement projects on the ground and, more importantly, establish a real presence in Washington, D.C.

Since the Founders Meeting in Alexandria I had been working to establish new relationships that could benefit NADCP. I had several meetings with the staff of the Robert Wood Johnson Foundation in Princeton, New Jersey, as well as a breakfast meeting with RWJ's program director at the Claremont Hotel in the Berkeley Hills. I gave presentations and provided documentation to establish the potential of drug courts to improve the nation's health. I ran into what continued to be a vexing problem for drug courts: how to convince healthcare providers of the health benefits of drug courts. Their interest was legitimate, but some were reluctant to fund drug courts—a criminal justice entity—and saw it as outside the RWJ Foundation' mission "to improve the health and health care of all Americans."

As if on cue, the Robert Wood Johnson Foundation came to our rescue, deciding after all to fund us. The RWJ Foundation, which was Community Anti-Drug Coalitions of America's (CADCA) main funding source, would funnel funds through CADCA to NADCP, providing an incubator for the startup of a Washington, D.C., office. We would receive approximately $150,000 a year for three years in startup costs, which were intended to cover two cubicles at the CADCA Alexandria offices, along with telephone service, office equipment, and other basics. Unfortunately, we would need at least double that amount to get a credible criminal justice organization off the ground.

During my original bout of Washington fever I had focused on working within the Clinton administration. Originally, I believed the drug court director would be a position of executive-level decision-making and one with funding of $29 million for fiscal year 1995–1996 and, fancifully, $1 billion over a five-year period. I had reason to believe that I would be offered the drug court director position. At the same time the Republican takeover of the House and Senate in the 1994 election made the position substantially less attractive than it previously had been. I was also beginning to think that the federal government might not be a good fit for me. I was used to acting aggressively and then living with the consequences, a character trait that continued to get me into trouble. I might not last very long as a government bureaucrat.

Finally, if I left NADCP, it would be rudderless. No one of particular stature working within the field was interested in leaving their home and position (judgeship) to work around the clock to establish NADCP as an important national drug court practitioner organization. I believe to this day that if I had walked away before the organization had gotten off the ground, NADCP would have disappeared without a trace.

Enter Pat Morris, a San Bernardino Drug Court judge with contacts on high. I'd met Pat at the first national drug court meeting in Miami Beach, circa December 1993. He was a mentor, pushing me in the right direction politically, making contacts for me within the California Administrative Office of the Courts (AOC), and introducing me to his good friends: California Chief Justice Ron George and AOC Director Bill Vickrey.

Pat encouraged me to assume the leadership of the national drug court movement. He strongly supported my move to D.C. to head up NADCP. He offered to help arrange for a one year's leave of absence from the Oakland bench for "educational purposes." As much as I appreciated Pat's support I was still unsure that it was the right decision.

I was presenting at a TASC conference held at an Orlando hotel in 1995 when I learned that the Appropriations Committee had reduced drug court funding from $29 million to some $6.5 million. I decided that building NADCP was the better path forward for both the drug court field and for me.

With that in mind I had two brief but important encounters at that conference. First, I ran into Tim Murray; we sat down for a candid conversation. I understood that we were both vying for the Drug Court director position at the Department of Justice. I offered to support his candidacy for it if he would support funding for NADCP. He seemed surprised at the offer but accepted.

Later that afternoon I spied Laurie Robinson at the hotel pool. Until that point I had only met her twice before. She was the director of the Office of Justice Programs (OJP) and the third-ranking assistant attorney general. Her agency would have responsibility for the administration and funding under the '94 Omnibus Crime Bill, drug courts included.

Laurie had a wonderful demeanor. She remained straight-forward, fair-minded, and seemingly oblivious to the conflicts around her. Such traits made her essential to the institutionalization of drug courts, someone less interested in political power than moving a reform agenda forward.

I told her that I was withdrawing my name from consideration for the drug court director position in favor of Tim Murray and that I thought I would be more useful to the field as president of NADCP. Up to that point she only knew me as a municipal court judge from California with aspirations to run OJP's drug court office. I took a deep breath and asked her if OJP would support NADCP's education and training projects. To my surprise she enthusiastically said that they would. Specifically, she mentioned her interest in developing standards for the field.

What might later be seen as a masterful strategic maneuver could also be seen as little more than opportunism. Going into the government had been a short-term goal to advance the drug court field and my career. With that opportunity diminished I turned to a vehicle for advancement outside the government, NADCP.[61]

I was now president of NADCP. I had built an organization of community-wide practitioners from across the country. It had strong bipartisan support locally and in Congress and had demonstrated its ability to marshal political support. It was positioned to work closely with government agencies; outside of government it could lobby for reform (and funding) yet make decisions and create projects that could be implemented quickly.

Most importantly, when administrations changed, the government had no power to directly affect NADCP personnel, nor its power, structure, or survival. Case in point: the Drug Court Office within the Office of Justice Programs was discontinued by the Bush administration in 2001, but to this day NADCP continues its close cooperation with DOJ, Health and Human Services, and other governmental agencies, as well as with its congressional allies.

Once I had secured both the Robert Wood Johnson Foundation's and Assistant Attorney General Laurie Robinson's commitment to support NADCP, I moved to request a one-year's leave of absence from my judicial

---

61 I had one other significant meeting at that Treatment Alternatives to Street Crime (TASC) conference in Orlando. The TASC Board of Directors asked me to make a presentation, so I spoke briefly on how drug courts and TASC programs could collaborate. Melody Heaps, then president of TASC's board and director of Chicago's TASC program, was the most powerful person in the room. I had visited her Chicago TASC program (TASC's flagship program) the previous year and had been impressed. She put it to me directly: Drug courts needed to be part of TASC; without a strong organization behind me, NADCP would never survive. I thanked her for the offer but demurred, noting that I would have to take the offer to the board—a board dominated by judges. Any talk of a merger with TASC stopped right there. Everyone knew judges to be notoriously jealous of their prerogatives. It was a position I was to utilize in deflecting the ambitions of more than one acquisitive organization.

position. I didn't want to give up my career as a judge to launch NADCP's office, and with Republican Pete Wilson as governor, it was unlikely that I, a liberal judge, would be reappointed to the bench.

Judge Morris took care of the details, dealing with the Judicial Council, which had to approve the leave, as well as Bill Vickrey and the chief justice. I would request and be granted a year's leave, constitutionally the longest period a California judge could be away from the bench.

My first exposure to the sharp elbows of D.C. life was dealing with the Denver-based Justice Management Institute (JMI). Barry Mahoney, its founder and director, was a close friend of the newly appointed drug court director at the DOJ, Tim Murray.

JMI trainings seemed to be the cost of doing business. After Tim Murray had apparently given the go-ahead to fund NADCP projects, I received a budget from JMI, which had previously been awarded overall training and education funding for drug courts. I had been led to believe and expected to receive sufficient funds to set up a bare-bones shop in D.C., having requested $250,000. The document faxed to Oakland showed NADCP receiving some $100,000 out of a $500,000 training budget.

I was floored. It was October of 1995 and I was preparing to leave for D.C. to hire an assistant director. I was requesting substantially less compensation than I was receiving as a judge in California, and my chief of staff was to receive approximately half that, for a grand total of $200,000. The money that Barry had put on the table was half that amount.

I stopped in Denver on my way to D.C. and sat down with Barry on his home veranda for a very direct conversation. When I told him that I had a revised budget that split OJP funding into two, he blanched and said that was impossible. I argued that we could provide the technical support and expertise required for the project. He said that he did not believe we had the experience or expertise to provide that assistance. We went round and round, with seemingly no resolution in the offing.

I told him that I would be meeting with Laurie Robinson in Washington within the next few days and would show her the proposed budgets and ask for her assistance. I knew I was going over the head of Drug Court Office Director Tim Murray to Laurie Robinson, also a friend of Barry Mahoney, but felt that it was critical to NADCP's survival. It was a trial lawyer's bluff, but I left Denver with an NADCP budget of approximately $200,000, enough to survive on along with the resources provided through the incubator funding.

The Justice Management Institute wasn't the only one setting up road-blocks that I had to overcome in establishing NADCP. With Tim Murray now the drug court director, he and I had meetings on how NADCP was to use its funding. He didn't think much of NADCP's capabilities—or mine, for that matter—but he agreed to limited support for NADCP.

He authorized NADCP's assistance in JMI trainings and my plans for regionally focused mentor courts. And then he surprised me: he told me he wanted NADCP to develop standards for the drug court field, apparently something on everyone's agenda, including Laurie Robinson's. Laurie was and would continue to be NADCP's and my guardian angel.

I was now president of the National Association of Drug Court Professionals and on my way to set up a Washington, D.C., office. I was on something of a roll, frequently interviewed by the media, presenting at conferences, and holding meetings with governmental, professional, and business elites. I was working twelve-plus hours a day. My wife was not happy about my workload or my plans to temporarily move to D.C., but at the time she supported me. I think she thought that if I could reach the top of the mountain, I would stop climbing.

It was hard to explain to her then, as it is to myself today, why I felt so committed to the field's success and my belief that I needed to lead. I suffered from Stanley Goldstein Syndrome: I was happiest as a judge presiding over my drug court. It was enormously demanding and emotionally draining work, and I loved it.

Then I was torn away from my calling.

That I found myself on the national stage, inspiring others to change the way they treated drug offenders, was surprising and exhilarating. This was more than ambition. I felt blessed to be given an opportunity few would know: to create an organization that would be an engine for criminal justice reform. I now had a vision of what a single individual with conviction, energy, and audacity could accomplish, and I intended to see that vision through.

CHAPTER 12

MISTER MAGIC

In October of 1995 I flew east to finalize preparations for the grand opening of NADCP. I had one overriding goal: to convince the governmental and organizational elites in D.C. that we were for real, that we were capable of providing the services and programs we had been touting the past two years, and that we could stand toe-to-toe with existing NGOs.

If there was one thing I was pretty sure of, it was that we weren't welcome at the dinner table. Organizations would test the loyalty of our practitioner members (read: judges), the soundness of our programs, and the capabilities of our staff. From time to time those organizations would offer to partner with us (read: take us over), but their clear preference was that we quietly go away. There just wasn't enough room at the table.

Actually, their assumptions about NADCP weren't far off. NADCP was, as said, built with smoke and mirrors. I would make claims as to our accomplishments and capabilities that were often (to be kind to myself) exaggerations; then we would go out and accomplish whatever we said we would, with an innovator's energy and focus. That included our publications, trainings, organizational innovations, programming, and conferences.

I had intentionally chosen an ambitious agenda for our first several months in D.C., which called for me to assume the role of political leader, lobbyist, educator, administrator, presenter, writer, propagandist, organizer, and conference planner. My ability to rise to the occasion would clearly be tested, and soon. I found myself working 12/7 and more, and there was always some unexpected emergency that needed to be dealt with.

Columbus Day weekend I interviewed fifteen-plus applicants for the position of chief of staff (although, given the reality, the title may have been a bit grandiose). One applicant stood out: Marc Pearce. He had a master's degree in business administration, an engaging personality, a keen intellect, and he was a pragmatist (reality had never been one of my strengths). He also had once stood before a judge, had been charged with drug possession, and had been given a second chance.

Marc handled our finances, was a wonderful sounding-board, and, unfortunately for him, an excellent editor (my computer skills at the time were nil, amounting to little more than placing sticky notes on computer monitors). NADCP's staff was complete—all two of us—as we approached January 1996.

I leased a ground-floor garden apartment with a bricked-in terrace, facing east for morning sun, which was critical to a Californian. It was on Polk Street in Alexandria, just two blocks from our incubator organization, CADCA, and one block from the Potomac River. I rented furniture and a car for the year. I was set.[62]

CADCA was led by its President Jim Copple and Vice President Nelson Cooney. I took care to deal with Jim as little as possible, as he tended to be intense and mercurial. Nelson was conservative by my lights—he had been on Drug Czar William Bennett's staff—but we agreed on more things than not. He became an important advisor and a good friend (his calm and sense of humor eased many a tense moment).[63]

One early incident demonstrated the pressures we were all under. During my first week on the job Jim Copple called me into his office (never a good sign). He opened by quietly telling me about his hopes for NADCP.

Suddenly, he began screaming at me—words to the effect of, "You'd better not screw this up," and "You're not getting a second chance," and "You and Marc better make sure you can deliver."

I was speechless.

Apparently, Marc and I weren't the only ones feeling the pressure for NADCP to succeed. I was a bit confused and shaken—we hadn't done anything for Jim to complain about. In fact, we hadn't done anything at all up to that point. I left Jim's office mystified about his anger and wondering whether his outburst might have something to do with our competitors (some bad-mouthing about Marc and myself had been making the rounds).

Stopping by Nelson's cubicle to tell him what had just happened, he said that it was just Jim's way and not to take it personally. Thinking back on that incident, Nelson was probably right; it was something like a preemptive strike.

---

62 Our office was located on Polk Street in Alexandria, Virginia, a fifteen-minute drive from Washington, D.C. For the purposes of this book, I will refer to it as the D.C. office.
63 Community Anti-Drug Coalitions of America was to play a central role in the development of NADCP from the Founders Meeting in 1994 until we left their umbrella and offices in 1997. In so many ways it proved to be a blessing, and my appreciation goes out to both organizations for their critical assistance at NADCP's inception.

Jim, expecting the worst and how it might reflect on CADCA and him, prepared us for adversity by trying to frighten us out of our wits.

We all had a lot to be worried about. We had four months to start up a functioning national organization, provide innovative education and training across the nation, and put on a major conference. That we would consistently come up with effective and innovative initiatives and complete our projects on time was something Jim had no way of knowing. And, I suppose, neither did we.

Even with Jim Copple spreading fear and woe, CADCA turned out to be a terrific workplace (I had a corner cubicle next to Nelson and Marc). It was a mostly open-plan space within a building with a large atrium at its center. It was two blocks from the Potomac River, on the north end of Alexandria, and about fifteen minutes from the White House. A wonderful path ran along the Potomac all the way to Mount Vernon, which I jogged frequently.

The beginnings of our new NADCP offices were inauspicious, to say the least. I arrived in D.C. on the first Wednesday in January of 1996. After two days of continuous snow, the storm stopped long enough for my plane to touch down. Almost immediately it began to snow again and continued for two days (the newspaper claimed it to be the worst snowstorm in 97 years).

I found my barren condo situated in Alexandria, Virginia, without a chair to sit on. I turned on the heat and, thankfully, found that it worked. I opened my luggage to unpack my belongings: no heavy clothes, gloves, or sweaters— mostly just muscle shirts, shorts, floppies, and such. Apparently, I had grabbed the wrong bag when leaving Oakland.

The condo manager advised that I shouldn't expect any deliveries or mail for at least a week, maybe two. The D.C. area was not prepared for even minimal snowfall. That first night I slept on the floor next to the heating ducts with Hawaiian shirts draped over me. It would be two weeks before I would have rental furniture delivered and almost as long for my personal effects to arrive.

But that was alright with me. Alexandria's streets were empty, with snow falling quietly on the Polk Street clock. I was mesmerized that first night as I wandered the streets of Alexandria in my heavy winter jacket, running shoes, and jeans.

The next day I walked the two blocks to NADCP's new offices, located at Community Anti-Drug Coalitions of America. Because the federal government had shut down due to the snow, I was the only one there. I enjoyed the quiet and took the opportunity to get organized so that we could move forward when the weather permitted.

It was during this slow time, with the federal government, schools, and CADCA offices closed, that I received my first official phone call. It was from Jose Cerda, my friend at the White House, welcoming me to D.C. After exchanging pleasantries he invited me to take part in a panel discussion on youth and drug abuse, to be hosted by President Clinton at a Maryland high school. An auspicious beginning for NADCP after all.

I arrived at the designated high school auditorium for the panel only to learn that President Clinton would lead the discussion with some fifteen national leaders and me. Among the panelists were Vice President Al Gore, Jesse Jackson, James Welch (CEO of General Electric), and other luminaries. I sat on the far right of a semicircular table with my heart pumping and a few notes scrawled on a napkin (the gist of which was probably the name of the organization I represented and my own name).

The president asked prepared questions, and the panel responded appropriately. Late in the discussion, when I was thinking I wouldn't have an opportunity to speak, I saw an opening and introduced myself and NADCP, then offered a somewhat wordy rejoinder to a previously asked question. I have no recollection of the question or answer, but from the attention paid to my response, I got the impression that I had passed the banality test.

But that's not the point of the story. I had previously met Bill Clinton at formal events. He knew me as a judge who played tenor sax and, given his own music history (he also played tenor sax), we related a bit.

I was serving as chair of the Oakland Arts Commission when Clinton was elected president. I wanted to do something special for him that might focus his attention on Oakland and actually get through some of the noise surrounding his inauguration. Thus, on behalf of Oakland Arts, I commissioned a gold-plated tenor saxophone mouthpiece for the new president (the product of master craftsman and alto sax player Fred Lamberson) inscribed with the words *William Jefferson Clinton, In Celebration* and the date of his inauguration, *January 20, 1993.*

The next problem was how to get the mouthpiece to him. I knew that every sax player's dream was to discover that special mouthpiece that would turn aimless noodling into threads of gold. If I could get that mouthpiece to the president, I knew he would play it.

Because at the time I was an Oakland judge with no connection to the White House, I paid a visit to Oakland Mayor Elihu Harris and asked if he could present the mouthpiece as a gift from the city of Oakland. He said he would. I was home when C-SPAN aired coverage of the U.S. Conference of Mayors with the new president as speaker. On screen was Oakland's Mayor, Elihu Harris, fighting his way through the throng of mayors to present what was unmistakably a clear plastic box containing a saxophone mouthpiece.

It was at that Maryland high school, approximately two years after that C-SPAN broadcast, that I spied the president standing alone on stage; an unusual occurrence. I screwed up my courage and approached.

When I introduced myself, he appeared to remember me: he smiled broadly and shook my hand. I asked him, "Have you gotten to play the gold-plated tenor saxophone mouthpiece presented by Oakland Mayor Elihu Harris?"

His eyes lit up. He slapped me on the back and hugged me and said in his southern drawl, "That's my favorite mouthpiece. I play it in the Blue Room all the time."

To say I was speechless would be an understatement. We continued to talk about saxophones, mouthpieces, and music. Eventually, we were swept up in a flood of eager spectators. I'd had my first real conversation with Bill Clinton and had spoken at a high-level gathering of national leaders. I was to be invited to many events at the White House, and I liked to think that that engraved mouthpiece had something to do with it.

With the snow in abatement, Marc and I began putting together our strategic plan for the year. A high priority for the organization was interaction with the White House, the Department of Justice, and Congress. We presented at or were part of a number of White House events, appeared at hearings on drug-court-related matters, and met with government officials, congressional members, and their staff members who were interested in the potential of the drug court.

Jose or other government officials often contacted me before 8:00 AM to request that I appear at a hearing or meeting by 10:00 AM. As I lived two blocks from CADCA offices in Alexandria, I could be in my Sunday best at a congressional hearing within an hour. My job was to wave the flag and establish NADCP in the minds of the Washington elite as a vibrant, aggressive, and credible community-based and judge-centric organization standing at the center of the drug court world.

At one White House gathering soon after I arrived in D.C., I was introduced to General Barry McCaffrey, the newly appointed director of the Office of National Drug Control Policy (ONDCP). He stood straight and tall, perhaps 5'10" and of moderate build. After I introduced myself he looked me up and down and spoke plainly. He told me right off that he wasn't convinced of the effectiveness of drug courts but that he was open to persuasion. I told him that was more than fair, that we only wanted to make sure he had relevant information and an opportunity to visit drug courts so he could make up his own mind. He said that was exactly what he would do.

I moved around the Second Floor Gallery, looking for anyone who might be of help to the new organization. I approached these White House gatherings with real trepidation, as mixing with the political elite was still difficult for me. Still, I put on my best smile and approached Donna Shalala, Secretary of Health and Human Services. I introduced myself as a judge and the president of the National Association of Drug Court Professionals. I expressed an interest in talking to her about drug courts. She looked at me as if I had two heads and kept on walking. I took the rejection and moved on to new potential contacts.

As has been written by many before, these "get-togethers" were mostly about meeting and greeting those who could advance your career, organization, or agenda. When the person you were talking to started peering over your shoulder, you knew your moment was over and that they were about to move on. It happened all the time.

INTERLUDE 5

HEDZOLEH SOUNDZ

I was playing regularly at blues club "Louie's Place" on Telegraph Avenue in Berkeley. One night, Pajo, a Ghanaian bass player, sat down next to me. He said he liked my playing and invited me to join his band.

His band was Hedzoleh Soundz. It had been the most popular band in Ghana, West Africa, during the 1970s. The great South African trumpet player Hugh Masekela released an enormously popular recording of their music, "Introducing Hedzoleh Soundz," in 1973 (that same year I had travelled through Ghana unawares). Masekela then toured Europe and the United States with

Hedzoleh Soundz as his backup band. They had crisscrossed the U.S., playing with the likes of the Pointer Sisters. Masekela and the band eventually parted company, apparently due to the band members' indulgences, and the band had washed up on Oakland's shores.

At the time I thought this could be my ticket out of criminal lawyering. We played our first gig at a club on San Pablo Avenue in Berkeley called "Ruthie's Inn." It was a disaster. We hadn't rehearsed (or maybe it just sounded that way). Half the musicians appeared to be playing in different keys.

But then again, certain songs came together almost magically. They were both enchanting and kick-ass. At times I felt as if I was floating above the bandstand. When this band was on, there was no way to be in the hall and not have a big grin on your face. I decided that this was a band that would make great music and that I wanted to be a part of. I stayed with the band and took over managing it with my friend John Webb.

Hedzoleh Soundz was to be a mixed blessing. The band members were extraordinary musicians but crazy. Sometimes they would walk out on the gig during a break and "forget" to come back.

Playing with them I became a better musician, though managing the band was a daunting experience. We performed several times a month. I rented the trap drums that Salas, the drummer, used for gigs. As predictably as Charlie Brown, Lucy, and the football, he would call me up on Friday afternoons to tell me he had hocked the drum set. Under most circumstances, if someone does that to you once, they never get to do it again. But Salas was a spectacular performer. He was the only trap drummer I knew who played with curved African sticks. He was a master musician and a hard person to fire. After several such incidents I took to carrying the drums around in my car to prevent Salas from hocking them to "buy milk for his children."

My stint as manager and musician with Hedzoleh Soundz came to an abrupt close after playing with the band for almost three years. We were working our way up to better-paying, more prestigious gigs and were to play the Great American Music Hall, a major music venue in San Francisco. I was concerned about the stress level in the band. With Hedzoleh Soundz anxiety often translated to substance abuse, especially alcohol. I kept my eye on Niama, our lead singer—all 4' 10" and 90 pounds of him. He took the stage after drinking a pint of gin and proceeded to do his worst show ever. He literally hung onto the mic to keep from falling. I quit the band that night.

CHAPTER 13

THE DAYS OF WINE AND ROSES

Once I had moved to D.C. my immediate challenge was to establish the NADCP Mentor Drug Court Network, which would link aspiring drug court practitioners to regional mentor sites across the nation. The process I envisioned would provide regional trainings at mentor drug court sites and visits to the courts themselves and with their practitioners. It wasn't so much a new concept as an amalgamation of a number of learning methodologies delivered via a regionally focused mentor court network.[64]

I would carry the NADCP flag and introduce myself and NADCP to a somewhat isolated drug court community, hoping to find great mentor sites while providing education and training along the way. Over the first several months I visited some twenty drug courts. I would go it alone, toting signage and educational materials. At one point I visited a half-dozen sites over a two-week period. I observed the court in action, consulted with the judge, then provided a half-day training for potential drug courts and their practitioners before moving on to the next drug court. Like many a serial traveler I would sometimes forget which city I was in and, on occasion, the audience I was addressing.

One of my most difficult tasks was critiquing the judge. Many seemed to feel they were doing a terrific job but weren't. It's hard to imagine a more difficult audience.

---

64 During NADCP's early years I was a part of the Justice Management Institute's Drug Court Trainings, which took place at NADCP mentor courts. The program typically consisted of two days of team-based training and a half-day visit to the mentor court (to observe the court in action and hold practitioner-based roundtable discussions). Local practitioners would volunteer to be team leaders and spend extra time with their professional colleagues. The mentor court judge was almost always a gracious host. Most importantly, the mentor court and its practitioners turned out to be extraordinarily effective advocates for drug court among their fellow prospective practitioners.

I learned to start the consultation with positive comments before easing into a discussion of a court's problems. I was often confronted with judges who would brush aside criticism or act as though they didn't hear them. It is a problem, unfortunately, that is not exclusively the province of judges.

I resisted attempts to water down the regionally based, practitioner-centric focus of NADCP, which I was convinced was one of our greatest strengths. A mutual admiration society was developing, with NADCP extolling the virtues of its drug courts and their leaders. At the same time those local drug court leaders advocated for NADCP and its agenda on the state and national levels. What made our drug court judges particularly effective was the fact that more than half (by my calculations) were former prosecutors. The combination of being a judge and former prosecutor proved to make for an extremely effective advocate.[65]

Relying on local drug court leaders could, of course, also pose a danger to a new field that had its share of flakes. Paul Anderson was an enormously popular district attorney and Payne County Drug Court leader in Stillwater, Oklahoma. He was a great talker, a wonderful advocate for drug courts, and a terrific traveling companion. He was also forced to resign as district attorney of Payne County, Oklahoma, in June of 1996, after being convicted of embezzling $84,000 from the county and sentenced to serve two years in state prison. We never attempted to decertify Stillwater as a mentor site though. Instead, we held our collective breath as the media, for the most part, ignored Paul's connection with drug court.

On the road I was always on the lookout for judges and others who had that special quality that makes for an exceptional drug court judge or practitioner. As an example, I was invited to Dallas–Fort Worth to talk about drug court and met a number of judges and other practitioners at my presentations. Judge John Creuzot of Dallas, a droll and seemingly humble charmer (who for the past 25 years has insisted on calling me "Judge") was a perfect example. He was intrigued by the concept but not sold on the idea of becoming a drug court judge. I met with him privately to convince him to start a drug court in Dallas.

---

65 Extraordinary practitioners, mostly judges, were taking the lead in their communities and across their states, people like Eugene Hamilton and Jay Carver of Washington, D.C.; Ron Reinstein of Phoenix; John Creuzot and Joel Bennett of Dallas and Austin; Jack Lehman and John Marr of Las Vegas; Steven Manley, Steven Marcus, Pat Morris, and Frank Hoover of San Jose, Los Angeles, San Bernardino, and Bakersfield; Claire McCaskill of Kansas City; John Schwartz and Robert Russell of Rochester and Buffalo; Jamey Weitzman of Baltimore; Bob Ziemian of Boston; Bill Meyer of Denver, and so many others.

John was one of the drug court movement's most impressive success stories. He became a highly successful and innovative drug court judge, and Dallas became a mentor site. Later, John applied his charm to the legislative and executive branches of government, successfully advocating for drug court expansion and, more generally, court-based rehabilitation, which helped make Texas a leader in prison reform. In 2018 he was elected district attorney of Dallas County.[66]

We put out a special monograph at the 1996 Conference, "NADCP Mentor Drug Court Network: A Regional Approach to Technical Assistance." The monograph described the available mentor courts and encouraged all interested parties to contact nearby mentor courts through our offices, visit them, meet with their drug court practitioners, and establish a mentoring relationship with that court. American University in D.C. informed us that hundreds of visits and thousands of visitors to those mentor court sites were to follow.[67]

The mentor court model made mentor drug courts and their practitioners the regional arms of NADCP's education and training program. A friendly competition emerged among drug courts to become a mentor site, as it had become something of an honor over time.

Finally, mentor courts were an effective educational alternative to the typical federal training pattern then in vogue, where consulting organizations with no expertise or experience in a field—sometimes derisively called "beltway bandits"—would apply for federal grants, receive funding, and hire practitioners to send into the field to provide minimal, short-term assistance.[68]

It was to be expected that non-profits, as well as academic organizations, would look wistfully at drug courts as a new field to colonize. These organizations would typically move into a field, absorb the training and education

---

66 While traveling across the nation I visited a number of potential mentor court sites. I was looking for geographic, offender, staff, and demographic diversity, as well as judicial and program effectiveness. Of the sites I visited in those early months, eight were found to be appropriate as mentor sites: San Jose, CA; Pensacola, FL; Louisville, KY; Kalamazoo, MI; Las Vegas, NV; Rochester, N.Y.; Stillwater, O.K.; and Washington, D.C.

67 By 1998 the DOJ Drug Court Office had funded the expansion of the mentor court network to fifteen drug courts (described in a monograph published for the 1998 national conference). In fact, the mentor court network was so successful that Assistant Attorney General and Director of the Office of Justice Programs Laurie Robinson told me she had used NADCP's mentor courts as a model for other DOJ projects.

68 My own progress as a trainer, presenter, and educator in the drug court field owed much to Barry Mahoney and his organization, JMI. Barry was one the smartest and most experienced judicial educators in the country—and undoubtedly the fastest talker. I watched him closely and took notes.

funds available, and distribute them strategically to cooperative practitioners. With the Clinton administration starting up, most in the field believed that drug court funding was on its way. And whoever controlled those funds would likely control the field.

Planning the D.C. national conference turned out to be more than a full-time job. While traveling across the country I was getting out the word to the field and organizing the conference agenda and its training sessions while searching for prospective conference presenters. I was lucky to have Marc as a partner. We spent hundreds of hours working on the conference agenda and presentations, knowing that this one event could make or break NADCP. We brought a temp on board to help with the increased clerical workload and relied on CADCP's conference planner to help us with conference logistics.[69]

I had been experimenting with a new format based on shows like "Oprah." I had good reason to try a new format. First of all, nearly everyone was bored with existing drug court presentations. Judges dominated as presenters, and their presentations tended to be judge-centric and somewhat duplicative. I felt that a more active moderator-focused format could work for an organization like ours, as we were just starting out, with relatively inexperienced present-ers and little research, science, or technical expertise to present in a formal presentation.

The "Oprah" format consisted of four or five experienced (and diverse) practitioners sitting at a table with stationary microphones and a modera-tor with a cordless mic. The moderator allowed each panelist five minutes to speak to the session topic. Beyond that the moderator was to take charge, asking probing questions and keeping answers focused and rejoinders short so that some heat and hopefully light would emerge.

At that point the discussion would be opened up and the moderator would include the audience in the general discussion. Above all else the moderator was to block any panelist's move from their shared table to the podium, which in most cases was the kiss of death to a lively discussion. The audience was often filled with drug court practitioners with useful information they were eager to share, and it wasn't unusual to discover new talent—future present-ers—in the audience.

---

69 Our conference was held at the Renaissance Hotel in Washington, D.C., May 9–12. Our plan called for seven tracks made up of five workshops each, for a total of 35 work-shops requiring approximately two hundred presenters. We sought presenters across the practitioner spectrum with a high level of experience, competence, and diversity (geo-graphic, gender, racial, and cultural).

We threw the conference open to sessions that had the potential for conflict and controversy. Even our least articulate panelists had opinions on sanctions and incentives, program eligibility, and treatment alternatives. We urged panelists to leave their presentations at home and show up without preplanned comments. Non-practitioners were passed over for practitioners when practicable, acknowledging that specialties would be dealt with through an expert's formal presentation, i.e., evaluations, data, drug testing, and research, among others.

We had used this format with mixed results at the first NADCP National Conference held January 8–11, 1995, at the Golden Nugget Hotel in the heart of downtown Las Vegas. We had over 400 attendees and perhaps a total of twenty workshops over the course of the four-day conference. The workshop rooms were small and crowded (with many audience members sitting on the floor and against the walls).[70]

We worked at embedding "community" into the very fabric of the conference. In the early days of the drug court movement I was able to cobble together a small coalition of activist drug court leaders from a number of courts nationwide. Engaging 200 practitioners as presenters at a single conference turned out to be an extraordinarily effective way to recognize the contributions of the many and build a sense of drug court community and loyalty to NADCP. It also helped that we were able to get federal agencies to foot the bill for presenters over the first few critical years.

In most jurisdictions, judges and other criminal justice leaders faced numerous obstacles and opponents to get a drug court off the ground. Our purpose was to provide common ground for all, encouraging the sharing of information and ideas while creating a support network for a geographically and culturally disparate group.[71]

_____

70 The crowded workshop conditions turned out to be a net positive, if getting to know and engage with one another was a goal, which it was. The one problem was that our moderators had difficulty with the format. They were mostly judges who monopolized the discussion, focused on their own experiences, or allowed presenters to give prepared presentations. I was determined not to let this happen in D.C. I had separate meetings with moderators and panelists and made sure everyone understood the ground rules: direct questions, short answers, and no long introductions or presentations by the moderator. The idea was to keep it a discussion and not a series of lectures.

71 During my tenure the conference typically featured two formal luncheons and a sumptuous dinner featuring live music and dancing on the last night of the conference. The events were mostly subsidized by sponsors. Our banquet at the Renaissance Hotel was an impressive gala, with many in gowns and tuxedos. The band itself was a terrific ten-piece ensemble whom I had enlisted. And, of course, I got to play a few tunes with the band.

By industry standards we were spending too much on our conferences and not realizing enough profit, but it was also part of the plan: create a dedicated core of followers in a sometimes hostile world, put on great conferences (involving as many practitioners as possible), and provide a sense of belonging and community for everyone.[72]

From the responses we received at the 1996 D.C. conference, we had achieved our goals. We had put on a first-class (even groundbreaking) conference. Approximately one thousand people attended (double the previous year), enormous enthusiasm was generated, and accolades were received. We had engaged our audience, excited our practitioners, convinced our detractors, and expanded our support base. As importantly, we had convinced the Washington elite that we were for real, that NADCP would be a force to be reckoned with.

Drug courts were encouraged to come as teams and bring along their skeptics: DAs, public defenders, legislators, sheriffs, etc. NADCP conferences earned a well-deserved reputation as the place where drug court teams coalesced, judges became human beings, and non-believers became converts.

People told me what an outstanding job I was doing at NADCP and how I was making an impact that no one believed possible. All I knew was that I was exhilarated by the events of the past year. I had navigated a one-year leave of absence, moved to D.C., established a legitimate organization with real accomplishments, and produced a much-heralded, innovative conference.

By moving across the country to live among strangers and fight for survival in a political jungle—with competitors plotting and hoping for my demise—I had also left my family. My wife had filed for divorce a month earlier, and I could no longer sleep through the night, resulting in a sinus infection that plagued me till winter's end.

At the close of the conference I talked to a Brazilian psychologist who was impressed by the event. She said I should be enormously proud of what I had accomplished in such a short period of time, that I had provided the leadership and vision to make the conference a huge success. At the time I had a hard time hearing her with all the distractions in my life. It didn't sink in. Even today it feels like a dream.

---

72 Complete contact information was provided to all participants as they left the conference.

CHAPTER 14

I GOT RHYTHM

The year 1997 proved to be a critical year for NADCP: a time to consolidate the gains of the previous activist years, focus on establishing a standardized drug court model, feature community partnerships, and institutionalize the drug court on local, state, and national levels.

As I approached the end of my first year as president of a fledgling non-profit, I had a decision to make. I had been granted a single year's leave of absence in order to go to D.C. and build an "education and training organization." That was my charge, and I had done better than I could have imagined, but the year was almost over, and I had to decide whether to stay or return to Oakland and my judgeship.

Beyond the finality of resigning from the bench at the age of 50 and giving up a judgeship that I had sacrificed so much to attain, I faced serious financial penalties should I stay in D.C. My pension would be frozen at eight years, rather than the full pension I would receive after standard retirement at twenty years, a reduction of some 75%. On top of that I would remain a municipal court judge, even though all municipal court judges in California were uniformly elevated to the superior court that year.[73]

Against those penalties I weighed the possibility of building an organization that could serve as the base for widespread reform of the criminal justice system. NADCP—now respected and even somewhat feared—was sitting at the table along with other organizations and putting on major conferences. We were working the hill as an effective lobbyist and were the subject of admiration and approval of politicians on both sides of the aisles. We were training drug court practitioners across the nation through NADCP's Mentor Drug

---

73 In 1996 the legislature put Proposition 220 on the ballot. Everyone expected the passage of the "Trial Court Consolidation Act," which would create a single court in California in 1997, the California Superior Court. It passed.

Court Network and making astonishing progress in expanding the number of courts in the field.

It was a painful decision to make, though one that was never really much in doubt. If I walked away from NADCP it would likely collapse like a house of cards, and I couldn't allow that. I wrote to Oakland's presiding judge at the time, Carlos Ynostroza, and Administrative Office of the Courts Director Bill Vickrey, resigning from the California bench.[74]

Conceptually, national standards would be at the heart of NADCP. By the end of 1996 the criminal justice system was growing to accept drug courts. We clearly ran the risk of having the field hijacked by other organizations, but the greater danger was always that the concept would be subverted and co-opted by existing state bureaucracies.

There was no question that drug court would be a major challenge for the court system. For too many the way to implement a reform was to do as little as possible. In the case of drug courts such a gestural approach might simply be adding drug court signage to the front of a court department and continue on as before. It has happened again and again over the history of court reform: the existing conventional approach usurps and swallows reform whole, resulting in little more than superficial change.

Developing fieldwide standards was critical to maintaining the integrity of the drug court model and an important way to move drug court reform forward. Laurie Robinson and Tim Murray wanted NADCP to promulgate standards, and so did I. Standards could be used to enlighten the field as to how a model drug court works, inform potential mentor court sites of the model's optimal features, and create parameters for future drug court grant applicants.

After NADCP's 1996 D.C. conference, Marc and I began to make plans to develop drug court standards that could be distributed at our 1997 L.A. conference. I was convinced that standards had to be the product of a democratic process, meaning not dominated by the traditional power brokers: judges and DAs. We chose twelve representatives diverse in profession, ethnicity, geography, gender, and background. Many others wanted to be on the committee, but we needed to limit the number of participants to those who had expertise, experience in the field, and the ability to do committee work.[75]

---

74 Largely on the back of our successes in 1996, we were to receive $30 million in funding for drug court grant programs for 1997–1998, more than four times the funding of our initial grant of $6.5 million in the 1995–1996 budget.

75 The members of the NADCP Standards Committee were: Bill Meyer, (Judge, Denver); Ed Brekke (Court Administrator, Los Angeles.); Jay Carver (Director, D.C.

My most important task was choosing the chairperson. Bill Meyer, an ex-assistant U.S. attorney and Denver's Drug Court judge who had been so important in the writing of NADCP's bylaws, was my choice for chair. He was extremely bright, hardworking, conscientious, an excellent mediator, and a good taskmaster. He agreed to be our Standards Project chair.

Vice chair of the committee, John Marr, was director of the Choices Group treatment program, which operated out of the Las Vegas Drug Court. John was a thoughtful and clear-thinking presence on the committee.

I had met a DOJ employee during funding talks at the Bureau of Justice Assistance during the Bush years who had impressed me. Jodi Foreman was no longer at the DOJ and had opted to form a one-woman consulting firm, Dogwood Institute, out of Charlottesville, Virginia. I contacted her and asked her to assist in pulling the standards together. She somewhat reluctantly accepted this long-distance assignment and turned out to be superb selection, hardworking and very outspoken about her view of the standards process. With the three most important players on board, we were ready to begin.

Our first meeting took place in Alexandria, and we had a full house. Ideas flew around the room. We were all too familiar with "standards" documents made up of hundreds of pages of small type that were almost impossible to navigate and were too often tossed aside. This document would be different: statements of principle followed by examples of those principles at work—no small print. It was to be a document you could read and absorb in an hour, nothing fancy or complicated, with the ten commandments of the drug court that could be easily understood and followed.[76]

It took more than one general meeting and several executive sessions with Bill, Jodi, John, and myself before the document approached its final form. We were on a tight schedule, pushing to complete the document by early

---

Pretrial Services Agency); Caroline Cooper (Director, Drug Court Clearinghouse, American U.); Jane Kennedy (Executive Director, TASC); Barry Mahoney (President, Justice Management Institute); John Marr (CEO, Choices Unlimited, Las Vegas); Carlos Martinez (Assistant Public Defender, Miami); Molly Merrigan (Assistant Prosecutor, Kansas City, M.O.); Ana Oliveira (Director, Samaritan Village, Briarwood, N.Y.); Roger Peters (Associate Professor, Florida Mental Health Institute, USF, Tampa); and Frank Tapia (Probation Officer, Oakland). In addition to myself (an ex officio member of the committee as NADCP President), Marilyn Roberts (Director, Drug Courts Program Office, DOJ) took part in the writing process.

76 I was determined to make "community" a cornerstone of drug court standards, using whatever leverage I had to inject community and partnership into nearly every key component and, finally, to be showcased in the final key component, #10: Forging partnerships among drug courts, public agencies, and community-based organizations generates local support and enhances drug court program effectiveness.

spring. Our '97 national conference was in May, and I wanted to make standards the focus of the entire conference. To do that the document had to be peer reviewed, approved by the DOJ, and published all before the event. Bill, Jodi, and John did a terrific job putting the document together in such a short period of time.[77]

It's hard to say what makes one document successful and another not so much, but whatever it was, the "Ten Key Components" had it. It became the drug court bible, found in virtually every drug court across the nation. It was referred to and relied on in discussions and arguments as to how to set up a drug court, and it was a continuing source of guidance to existing programs (and, importantly, used as eligibility criteria for federal and state drug court funding grants across the nation).

It was followed by drug courts throughout the U.S., particularly since NADCP had engendered so much good will from its members, the practitioners. By acknowledging their expertise and experience, by involving them (by the hundreds) in our panel discussions and presentations, by involving their courts as mentor sites (a status to which many courts aspired), we were able to create an environment and a community in which the "Ten Key Components" could take root and thrive.[78]

One of the decisions made pre-conference in 1998 that had enormous ramifications was to directly take on the issue of emerging state drug court organizations and state agencies responsible for drug court administration.

NADCP's prime focuses up till this point were national projects (i.e., the "Ten Key Components" and the National Mentor Drug Court Network). Courts were, in the end, mostly state structures, and states needed to be involved as principle partners. It was already happening in California, New York, and a few other states where steps were being taken to recognize, regulate, and fund drug courts.

We could very easily end up in a tug-of-war with those state judicial agencies and emerging state drug court associations if we didn't act preemptively.

---

77 The work of the Standards Committee was split into two sub-committees. Bill led the Standards Committee's subcommittee on criminal justice issues, and John Marr chaired the Standards Committee's treatment subcommittee.

78 The document, "Defining Drug Courts: The Ten Key Components," was reviewed, approved, and published before our third NADCP conference in Los Angeles. I had a special plan: the theme of the conference was very clearly focused on drug court standards, so instructions were sent out to presenters well ahead of the conference, informing them that whatever the topic, they were to relate the presentation or panel to the "Ten Key Components," which were distributed at the event.

States had to be recognized, respected, and involved in the drug court movement. To me, now was the time and L.A. was the place.

We established the Congress of State Drug Court Associations at the 1997 L.A. conference. Towards the end we had our first and only conference-wide, state-based organizational meeting. I offered all state organizations membership in the newly minted Congress of State Drug Court Associations. It was my intention to convene the congress twice a year (initially, once a year in New Orleans, expenses paid, and the second at the national conference).

By the end of the conference something in the neighborhood of 30 states had committed to forming state associations and to be part of NADCP's Congress of State Drug Court Associations.[79]

The 1997 California conference was critical to the future of NADCP, with its new programs, organizations, and ventures to bear fruit for a decade and more.

Once again our national conference proved to be a huge success (our only problem was that the session rooms were too small for the number of participants, some 1,400 attendees). We had focused on standards (the "Ten Key Components") that would live on as a testament to the organization's mission twenty years after they were written. We had begun a critical process of decentralization, with the purpose of sharing power with state organizations through the Congress of State Drug Court Associations, and for the first time at a national conference, our keynote speaker, Andrew Welles of the United Nations, introduced drug court to an international audience.

We were sited at the Biltmore Hotel in Los Angeles, the most fabulous venue we were to occupy over our twenty-five-year conference history. We also hosted the most amazing, heart-stopping banquet I have ever been to, either as host or guest. It was an extraordinary event held at Grand Union Station. The letters N-A-D-C-P were projected onto the station's walls with colored laser beams. Hors d'oeuvres and dinner were served outside in the Grand Union Station's fabulous gardens. Actor-composer Paul Williams graciously hosted the festivities with celebrity guests—while singer Kenny Rankin and many of L.A.'s finest musicians entertained—with dancing taking place inside the station, alongside overflowing dessert tables.

---

79 We owed much of the congress's considerable success to Judge Bill Hunter of Jefferson County, Louisiana. Bill had no problem convincing me that delegates would jump at the chance to visit New Orleans. Bill was to be a wonderfully generous host, leading us all on down-home tours of New Orleans cuisine and nightlife, which cemented New Orleans as the congress conference site for years to come.

It was in Las Vegas in 1995, at our first-annual NADCP Drug Court Conference, that we learned just how sobering a conference could be. Though the conference was a success, by the third and last day, attendees had largely departed (this was Las Vegas, after all) for more attractive venues. Just a few die-hards were left to close the show at noon on the fourth day.

After Las Vegas the plan was to change our closing session in a major way. We planned to have more participants occupying their seats at the end of the conference than at its beginning. We had a mission that would appeal to many celebrities, who often had substance abuse problems of their own: we would invite famous names to close out the conference with their personal stories.

While in L.A., preparing for the 1997 conference, I had the good fortune to be introduced to Bob Timmons, drug counselor to the stars. Bob was to become a good friend of drug courts and NADCP. He, in turn, introduced NADCP to MAD, Musicians Against Drugs. Through these new friends we were able to reach out to Paul Williams and a coterie of previously drug-dependent celebrities and musicians who came to know and support NADCP over the years.

One fly was stuck in the L.A. ointment, however. Robert Downey Jr. had promised to be our closing speaker, but at the last minute his manager had written a letter of regret. James Caan gracefully accepted Bob Timmons's entreaty to be our closing celebrity speaker. He spoke brilliantly, holding the attendees spellbound until the last minutes of the conference. I still recall his parting words: that he had done harm to many, and this talk was an attempt at righting the wrongs he had done.

AMEN.

It was our second year under CADCA financial control, and I was having a hard time getting budget numbers from them. When I did I understood that we were being charged full price for everything from telephone service and faxes to rent and staff assistance. That was understandable but not as much of a surprise as the financials from the L.A. conference were. The costs were high but reasonable for L.A. and a hotel as splendid as the Biltmore, but the spending on the banquet at L.A.'s Grand Central Station was astonishing: CADCA's conference director had spent $75,000 of our conference profits on a banquet without ever consulting with Marc or myself, and that was after repeated requests to see proposed expenditures.

I was shattered. We were trying to build an effective reform organization but instead were spending the funds from our very successful conference on a party. At that point I decided that we would be leaving CADCA.[80]

Our parting from CADCA was amicable. Both Jim Copple and Nelson Cooney had already left CADCA. Jim and his board had gone their separate ways. He was one of those people who always landed on his feet, and he was soon working for another non-profit. Nelson Cooney, who had been a great friend to NADCP and myself, went on to be a founding partner in Blue Sand Securities, an investment firm.

---

[80] An office just one flight down and across the hall in the very same building was available; we took it. It had room for 6–8 staff. Over the next several years we broke out a wall and expanded farther for an ever-increasing staff: over twenty by 2001.

INTERLUDE 6

WEST AFRICAN HIGHLIFE MUSIC

In the early '80s the worldbeat sound took the East Bay by storm. Paul Simon wouldn't unveil his extraordinary paean to African music, "Graceland," until 1986, yet bands like Hedzoleh Soundz, Mapenzi, O. J. Ekemote, and Zulu Spear had already introduced African rhythms, multiple guitars, and jazzy horn sections to the local music scene. It was also called African highlife music, and it had a wondrous, driving sound that lifted you up. It moved rhythmically, one major progression upon another, four simple major chords going round and round, building to a crescendo. And the wonderful thing about this music was that it made you happy. And it made you want to dance.

The club Ashkenaz on San Pablo Avenue in North Berkeley had been a folk-dance haven since the '70s. Mostly dedicated to Israeli and Balkan dances, it had a large wooden floor that was made for dancing. Balkan dancing on New Year's Eve is a tradition from pre-worldbeat Ashkenaz that survives to this day.

African highlife bands would call Ashkenaz home in the '80s. African musicians, much like blues players, loved to share the music, creating a groove and building their sound together. And it happened every weekend at Ashkenaz, with African and American musicians sharing the stage and that space in time.

The new edition of Hedzoleh Soundz had its first real gig at Ashkenaz in 1983, and it was a joyous affair. Over 400 paying customers crowded into the club to dance to the exciting music of great Ghanaian musicians like James Kwaku Morton, Samuel Nortey, Isaac Asante, and Nat Hammond.

I met with the club owner, David Nadel, at the end of that unusually profitable night for the struggling band and dance club. David would hire us to play at Ashkenaz on a monthly basis.

I would sometimes visit David in his tiny apartment above the Ashkenaz stage, accessible only through a retractable staircase. He was an eccentric in an eccentric city. He was the only club owner I ever knew who would write political diatribes—focusing mostly on UC Berkeley—on his club's bathroom walls. A radical with integrity, he refused to make money off holidays that other clubs thrived on. Sadly, I was in Washington, D.C., when I learned that David had been murdered in Ashkenaz by a drunk with a knife. The club and its community still celebrates his life each December.

In 1985 I was invited to play in the horn section of a new band, Kotoja, led by Keni Okulolo, the band's leader, bass player, songwriter, and lead singer. Keni had played bass with Nigerian highlife icon Fela Kuti for many years. I played with Kotoja until I took the bench as a judge in 1989.

One of the most satisfying experiences of my judicial career was the act of joining two persons in matrimony. I have done it hundreds of times over my long career, but few matched the delight in marrying drummer Jeffrey to guitarist Cynthia on stage, followed by a Kotoja performance.

Playing music with Kotoja was a highlight of my music career. But with my energies refocused on the court, and soon on drug courts, I wouldn't have much time left over for music. That would be the end of my so-called music career until my arrival in D.C. in 1996.

CHAPTER 15

IMAGINATION

We were coming up on the 1998 Annual Conference in D.C., and I was getting desperate: we hadn't found a celebrity guest for the conference closing session. Davida Coady, an epidemiologist and the director of Options, Inc., an excellent drug treatment program in Berkeley, California, came to our rescue.

Davida had been an anti-war activist when she met actor and fellow activist Martin Sheen in Nicaragua during the Sandinista Revolution. Over the years she had become a close friend and advisor to Martin. She suggested I extend an invitation to him to speak at the conference to be held in D.C. on the other side of the continent from his home in L.A.—in just a few weeks. I didn't expect a positive reply, or any reply for that matter. To my relief and delight, Davida told me that Martin had agreed to be our celebrity speaker.

Before Martin was to take the stage I went looking for him. I was told he would be in the restaurant at the Renaissance Hotel. I saw him sitting over coffee with another man who looked familiar. I introduced myself to Martin and then to the well-dressed man sitting by his side. The man had gray hair, a ruddy complexion, a stout frame, and a playful smile. I couldn't quite place him, though I thought I knew him from the Oakland court.

When I asked if he was a probation officer from Oakland, he broke out in a broad smile. He cheerfully introduced himself as a frequent flyer on Alameda County's "Drug and Alcohol Merry-Go-Round." Only then did I realize that this impressive man had appeared slovenly and unkempt in court on drug and alcohol charges on dozens of occasions over the years. He had only recently found sobriety through Judge Carol Brosnahan's Berkeley Court Rehabilitation Program. His name was Tom Gorham, and he was an associate of Dr. Davida Coady, the epidemiologist who ran the Options, Inc., treatment program in Berkeley.

Martin Sheen turned out to be a terrific speaker. He had directly experienced the impact of drug courts. Though he had given up alcohol some fifteen years before, his son Charlie had had a cocaine dependency. On more than one occasion Charlie had been taken to the hospital following an overdose.

When Charlie had refused to allow his father to visit him in the hospital, Martin decided it was time to reel Charlie in. He contacted his attorney and through him reached out to the district attorney and probation officer who were supervising Charlie on a domestic violence offense. Charlie was arraigned in court the next day before an L.A. judge, charged with violating his probation, and put into a drug treatment program as a condition of modified terms of probation. Charlie fared much better in rehab than anyone expected and graduated from his court program.

Partially because of that experience Martin was to become NADCP's champion. He helped us make substantial inroads into the celebrity community, assisting us in finding future celebrity speakers. He was a powerful advocate for drug courts and a frequent celebrity closing speaker, which by then had become an integral part of every NADCP national conference.

The truly remarkable part of this story is that Tom Gorham went on to become the CEO of Options, Inc., received his Doctorate in Rehabilitation Counseling, and married Dr. Davida Coady at the Berkeley home of his once supervising drug court judge, Carol Brosnahan, who also presided over the marriage ceremony.

Though an extraordinary story, it made me think of the tens of the thousands of offenders (if not hundreds of thousands) misdiagnosed by judges, district attorneys, defense counsel, probation officers, and treatment providers every year. It reminded me that neither I nor my brethren were seers, that we often made serious errors of judgment about an offender's potential for successful rehabilitation.

From almost the beginning of NADCP I had pictured some arm of the organization dedicated to academic endeavors, evaluations, and research projects. It was a side of NADCP that was clearly missing.

After our 1997 conference in D.C. I took stock of what had been accomplished. NADCP was clearly on the map in the nation's capital. It had supporters among both Democratic and Republican leadership. We had more than doubled federal drug court funding over the previous year, and we were increasing the number of drug courts exponentially. We were creating partnerships with state organizations and judicial and executive agencies, our conferences and mentor court trainings were breaking new ground and pulling the field together, and now we had our own offices and an expanding staff.

The one area where we had not made much headway was in establishing NADCP as a source for credible research and scientific information. We also weren't doing the sophisticated training and education in the field that we needed to do. To some extent research, education, and information resources were flowing to American University's Justice Programs Office because it had a university's imprimatur. It was critical to somehow create our own "Good Housekeeping Seal of Approval."

For the first time I found staff reluctant to move forward on a major project. I was surprised but also aware that we were both understaffed and overworked. I had difficulty accepting the fact that drug court was not a mission for all NADCP staff. This was the first time I can recall that senior staff had a serious debate as to how far and how big an organization NADCP ought to be.

My position was that this was a once-in-a-lifetime opportunity, that we had the chance to be part of a historic reform within the criminal justice system, and that we had to push our reform initiative as far as we could. I tried to motivate staff by reminding them that being there at the genesis of the drug court movement was an honor and a privilege that few would know. Of course, some disagreed but didn't necessarily say so out loud.

I gave everyone who came on staff the same speech, telling them that this was more than a job and that if they wanted to work nine to five, positions were to be had at other non-profit organizations. More than a few took my advice to heart and declined to join NADCP.

We were an organization with a mission. We moved ahead with the National Drug Court Institute project. I didn't understand until then just how important having staff fully committed to one's organizational goals was. I found that the best I could do to build momentum when staff wanted to slow down was to lead by example: working longer hours and making sure that I was the one to turn the lights off at the end of the day.

I came up with the name the National Drug Court Institute (NDCI); that was the easy part. It was pretty conventional, but that was just the sort of thing we needed: a mainstream, science-based institute. Before I did anything else I created a brochure touting NDCI as the scientific, evaluative, and educational arm of NADCP. I described NDCI as being an independent organization affiliated with NADCP, because practitioner-based organizations didn't get a lot of respect when it came to science-based research and education. The quiet reality was that NDCI existed as an empty room at the NADCP offices, with its symbol over the door.

That symbol itself proved to be more of a headache than we'd anticipated. NADCP's enormously successful logo had been gifted to me by Nelson Cooney of CADCA in 1994, after the Founders Meeting in Alexandria. We hired the same graphic artist to design the NDCI insignia. This time we had a much harder time finding the right symbol. Marc Pearce, now director of NADCP, and I literally looked at hundreds of possibilities, but none spoke of honesty, integrity, and science the way it needed to.

Desperate for a resolution I sat in my office late one night, looking over a text on Greek statuary, and there she was, the statue of a Greek goddess holding a goblet in one hand and grapes in the other.[81]

I had plans to make NADCP's June 1998 conference as special an event for NDCI as 1997 had been for the "Ten Key Components" and the Congress of Drug Court Associations. But it required having an institute in place (or at least the facade of one) as soon as possible to attract funding for the initial projects I hoped to trumpet at the 1998 conference.

The federal government's Office of National Drug Control Policy (ONDCP) was an independent agency under the jurisdiction of the White House. Its director, a cabinet officer, was popularly known as the Drug Czar. At the time its director was retired four-star General Barry McCaffrey.

I had met General McCaffrey early on, in 1996, when we were both recently arrived in D.C., and he had promised to look over the drug court model. As he explored and studied our model and visited drug courts, he became a committed supporter. As Drug Czar, General McCaffrey often spoke at our conferences and on more than one occasion described drug courts as "one of the monumental changes in social justice in this country since World War II," a message that I would carry with me to audiences near and far.

General McCaffrey was the first general I ever had any dealings with. I was a bit intimidated. His staff considered him brilliant but demanding. I visited with the general on a regular basis and found him to be forthright, friendly, and open to new ideas. And I had one.

I broached the idea of a committed congressional funding source for NDCI. General McCaffrey liked the idea and assigned two senior ONDCP

---

81 I can't say I recall which Greek goddess it was, but it worked for me. A simple modification substituted a book and the caduceus (the Greek symbol for the healing arts) for a goblet and grapes. The result was a stunning symbol with the propriety and integrity we'd hoped for. If delivered by a rehabilitated goddess, so be it.

staffers, John Carnevale and Ross Deck (then with the Planning Budget and Research Section at ONDCP), to examine its feasibility. They were thorough, enthusiastic, and extremely helpful in our quest for ONDCP funding. They presented their analysis of the institute's prospects to General McCaffrey.

General McCaffrey decided to move forward and announce, at a White House event, an ONDCP–NADCP partnership in founding NDCI. I couldn't have been more pleased. We were given a date when the Roosevelt Room would be available. We hoped the president would be available for the inaugural event. As it turned out the president, vice president, and attorney general were out of town, but we were well served at the ceremony by General McCaffrey and Assistant Attorney General Laurie Robinson.

On December 10, 1997, chairs were set up in the Roosevelt Room of the White House and perhaps fifty people were ushered in for the inaugural Ceremony.[82] The Robert Wood Johnson Foundation was represented by its CEO, Steven Schroeder, and CADCA by its acting President, Nelson Cooney. NADCP was represented by current chair Pat Morris, past chair Claire McCaskill, and myself, as well as NADCP's new director, Marc Pearce. The speeches were thankfully short; a brief press conference took place outside the White House, at which most of the principle figures spoke.

I wanted NDCI's first project to be relatively simple—one that broke few conventional rules and had an easily recognizable format. It was important that we produced a physical product we could hand out at our 1998 conference in D.C. The option I believed would be most acceptable to the field was that of a respectable legal journal, though this journal's focus would also be science-based. We called it the *National Drug Court Institute Review*. Because I wanted the *Review* to resemble publications judges and lawyers were generally familiar with, it had footnotes, headnotes (a brief summary of a particular point of law), and a cumulative index, all conventional features in legal publications. Hopefully, this would provide the NDCI articles the appearance of seriousness, respectability, and importance.

Unlike most reviews, documents, and publications I came across at conferences, Volume I of the *Review* would be found inside a handsome, green, loose-leaf binder (intended for the first four volumes). The publication's name and insignia on the volume were to be in gold leaf, a handsome addition to any legal bookcase. In that way I hoped to avoid the fate of 90% of conference literature: dumped into the circular file, unloved and unread.

82 See C-SPAN's coverage from Dec 10, 1997, "Drug Court Initiative," at https://www.c-span.org/video/?96425-1/drug-court-initiative.

I cast about for funding to implement my plans for an NDCI *Review*. I had few accessible sources for unrestricted funds. The one that offered the most potential was the Robert Wood Johnson Foundation. They had sent a representative to our 1997 conference who had been seemingly impressed by the energy, excitement, and substance of what we were doing. I got back in touch with the RWJ rep and explained our need for $50,000 to print and publish what was to be our first NDCI project, the NDCI *Review*. Someone at the Johnson Foundation said yes, and we were on our way.

I convened an editorial meeting of writers and researchers on relatively short notice in early 1998 to help create an agenda for the *Review*. They included Dr. Steven Belenko, Dr. Kenneth D. Robinson, Dr. Sally L. Satel, NADCP attorney Susan P. Weinstein, and myself. I was trying to produce a publication, and we had precious little time to do it. That first volume needed to be special.[83]

NDCI
NATIONAL DRUG
COURT INSTITUTE

By far the most critical material product in Volume I of the NDCI *Review* was to be a comprehensive meta-analysis on the effectiveness of drug courts. Too often I had met with congressional, court, or other government authorities skeptical of drug courts who insisted on seeing the hard research. Though I provided individual research documents supporting drug courts, most indications were that they went unread.

Part of the problem was a natural skepticism of evaluations that covered a relatively short period; in this case, the three years or less most drug courts had been around. We decided to turn that three-year limitation into a positive for the *Review* by focusing an article on the period during which a drug court participant was under court supervision, typically one to three years. With the *Review* coming on line, we had the opportunity to put out a special publication: easily read, relatively brief, and digestible.

---

83 After our editorial meeting we had our agenda, but the Review still had to be written and published. The writing of the first Review was done by Dr. Steven Belenko, Dr. Kenneth Robinson, Dr. Sally Satel, Michelle Shaw, and myself.

The challenge was finding the right writer and organization to produce the article. I asked Steven Belenko, a highly respected researcher working with Columbia University's National Center on Addiction and Substance Abuse (CASA), if he would be interested in having his research showcased in the layman's format envisioned for the NDCI *Review*'s first volume. We discussed issues that were important to the field and agreed upon the question "What could we learn from a meta-analysis of drug court research about participants while in a drug court program?"[84]

Published in 1998, the resulting study was "Research on Drug Courts: A Critical Review" (hereafter "The CASA Study") by Steven Belenko, PhD. It was the first major academic review and analysis of drug court research up to that time (based upon some 30 drug court evaluations). The finding was right out front in the introduction: "Drug use and criminal behavior are substantially reduced while offenders are participating in drug court."

It was published in the inaugural NDCI *Review* as the lead article, as well as a forty-four-page monograph distributed freely at the D.C. conference. Beyond that, over the next few years, some 30,000 copies of the research monograph were widely distributed by NADCP. In a world of short attention spans it was the right publication for its time. "The CASA Study" was a huge asset for advocates of drug courts. It was the first NADCP research publication to go "viral," having more impact than any drug court research document before or since.

While finishing the editing of our first *Review* I started to search for a manager for the NDCI. Any number of drug court practitioners were willing to come to D.C. to work for NADCP in a management position, but one young man in particular had made a major impression upon me.

I was crisscrossing the U.S. in 1996, scoping out drug court mentor sites for trainings and regional stars to showcase in D.C. and elsewhere. Stillwater, Oklahoma was on the list, and I arrived at Tulsa's airport, the closest major city to Stillwater, sometime after midnight. I was wondering how I would get to a hotel in Tulsa when a cheerful, polite, and deferential young man approached me.

He introduced himself as West Huddleston. He was there to be my host and driver for my stay in Oklahoma. And I was delighted to meet him, as I had no idea how I would get to my hotel from a deserted airport after midnight.

---

84 Dr. Belenko was promised complete independence and control in producing the document, and NDCI had agreed to publish the research in Volume I, no matter the findings.

The next morning West drove me through what appeared to be a desert to Stillwater, a small town seemingly in the middle of nowhere. It had a drug court that met in the evenings—an innovation worth noting—and other features that would diversify the drug court mentor system. That little town sat in a rural setting in a conservative state in Middle America, a part of the country without many mentor sites or drug courts.

West and I hit it off and became friends. He was a good traveling companion. I would see him at trainings and conferences from time to time (we often started the day with a run). I began to find room for him at conferences as part of our training staff.

In May of 1998, just weeks before the D.C. conference, West Huddleston reported for work as NDCI's first deputy director, along with his fiancée Michelle Shaw, who helped us complete our work on the *Review*. An enormous amount of logistic, editorial, and detail work were yet to be completed before we could go to press. West and Michelle dove in headfirst, and because of their efforts, which included a number of all-nighters, we managed to finish and deliver the *Review* on time for the conference.

Once again the 1998 D.C. conference exceeded all expectations: over 1,800 participants, fifteen training tracks, extraordinary speakers, a continuing emphasis on local and regional leadership, and a Congress of State Drug Court Associations meeting, as well as individual jurisdiction and state association meetings and a new emphasis on law enforcement involvement in the drug court movement.[85]

By that time we had introduced a number of innovations to the field, none more important than the National Drug Court Institute. The Washington elite were there, as was the federal government, with ONDCP director General McCaffrey giving the premiere plenary speech.

Though West was new to NADCP and had not been part of the development of NDCI projects to that point, I wanted to recognize the hard work that he and Michelle had put into finalizing publication of the NDCI *Review*. I put both West and Michelle on the *Review*'s editorial board.

I also gave West the opportunity to showcase the NDCI *Review*—and himself—to the field at the first plenary session of the conference. At first he was reluctant to speak to the two-thousand-plus attendees present at the session, but I urged him to do it. He did a fine job.

---

85 With funding assistance from the DOJ's Community Policing Division, then under Director Joe Brann, we added an NADCP staffer with a law enforcement background and expanded our mentor court system to include sites with substantial law enforcement connections.

And while it may be delusional, what I remember most about the 1998 D.C. conference were two thousand attendees heading home clutching Volume I of the NDCI *Review*—with its green binder and gold-leaf inscription—a bit more tightly than other reading material.

We wanted to roll out the National Drug Court Institute with a bang and apparently had succeeded. Years later, when I returned to California as an assigned, or senior, judge, I was to find that green NDCI binder in more than a few judge's chambers.

Landing substantial ONDCP funding was to become senior staff's number-one priority. West Huddleston, NADCP lawyer Susan Weinstein, and I spent a good deal of time with ONDCP and congressional leadership, discussing how to access ONDCP congressional funding (through what was called a "congressional earmark").

I received the news in a phone booth at Reagan Airport: we would receive $2 million in ONDCP funding for NDCI's next two years and $1 million a year thereafter (until we didn't). I made up my mind right then: we would spend the $2 million appropriation in NDCI's first funded year, 1999, and ask for another $1 million the following year. I felt our mission was too important to ration resources when we needed them most. The NDCI would focus the drug court field on scientific issues too often neglected or ignored.

Looking back on the accomplishments of 1998, the first full year of NDCI, it's hard to fathom just how many challenges we took on and how much we accomplished in such a short period of time. It was already NADCP's trademark, and it demanded near-total dedication and commitment.

I often worked eighty-plus hours a week and expected the same from my staff. I was delighted that our new NDCI deputy director had shown so much promise in his first months with us. He had a strong work ethic and commitment to the cause, and that would be the beginning of both successes and conflicts to come.

CHAPTER 16

WAVE

By 1999 the drug court field was akin to a giant wave. It was my fourth year running NADCP's D.C. office. I spent much of my time crisscrossing the country, laying the groundwork for a national criminal justice reform movement. At the same time I was hanging on for dear life during the most exhausting and exhilarating period of my career.

When riding a wave there occurs a moment when you reach the crest and are on top of the world. At the same time you are aware that the wave will inevitably break. That's what it felt like to be leading the drug court movement in the late '90s. Getting ready for the dismount, or in my case the exit from NADCP/NDCI, was as difficult as the ride itself.

As the founder of NADCP and NDCI, I believed I was leading the most far-reaching criminal justice reform movement in more than a generation, driving the organization towards a distinct vision, if one that only existed in my own mind. In retrospect others seem to agree. In her 2010 book *How Information Matters*, Professor Kathleen Hale of Auburn University focused entirely on NADCP, the "champion" non-profit organization. Professor Hale describes the National Association of Drug Court Professionals as "the best among extraordinary organizations; whose structure, initiatives, strategies, and planning define excellence in the non-profit world."

Long term, my vision was of NDCI taking a leadership role in the larger criminal justice reform movement and setting up long-term projects and hopefully reform institutes to deal with critical issues, such as systemic approaches to drug abuse and criminality, the decriminalization of the drug user, and alternatives to prison and incarceration for less serious offenders.

There was an explosion in media attention interest surrounding NADCP and drug courts. To my mind, that was a causal factor in the extraordinary change in attitudes towards drug users over the last 25 years. On many a

Sunday morning I would run the ten miles from my home in Alexandria, along the Potomac River, across the Arlington Memorial Bridge, to the Washington Mall and up the stairs of the Lincoln Monument. Like Rocky Balboa I felt I had come so far and the reward lay just beyond my reach.

I saw NDCI monographs as a critical step in the development of far-reaching criminal justice reforms. It was my hope that NDCI could create enough attention and activity around prospective reforms that we would attract investment and involvement from federal agencies, state governments, individual courts, and private investors. The funding could be used to establish projects and institutes at NADCP dedicated to reforms important to both the organization and the larger criminal justice system. It was an ambitious agenda, but I believed it doable.[86]

I, along with West, led focus groups that were the basis for the monographs. We saw the drug court as a harbinger of courts to come: problem-solving courts, which reflected the drug court model but had a broader impact on the criminal justice system.

With that in mind we launched three focus groups in 1998–1999, expanding on the drug court model. The first focus group, held in November 1998, dealt with an early offshoot of the drug court movement, the DWI court, or driving-under-the-influence court. It was shortly followed by a monograph, "DWI/Drug Courts: Defining a National Strategy," published in March of 1999.

The next topic was more ambitious: focusing on drug court systems and the need to develop more sophisticated means of sentencing drug offenders to appropriate rehabilitation, supervision, and possibly custody. Monograph No. 2 of the series, "Development and Implementation of Drug Court Systems," was published in May of 1999. It presaged in many ways the increased interest in evidence-based sentencing, sentencing systems that deal with all criminal offenders.

In retrospect our most important monograph was "Reentry Drug Courts." It was the first publication to deal with this nascent field when there were few existing models for reentry courts. I was fascinated by their potential as sentencing courts with broader applications for the future. Rather than conducting a single focus group session dealing with the concept, as we did for other topics, we held two sessions that dealt separately with jail and prison reentry.[87]

---

86 We mailed out, on average, one NDCI publication every month in 1999, including fact-finding documents, the NDCI Review, newsletters, and monographs.

87 The first of two focus groups, Jail-Based Reentry Court, was held in Washington, D.C., April 6–7,1999. We invited some twenty practitioners from Broward County, F.L.; Los Angeles, C.A.; San Bernardino County, C.A.; and Uinta County, W.Y. Other practitioners and experts in the field were invited to be part of the audience. Similarly, the

The key concept here is for the same court and court personnel to seamlessly monitor the offender's progress from first contact—whether at arraignment, sentencing, in custody rehabilitation, or upon release into the community—until the offender is discharged from the court's supervision.[88]

This monograph, more than any other, focused national attention on the plight of offenders coming out of our prisons and jails without adequate assistance, resources, or monitoring, services that courts were capable of providing if given the authority to do so.

Today's focus on mass incarceration was in many ways anticipated by NDCI's thinking about reentry courts. Reentry courts were intended to engage those leaving prisons in court-based rehabilitation but also offered less serious offenders that opportunity, either immediately before entering prison or after a brief prison term.[89]

The new NDCI trainings were important to the field in a number of ways. They would be discipline or practitioner specific, meaning judges working with judges, DAs with DAs, and defense attorneys, supervision personnel, treatment providers, and so forth without their fellow practitioners from back home being present. They would also rely heavily on video learning. The previous five years had taught me what worked when teaching criminal justice practitioners (and judges in particular): they learned best when engaged in discussion after they had observed reality-based demonstrations, whether as observers of court sessions or videos of such sessions.[90]

---

second focus group held May 11–12, 1999, featured four states that had developed statewide reentry court initiatives, transitioning state prisoners back into the community through the courts: Florida, Missouri, Nevada, and Oklahoma.

88 The initiative being tested in a number of jurisdictions offered several promising variations that we wanted to bring to the attention of the criminal justice community. Those sentenced to incarceration could (1) have their term suspended and be supervised through the reentry court, without ever entering into custody; (2) serve a brief term in prison—receiving treatment in custody—to be returned to the same court for resentencing by the reentry court; and (3) be sentenced to prison, serving their full term—while receiving incentives for rehabilitation completed in custody—and seamlessly placed back into a reentry court program.

89 Within a short time after the focus group we would follow up with a monograph outlining the usefulness of the reform and descriptions of its successful implementation at model court sites, distributing 10,000 monographs on the reform across the nation.

90 At that point I sat down and planned the first discipline-based training, the judicial practitioner training set for a few months out. After putting together the training schedule, I sequestered myself for two days in Taos, N.M. (after a mentor site visit to Las Cruces) and wrote the training curriculum. The first NDCI Practitioner-Based

Visual aids were at the heart of the training and often not easily assembled. My idea was that every session—be it Incentives, Sanctions, or Drug Testing—would be followed by 8–10 short video clips from drug courts around the country. To one extent or another they displayed the concepts that judges (or other practitioner training groups) would be working with.

Discussions were moderated by an experienced drug court judge doing double-duty as a presenter and training leader for a group of 6–8 drug court student judges over the duration of the training. To my mind, the trainings would succeed or fail on the basis of the video portion of our trainings.[91]

The student judges became engaged and generally achieved a visceral understanding of the drug court topic by watching and discussing the videos in small groups. It was the most innovative part of the training and the segment that students appreciated most.

West handled the planning for and implementation of the Discipline-Based Trainings for Adults, as well as Juvenile Drug Court Coordinators, Treatment Providers, Prosecutors, Defense Attorneys, and Community Supervision. In all, ten weeklong, discipline-based trainings were held in 1999.

NDCI's research project also made significant progress in its first year. We convened and presided over a Research and Dissemination Committee made up of practitioners, researchers, scientists, and others to take on the task of devising ways to get existing research to the field (something discernibly absent).[92]

Though I had difficulty admitting it at the time, the field was moving beyond what I could personally supervise. I didn't know that "HR" stood for human resources until my final year as NADCP President. I wasn't used to dealing

---

Training was held as planned from October 18–21, 1998, at George Mason Law School in Arlington, V.A. (literally down the road from NADCP).

91 The video project idea had grown out of my experience as a drug court judge, as well as from watching other drug court judges at work. The segments had to be short enough to maintain the students' interest and relevant enough that a small group of judges could analyze the effectiveness of the participating judges (or other practitioners) in the video. I spent hundreds of hours reviewing drug court segments. In the end I selected and edited some 100 videos on twelve topics. It was objectively a simple process but one that took months to complete, with VCR cassettes delivered to the first training held at George Mason University in Alexandria literally minutes before they were to be used.

92 The NDCI–NIDA research planning sessions held in September of 1998 bore fruit in 1999, with the development of a partnership with the National Institute of Drug Abuse (NIDA). As part of the NDCI–NIDA Joint Research Standardization Project, a research and evaluation workshop took place in D.C. from October 18–19, 1999, to launch the development of much-needed standardized research tools that the entire field could rely on.

with boards, committees, and administrators. During my first years as president I had Claire McCaskill as board vice chair and then chair, running interference for me with the board. I had ideas I believed needed to be actualized and wasn't much interested in what conventional managers thought. When Claire left the board to run for statewide office in 1998, I discovered that the board found my style of leadership abrasive. West joked that he learned to "never accept 'no' as an answer" from me.

Still, the sheer numbers of drug court professionals and participants in the field required management skills and an ability to deal with bureaucracy that I mostly refused to accept or acknowledge at the time. As the exponential growth of NADCP forced me to give up areas of responsibility, whether for planning, personnel selection, conference planning, or other management areas, I felt the organization slipping from my control. By the same token I believed with each concession that the organization became less accountable and less effective.

I had a problem with no real solution. I could break down bureaucratic walls and build new, more effective constructs; I could lead reform-minded pioneers in creating a new paradigm; I could affect the perception of the public through the media. But as more and more practitioners joined the movement, the movement became more unwieldy and bureaucratic, a dilemma that not many would envy: go create a movement and lead it to success, knowing that in doing so, you are ultimately rendering yourself irrelevant.

The solution, if one could call it that, was to accept the idea that less responsibility and accountability was ok, that no one could control so many levers at the same time, that one has to delegate as best as one can and pray for the best, that I ultimately couldn't control it all, so why try? Those who do best in that environment are often those who care less, and perhaps that is how the system works best.

The extraordinary increase in drug court participation and success was reflected in our national conferences. Attendance at our first Annual NADC Drug Court Conference Las Vegas in 1995 was something over 400. By 1999 attendance at our fifth-annual drug court conference at the Tropicana Hotel in Miami Beach, Florida, had shot up to 2,100.

As described earlier the national conference had traditionally been the place where the drug court community met and recharged for the coming year. Our leadership gatherings in the Presidential Suite were gala events where leading judges and others could meet as equals and share their experiences, problems, and hopes for the future. It provided sustenance and commiseration for the lonely few who were willing to brave the derision of dismissive colleagues. It was our shelter from the storm.

By 1999 the national conference no longer was the place where you met other practitioners and had instead become a somewhat impersonal gathering. So many people were attending the Miami Beach Conference at the Tropicana Hotel that you were more likely to spend time with friends and colleagues from back home than make new friends. Nor was it the place where you swapped stories and information among the drug court community. You probably did that at a more intimate state drug court association meeting with colleagues from your home state. As well, attendance noticeably shrank at the tail end of the conference, a logical consequence of putting on a three-day event at a Miami Beach hotel in June.

The conference had outgrown its original purpose of providing community and instead provided critical assistance, information, and ideas for practitioners and others to take home. Much of the important work of NADCP was happening away from the annual conference at NADCP trainings, focus groups, state conferences, judicial education seminars, and so forth.

I missed the personal contact with practitioners (and especially judges) who had been in the field since its inception. One by one they retired or moved away from the drug court field. The overwhelming number of NADCP conference participants (and new board members) knew little about me except that I was NADCP's founder, a title that, with time, had a somewhat hollow ring.

I believed at the time that standing in the background and pushing others to the forefront was the most effective way to broaden our national leadership and prepare for the day when I was no longer on the national stage. Few understood what it took for me personally to get us where we were, and I resigned myself to that reality.

Through the 1998 D.C. conference I retained final control of all plenary sessions, tracks, workshops, moderators, and panelists. It wasn't until then that I realized I couldn't handle the increasing numbers of tracks, workshops, and presenters, along with my new responsibilities as NDCI's executive director. In 1999 I began the process of delegating authority over conference presentations, sharing it with NADCP staff.

NADCP also began to move away from the "Oprah" model of presentation. With the growing sophistication of both presenters and audiences, we saw an increasing demand for more technical information and less use for the general expertise available through panel discussions. After the 1998 event, panel discussions dropped to 50% or less of presentations, and that was ok: it had served its purpose in establishing a strong connection between NADCP and perhaps one thousand panelists over a five-year period, as well as in providing the excitement, motivation, and illumination of ideas that panel discussions can generate in a new field.

Our conference was becoming a major national criminal justice event. We hired an outside conference planner for the first time, Jackie Sheehey, who did a wonderful job. I continued to meet with organizers from the host city to get their input on what local innovations and personalities the conference might highlight.

I tried to involve staff in the planning of the conference, asking them to take responsibility for at least one training track topic and the attending workshops. Some took the assignment more seriously than others. Still, I exerted much less control over the conference than I had ever done before.

Most weekends I was on the road, to or from a conference or meeting or at NADCP's offices, responding to correspondence or planning new strategies for the organization. I was recently divorced, with little social connection to D.C. society. It was far easier for me to bury myself in my work than deal with the outside world.

I had been working something close to 80 hours a week for almost ten years. My doctor diagnosed a serious non-specific fatigue condition. I couldn't see doing this for much longer. I began to think about an exit plan and my return to California.

Recognizing that I couldn't do it all was made less painful given the staff's capabilities at NADCP. Marc Pearce had been my "go-to guy." He was there when a problem needed fixing or a project needed direction. He worked long hours with little credit. Marc was now director of NADCP, a title he well deserved. My focus had turned to establishing NDCI's credibility, and I was delighted to have someone of Marc's capabilities at the helm of NADCP.

I believed that Marc would have made a worthy successor. Understandably, his passion for the job diminished as his personal life and family demanded more of his time. After giving so much to the organization in its early years he decided that he had given enough. He told me that his family was more important than his job at that point in his life, and I couldn't disagree with him. He handed me his letter of resignation.

Marc had been at the heart of NADCP since day one, and it was hard to see him go. He had been an indispensable presence, both as a partner and co-strategist during NADCP's early days. He will always be the brother with whom I dreamed of what could be.

I believed that West showed the most promise of any of our senior staff. To be honest, what was most attractive about him was that he was a strong ally among senior staff in my push to set organizational goals—and achieve them. West's support for my plan to pick up the pace caused major friction between him and other staff members who were looking forward to slowing it down. We were to have several rancorous management meetings on the feasibility of continuing our aggressive strategy to develop NDCI.

West had proved himself to be an exceptional deputy director at NDCI. He learned quickly and followed my lead with ease. He had an appetite for work that rivaled my own and was the only staffer who would run miles with me along the Potomac in knee-deep snow. Importantly, he had an almost insatiable drive to accomplish the impossible, which an exceptional reform leader has to have.

He also had an ability to manage bureaucratic complexities. He paid attention to details and could handle administrative tasks better than anyone else on staff. He drew up NDCI's budgets and grant requests to both the DOJ and the Office of National Drug Control Policy. It was stuff I had little aptitude for and even less interest in.

I took him to high-level meetings with ONDCP director General McCaffrey and other national leaders. I had been acting director of NDCI since its inception in December of 1997. In 1999 I became executive director of NDCI and moved West from deputy director to director of NDCI as part of my strategy to put him in a position to assume leadership of NADCP when the time was right. I was preparing to let go.[93]

---

93 Let me add a critical caveat here. NADCP and NDCI had exceptional staff who worked long hours with little acknowledgement or financial reward. They did the lion's share of the day-to-day work that allowed us to build a national organization and movement. Though some on senior staff were cynical about attaining our goals, the great majority of staff were deeply committed to the organization and saw our achievements as theirs, as they truly were.

PART IV
COMING DOWN
FROM THE MOUNTAIN

Presenting an award to a San Francisco Parole Reentry Court participant.

Celebrating the first NDCI judicial training. From left to right: judges Bill Meyer, Jeffrey Tauber, Robert Russell, Sue Finlay.

A WORLD ANESTHETIZED BY DRUGS

I was awaiting the start of my judicial career, with time to travel after my election to the Oakland bench. During my trip to the South Seas the chief justice of Fiji granted me the opportunity to visit the main jail facility. I was treated with respect and deference, and as a special honor I was invited to visit the guards' own housing unit to participate in a traditional Kava ceremony.

I also visited other communities where kava was used in the traditional fashion, with the kava ceremonial experience part of a family or village celebration. But with the modern world intruding on village life it had become endemic to many communities and was used everywhere and much of the time.

That explanation was brought home to me when I met a native Fijian on a bus. He invited me to his home to drink kava. He said he drank it every day, as there were no jobs, no money for a wife, and nothing to do but drink. He was drug dependent, with no apparent way out of his dilemma.

That is what I sometimes think is happening across the world: people using drug to anesthetize themselves from boredom and lack of opportunity and community—no job or prospects of one, no money to start a family or marry, and nothing much to do. Within a generation a ceremonial substance—admittedly hallucinogenic and possibly addictive—had become an acceptable part of the daily lives of an entire region of the world.

On that South Seas journey I began to seriously think about the value, nature, and consequences of drug use around the world.

CHAPTER 17

FLY ME TO THE MOON

The Oakland Drug Court graduation I remember best is not one I presided over. It was held nearly a decade after the Oakland Drug Court's creation. I had just arrived from Washington, D.C., and I was to be a guest speaker at a graduation ceremony. I watched from the jury box as graduates came forward to receive awards and praise from members of the community. What was so special about that ceremony was its closing.

An African-American woman stepped forward and led the congregation—that was what it most resembled—in singing the pop-gospel song "I Believe I Can Fly." In attendance were officials from the mayor's office, county government, the sheriff's office, the district attorney's and public defender's offices, and from agencies and organizations across the criminal justice and treatment spectrum. As the singer's powerful, gospel-drenched voice filled the room, everyone joined hands, swayed to the music, and sang the chorus with her. The display of emotion and joy was unlike any I had experienced in a courtroom.

I sat in that Oakland jury box, basking in the glow of the moment, amazed at all that had come to pass over the past decade: the creation of the Oakland Drug Court; the growth of California drug courts to well over one hundred; the establishment of NADCP, NDCI, and a plethora of state drug court organizations; an explosion in the number of drug courts nationally (approaching one thousand); and the unprecedented acceptance of a criminal justice reform—drug courts—by the nation's media and political establishment.

It was the high point of the Oakland Drug Court program, which had helped spearhead the drug court movement in California and across the nation. The Oakland Drug Court had seen great success and then met serious resistance from within the Alameda County bureaucracy, especially from the court and probation department. Ultimately, some five years after that spiritual display of court commitment and community power, the Oakland Drug Court would disappear entirely. Fittingly, I was there at the end of the program, as I had been at its inception. As an assigned judge I was sitting in for Oakland Drug Court judge Jacqueline Taber in an Oakland Drug Court that was a shadow of its former self, with a dozen participants sitting in a nearly empty courtroom. It was to shut down within days.

The Oakland Drug Court's demise pointed up the vagaries of criminal justice reform and drug court continuity, how drug courts could reach heights of popularity and effectiveness under powerful judicial and community leadership and then disappear entirely when that leadership waned. NADCP had succeeded in creating a movement of nearly one thousand drug courts, but their viability remained very much in doubt.

One only needed to look at the fortunes of the original dozen or so drug courts existing prior to NADCP's formation. They all began with great promise. While all had initial success, half of those drug courts withered on the vine. Drug courts in Bakersfield, California; St. Joseph, Michigan; Chicago, Illinois; Denver, Colorado; Oakland, California; and Portland, Oregon, were either to disappear entirely or were to fail, only be resuscitated over time. Meanwhile, other founding drug courts matured, expanded, and thrived. Miami and Fort Lauderdale, Florida; Kalamazoo, Michigan; Kansas City, Missouri; Las Vegas, Nevada; and San Bernardino, California, are just a few of the courts that grew stronger and more successful while expanding the populations they served and increasing their impact on their communities.

It was clear that criminal justice reforms could disappear almost as quickly as they appeared, unless they were deeply embedded within government institutions. Drug courts needed to be integrated into the very fabric of state court establishments so they couldn't be eliminated at the whim of bureaucrats or during the first economic downturn. I began to focus on a project that could lead to the drug court model's ultimate integration into state court institutions across the nation.

Part of this understanding came as the result of discussions with friend and mentor Judge Susan Finlay. She had been the dean of the California Judicial College and was a respected judicial educator and a former drug court judge. In 1999 she joined NADCP as NDCI's director of education. She was to be an invaluable advisor. Out of our conversations came a vision of NADCP as an organization that would work with state legislative, executive, and judicial leaders to achieve a critical level of drug court integration in state court bureaucracies.

There was controversy in the field, especially among drug court judges, as to whether formal state involvement in the nascent drug court field would benefit the movement. To my mind, it clearly had been beneficial in California, where Bill Vickrey and the Administrative Office of the Courts (AOC) had provided critical support for California drug courts. While some of my colleagues had reservations, the arguments for state involvement in the drug court movement won out.

Judge Finlay introduced me to Judge Roger Warren, a former California judge and president of the prestigious National Center for State Courts (NCSC). He was a skeptic and, according to Susan, had a "lock 'em up" mentality before being exposed to drug courts. As a matter of fact, the NCSC, as well as most state court administrations, had a long history of skepticism when it came to specialized courts such as drug courts. With Susan providing him with relevant information, research, and encouragement, Roger became a convert and then a strong advocate who provided critical assistance to the burgeoning drug court field.

I knew of Roger's reputation as an outstanding presiding judge on the Sacramento Superior Court. He had only recently become president of the National Center for State Courts (NCSC). We met for the first time at a restaurant in Alexandria on the Potomac River. We had the first of many conversations on drug courts and their future. We became friends and collaborators. Roger would come to see in the drug court field an exciting new direction in criminal court sentencing. Later, he was to write extensively on evidence-based sentencing and how drug courts were its critical antecedent.

Part of Roger's responsibilities as president of NCSC was to act as coordinator for the Conference of Chief Justices (CCJ) and the Conference of State Court Administrators (COSCA), which included all the chief justices of state supreme courts and their senior administrators. Roger turned out to be one of our most important allies, opening the door to NCSC and the prospect of formal recognition from the nation's chief justices and their court administrators.[94]

The genesis of CCJ's and COSCA's recognition of drug courts went back at least a year prior, to its passage. Roger Warren had arranged for me to speak on behalf of drug courts to a joint meeting of both the CCJ and COSCA boards at the offices of the California Administrative Office of the Courts in

---

94 Roger was to be the Plenary Speaker at our first NDCI Judge Practitioner Training held at George Mason University in Alexandria, V.A., October 18–23, 1998, and arranged for NCSC to partner with NADCP on numerous trainings and educational conferences at their campus in Williamsburg, V.A.

San Francisco. I was particularly nervous, well aware that CCJ and COSCA, as well as NCSC, would be critical components in the institutionalization of drug courts across the nation.

There were perhaps twenty men and women around a long conference table. They looked somewhat skeptical. I spoke briefly about the explosive impact of drug courts on the criminal justice system, the need for state funding, and administrative guidance for drug courts.

They listened quietly at first. When I stressed the importance of CCJ and COSCA getting out in front of this wave of reform, I sensed some discomfit in the room. When I suggested that the alternative to working with drug court leaders might be state judicial administrations finding themselves swamped by the drug court reform movement, I had their attention.

I may have made a convincing case to get drug courts on that year's conference agendas; then again, it is more likely that Chief Justice Ron George, AOC Director Bill Vickrey, and NCSC President Roger Warren—who coincidentally were all presidents of their respective organizations that year—had intervened.

Perhaps a dozen judicial leaders gathered in Florida to draft a relevant therapeutic justice resolution at a critical meeting of the CCJ–COSCA Task Force on Therapeutic Justice. The results of that meeting were to be presented as a joint resolution at the annual CCJ–COSCA conference, to be held in Rapid City, South Dakota, that year. I believe that the only non CCJ–COSCA participants present were Marilyn Roberts, director of the Drug Court Office representing the Department of Justice, and myself, representing NADCP/NDCI.[95]

Under the leadership of Dan Becker, Utah's state court administrator, a draft of the historic resolution was hammered out: a broad document endorsing what were to be called "problem-solving courts."[96] I pressed for specific inclusion of a statement regarding drug-court principles, one that provided a definition and description of the drug court as the model and template for

---

95 Dan Becker was made co-chair of the CCJ–COSCA Joint Task force on Therapeutic Justice, one of the first joint committees to be established under the leadership of then president of COSCA, Bill Vickrey. See a Dan Becker interview from 2001 at: www.reentrycourtsolutions.com/pioneering-documents/ccjcosca-resolutions/genesis-of-the-cjccosca-resolution/.

96 At the time Marilyn Roberts was the director of the DOJ/OJP Office of Drug Courts. She offered the DOJ's support for the resolution and the name "problem-solving courts" on behalf of Attorney General Janet Reno. Marilyn was an important partner during the field's early stages, providing critical leadership, support, and funding to NADCP and the field, and was a supportive presence at many drug court events.

problem-solving courts. One AOC director was strongly opposed to focusing so much attention on drug courts, arguing for a new, broader, undefined universal model. She was joined in opposition to my amendment by others at the meeting.

I saw the inclusion of a broad drug court definition in the resolution as critical to the continuing evolution and expansion of the drug court model as a national institution. I argued that the resolution would have little impact should it provide a vacuous, ill-defined description of a new problem-solving court construct, one that did not exist in the real world. Though the discussion was heated at times, the inclusion of the drug court principles ultimately gained favor. The proposed resolution, which included the so-called drug court principles, was accepted by the subcommittee. That afternoon drug courts became the prospective model for problem-solving courts.

Both the Conference of Chief Justices (CCJ) and the Conference of State Court Administrators (COSCA) passed the resolution unanimously on August 3, 2000, at their Rapid City, South Dakota, Annual Meeting.

A press release I wrote after the resolution's unanimous passage reads:

> *An extraordinary document has taken its place in the history of the Drug Reform Movement. It is the work of both the Conference of Chief Justices (CCJ) and the Conference of State Court Administrators (COSCA). CCJ Resolution 22 and COSCA Resolution 4 jointly endorse the concept of Drug Courts and Problem-Solving Courts structured on the Drug Court model. In unanimously passing the joint resolution, all fifty Chief Justices and State Court Administrators have made clear their intention of making the Drug Court concept the lynchpin of the criminal courts in the future. CCJ and COSCA recognized through their resolution that "well-functioning Drug Courts represent the best practice" of the problem solving court model and resolved to "advance the application and methods of Drug Courts into ongoing court operations."*

With that declaration, the judicial leadership of this nation put itself on record as supporting the integration of Drug Courts and Drug Court systems into mainstream court operations. Further, the Chief Justices and State Court Administrators resolved to promote "the broad integration over the next decade of the principles and methods employed in Problem-Solving Courts into the administration of justice.." and to "advocate for the resources necessary to advance and apply the principles of Problem-Solving Courts in the general courts systems of the various states."[97]

Even before my arrival in D.C. I believed that NADCP needed to be at the center of a movement with broader parameters than the traditional drug court model. The more I became aware of the realities of the nation's state criminal justice systems, the more I became convinced NADCP/NDCI should provide assistance and guidance to other related courts and fields developing across the nation. A plethora of specialty courts were to be modeled after the drug court and would need assistance (e.g., mental health, DWI, reentry, domestic violence, prostitution, elder abuse, and homeless, as well as adult, family and juvenile drug courts, to name a few).

The drug court model would obviously be most effective if it reached those most in need, many of whom were in state and federal prison systems. I was particularly interested in the possibility of the drug court model being used with non-drug-dependent prisoners. I saw the development of NDCI (NADCP's science- and research-based arm) as a means of shifting gears towards broader national policy goals, as well as towards trainings with more sophisticated and effective techniques.

I understood the importance but also the limitations of collaborating. Most organizations didn't make a move without the approval of a host of other organizations and agencies (something about being inclusive, no matter the cost). That hadn't been a possibility when I'd arrived in D.C. in 1996. Most were hostile to what they perceived as an aggressive new competitor. Yet, our initial isolation probably worked for us, as it allowed NADCP to move independently and in new directions, creating innovative projects.

That had changed. Now we were a respected organization, having proven ourselves worthy in a relatively short period of time. We'd made substantial efforts to collaborate with the Federal Probation Department and the Federal Department of Prisons, as well as with reform organizations such as the Prison Project and the Drug Policy Institute. Unfortunately, with little response. We'd had limited contact with the Department of Transportation's Highway Safety Section, the Health and Human Services Mental Health Division, and the Office of Juvenile Justice Programs. I was looking for new ways to expand the parameters of drug courts as a means to reform existing criminal justice institutions.

---

97 CCJ Resolution 22/COSCA Resolution 4 can be found at: https://ccj.ncsc.org/~/media/Microsites/Files/CCJ/Resolutions/08032000-In-Support-of-Problem-Solving-Courts.ashx.

That we were not able to connect with many organizations was a product of who we were and, I suppose, who I was. There was, at best, begrudging respect from organizations such as TASC, which had been marginalized by NADCP's rise in the hierarchy of criminal justice reform. I was not "one of the boys," as I had arrived in D.C. just four years before and was, to a significant extent, leading criminal justice drug reform efforts in D.C.

To be fair I was part of the problem. I was protective of the drug court reform mission and wary of other organizations and government agencies using drug courts and NADCP for their own purposes. Some would say I was uncooperative, overly protective of the field, or just a jerk.

Drug courts were already being misused by many jurisdictions who'd adopted the name but not the reform, using the drug court imprimatur to continue punitive responses to drug usage or simply to disguise their disinterest in reform of any kind. I wasn't about to let NADCP get into bed with what I considered to be bureaucratic and, to some extent, calcified organizations that cared more about protocol than people.

Drug court institutionalization was to be the last major project that I initiated and saw to completion during my tenure as NADCP president, NDCI executive director, and leader of the drug court (now problem-solving court) movement. It ultimately may have been my most important contribution to the drug court movement and criminal justice reform.

I had plans to develop model state legislation, administrative procedures, and drug court standards through NDCI. It appeared critical for NADCP/NDCI to be a guide and partner with state court administrations as they developed procedures for the integration of drug courts into their bureaucracies. Drug court judges still feared that state judiciaries would bureaucratize what was a grassroots and still-evolving reform, and such worry needed to be allayed.

Perhaps my greatest regret was that I wouldn't have the opportunity to move the drug court model into a more expansive modality, dealing with other offenders and specifically those returning from jails and prisons. I was moving towards a model that could encompass all who return from custody, no matter the offense—in effect a "reentry court for all" (later called an "evidence-based" approach to sentencing).

Importantly, states throughout the nation were now committed by their chief justices to develop their own administrative, procedural, and financial plans for the drug court and problem-solving courts to come. Today, twenty years after that CJC/COSCA resolution, statewide judicial and executive offices across the nation are dedicated to the education, training, and, critically, the funding of drug and problem-solving courts.[98]

My experience in pushing for the expansion of drug courts and in protecting the drug court's autonomy began to take its toll on me personally and on my ability to lead the field. My take-no-prisoners style did not find a warm response from rivals and bureaucrats who were used to more compromise and less passion in criminal justice advocates. Apparently, I was still an outsider.

---

98 There have been over fifty joint resolutions affirming and expanding CCJ and COSCA support for drug and problem-solving courts since their initial adoption in 2000. For more information and to browse the archives, visit https://ccj.ncsc.org.

CHAPTER 18

BUT NOT FOR ME

One morning in early 2000 I sat talking over coffee with Nelson Cooney, a friend and NADCP board member, at a corner table in the Royal Cafe, just a block from NADCP's offices in Alexandria.

We were discussing my plans for the future. Nelson knew that I intended to exit NADCP on my tenth anniversary as president in 2004. Nelson asked me when I intended to make it known that I was going to retire.

The more critical issue was who would take over as head of NADCP/ NDCI. Looking around the drug court and related fields, I knew dozens of exceptional leaders but few who had the potential to lead NADCP. Those who were capable weren't interested in leaving their positions or homes to work around the clock in D.C., chasing a dream and probably a pay cut.

Nelson and I had discussed the possibility of elevating West Huddleston to head up NADCP and NDCI. He suggested that rather than wait, I announce West's elevation to vice president of NADCP immediately, giving the field the opportunity to get to know him as heir apparent.

I agreed with him and announced West's promotion that same day. Unfortunately, that caused problems with senior staffers who had been with the organization longer and had stronger resumes. They also lacked the passion, leadership qualities, and appetite for hard work I believed necessary to keep NADCP at the forefront of a major reform movement. I had no idea that in impulsively elevating West, I was poking a hornet's nest and would suffer the consequences.

I went to the 2000 San Francisco NADCP Conference hoping for the proverbial hometown welcome. The three-thousand attendees at the San Francisco Conference were proof enough of the success of the organization and movement.

I was on a roll—or so I thought. We had established NADCP as the leader and focus for drug court and criminal justice reform activity in the U.S. and abroad. NDCI had been sanctified at a very special ceremony in the Roosevelt Room at the White House presided over by Drug Czar General McCaffrey.

Close to one thousand drug courts were operating in the U.S. and another 500 or so being planned. NDCI had begun to churn out publications—importantly, the NDCI *Review*—as well as monographs on important new topics (such as DUI courts, drug court systems, and reentry courts) that were being distributed all over the country.

The expected ratification of the historic "Problem-Solving Court Resolution" by State Chief Justices and State Court Administrators was just a couple of months off.

I was exhausted and overwhelmed by the workload, but I could see the light at the end of the tunnel. I had every reason to believe it was the right decision to promote West to vice president. I told him that I intended to retire and wanted him to be there to take over for me.

The bitter recriminations among senior staff about West's anticipated elevation to president prompted accusations that I had acted unilaterally. It did not sit well with them, and they went over my head and complained to board members. Senior staff were allied against the one staffer who had real promise as the future leader of NADCP. I knew little about office infighting, but I was about to find out.

To some extent there was a basis for senior staff's criticism. I was pushing the organization and its staff hard to achieve change in the criminal justice system. West, alone among senior staff, supported that aggressive stance and in turn was angrily denounced by the others. Keeping him at NADCP was critical to its continued success and, importantly for me, a way to transition out of the leadership without sacrificing the future of the drug court field.

At the San Francisco conference, Chairman Pat Morris, the San Bernardino County Superior Court judge, opened up the meeting to discussion. I expected kudos from the board for another remarkable year of innovation and progress. Instead, I was accused by several board members of being financially irresponsible—specifically, of making a short-term, no-interest personal loan of $100,000 to NADCP to pay staff salaries and other critical expenses while awaiting government grant payments.

Apparently, this was a violation of some governmental policy or regulation. At the time of the loan the only alternative was letting staff go and mothballing vital projects. I had done what I considered necessary for the well-being of NADCP and was being bludgeoned for what most people would consider a good deed done.

My free-wheeling leadership of NADCP and approach to reform was now being seriously challenged. I had made enemies among senior staff, and they in turn had undermined the board's confidence in me, arguing that my leadership needed to be reined in. The fact that that approach was what got us to the top of the mountain was apparently less important.

NADCP had become the organization I had dreamed of building: an accepted institution and a part of the Washington establishment. The reality was that after the San Francisco conference, I was considered a problem by the NADCP board. I became, for want of a better phrase, a lame duck president.

When I was building NADCP I had little concern for the whims of the board. Once Claire McCaskill left as chair, it became obvious that I had taken the board beyond their comfort level. In so doing I had somehow gone from father of the drug court movement to being replaceable. It became apparent that no new initiatives would be approved on my watch. I decided it was best for me to concede the inevitable and accept early retirement.

I met West at a bagel shop on King Street, a favorite place for coffee after a Potomac River run. I told him that I had talked to friends, experienced Washingtonians, and they told me the smart move was to step down before I was forced out.

West appeared stricken. He wanted to fight. He said, "Let's leave together and set up our own organization."

Tears welled up in my eyes. I was moved by his offer. But I knew that would be a mistake. I didn't want to further weaken NADCP by removing what in reality were its two mainstays, nor compete with or diminish the organization that I had worked so hard to create.

West needed to stay at NADCP. His outsized charm and drive would maintain NADCP as a major presence in the field, but his possible selection as my successor was a moot point. He was too young and too new to the job to vie for NADCP leadership at that point in his career.

I submitted my resignation letter and formally resigned as president of NADCP in 2001. I received many heartfelt letters of appreciation from both government and private individuals. Their kind words made withdrawal somewhat less painful.

I remained on the board of NADCP as an emeritus member to monitor the organization and help West stay on his leadership track. He had been a protege and trusted colleague and remained a close friend, and I felt that

I owed him my full support as he navigated his way towards leadership of NADCP.

My last significant responsibility was to assist in the selection of its new leader. I screened dozens of resumes with members of a selection committee comprised of board members. While most of the applicants appeared to be limited in experience, expertise, and background, we ultimately came down to a single applicant who had all the qualities that we had hoped for. She had been the first drug court judge in Gary, Indiana, and an appointed Indiana attorney general. She also had a wonderful, low-key managerial style, more in keeping with NADCP's new leadership profile. With Judge Karen Freeman-Wilson's ascension to the leadership of NADCP, I began to look for other avenues for my energies.[99]

---

99 According to the National Institute of Justice, at the end of the field's first five-year period (1989–1993), a total of 19 drug courts were established. From 1994 (when NADCP was founded) until the end of 2001, there were a total of 828 drug courts established (for a total of 847). American University's drug court program estimated there were an additional 450 drug courts in the planning stages in December of 2001.

INTERLUDE 7

JAZZ ON THE ALEXANDRIA PIER

Washington, D.C., had a colorful music scene that I could disappear into when work became too intense or life too painful. For some reason there was a dearth of saxophone players in the D.C. area, and I found gig work often, mostly in blues and R&B bands. It was a chance to let go of my troubles for an evening.

When my wife told me she was divorcing me, my reaction was to hang out at music jams across the D.C. area late into the night. I was burning the candle at both ends. I was also lucky to cross paths with a terrific piano-playing blues singer named Jazzy Blue.

Jazzy Blue and I played gigs all over the D.C. area, but our favorite was Friday night at the club Bojangles in Georgetown. During hot summer evenings Jazzy would bang out a rock and roll tune, and I would play my sax on the sidewalk as the crowd spilled out of the club, dancing onto M Street.

Jazzy encouraged me "to free my soul" and get out under the stars to play what was in my heart. It was the one achievement that eluded me. I was intimidated when playing my sax without any accompaniment, especially in front of a crowd. I wanted to play solo saxophone on the Alexandria Pier on the Potomac River, under the night sky.

The Alexandria Pier was where I really learned to play jazz. The transition from the blues to jazz wasn't easy, but I found that if I let go, it could open myself up to the music. I'd felt that way at times as an attorney, in final argument before a jury, reaching deep. And I experienced it when I played jazz, especially jazz ballads: a feeling of surrender, of stripping down to a place where you are most vulnerable.

Sometimes, on a Saturday evening, a dozen entertainers would perform on the Pier, everyone from jazz singers to blues musicians, pop bands, clowns, dancers, and wine glass players. I would show up after the regular entertainment and play jazz on the Pier after midnight with the moon mirrored on the Potomac River and my saxophone the only sound.

At times I felt split down the middle, much like I did when I took the bench at 8:30 in the morning after finishing an African jazz gig at 1:00 AM. I might be at the White House or the House or Senate building testifying at a hearing during the day, but in late evening you could often find me playing jazz on the pier. I wondered what the tourists dropping dollar bills in my sax case and my fellow musicians would think if they knew where I had spent my day.

CHAPTER 19

I CAN'T GET STARTED

At the age of fifty-five, I had reached the top of my game, and had been benched before the finals. Cutting ties and walking away from NADCP would have been the more rational path. But the organization had become so much a part of who I was that I couldn't leave until I saw that it was in good hands and would survive. So I went to board meetings and conferences as an emeritus member, enduring quizzical looks as to why I was still hanging around. I fought to remain relevant in a world that seemed intent on passing me by.

The 2001 Annual NADCP Conference was held in New Orleans. I was presented with the first Stanley Goldstein Drug Court Hall of Fame award for "extraordinary leadership and distinguished service."

Personally, this was a trying time. I was struggling to get my new non-profit organization, the Center for Problem-Solving Courts (CPSC), off the ground, working solo out of my condo on Polk Street in Alexandria.[100]

I believed that I had a part to play in the expansion of problem-solving courts and in establishing their relevance as a critical criminal justice reform, independent of drug courts. To my mind, the importance of a little-noted offshoot of drug courts, the reentry court, would be of primary interest going forward. And I hoped that the NDCI monograph that West and I had written in 1999, "Reentry Drug Courts," would open the door to exploration of that sentencing concept.

---

100 I wrote a monograph focusing on the reform of existing drug laws entitled "Rational Drug Policy Reform: A Resource Guide," which was published by CPSC and distributed at the 2001 NADCP Conference in New Orleans. Among other drug reform proposals was the reduction of all simple drug possession offenses to "misdemeanors, with no custody imposed."

The one area in which I was to maintain an active involvement after my resignation from NADCP was the international drug court field. I had visited over 70 countries. Probably the most important information I have processed from those experiences was that the people I met all over the world were decent, kind, and generous to travelers. I also developed a strong antipathy to government corruption and bureaucracy, which I met nearly everywhere.

From the army officer in Ethiopia who put an AR-16 to my head when I didn't move fast enough in leaving a bus (the fourth stop and frisk in an hour), to the Indian minister in New Delhi who wouldn't allow delegates to see a U.N. resolution before its unanimous passing, to the postal workers who routinely ripped un-cancelled stamps off my letters, to the court clerk in Trinidad who had me detained (on whose orders I never learned) because I was watching an open court hearing, I'd had a good deal of suspicion when dealing with the government officials I'd met in the third world.[101]

I made several trips abroad in 2001, the most illuminating being my second state-department-sponsored trip to Brazil. In many ways my trips overseas were more instructive to me than they were to my audiences. I learned of the difficulty in finding financial and rehabilitation resources believed necessary for drug courts in third-world countries. I also learned how different cultures see drug usage. The U.S. had become the center of anti-drug sentiment (as long as the drug isn't alcohol or labeled for medicinal purposes). This is not necessarily the attitude of cultures I have observed during my trips around the world.[102]

---

101 Shortly after becoming president of NADCP in 1994, I made my first presentation at the U.N. Conference on Communities in the Global Drug Problem (May 18, 1994). I was to present to the NGO section of the U.N. on several occasions as NADCP's president and the movement's leader. I took more than twenty trips abroad over the course of a decade to promote the drug court concept.

102 NADCP's most important international ally was Andrew Wells, a representative for the United Nations Office on Drugs and Crime. I had the good fortune to meet Andrew at a conference in New Delhi, where U.N. policy was to be drafted for the year 2000, entitled "United Nations Conference on the Global Drug problem." With the help of Andrew and others I was able to convince the drafting committee to include a section in the policy statement approving court-ordered treatment as an alternative to incarceration. The story behind the writing of that U.N. resolution deserves a brief description. About a dozen mostly Western delegates, of the 400-plus participants at the New Delhi conference, retired to a suite where the resolution was written overnight. To my knowledge, no one at the conference saw the final draft except for those who wrote it. What is truly amazing is that when it was called to a vote the following day, before some 400 delegates, one delegate stood up and demanded to see the document before he voted on it. His colleagues shouted him down and the resolution that was to be presented to the

In 1998 I was asked to assist in the formation of drug courts in the Pacific region. I flew to Guam to make a series of presentations and meet with the Pacific Island judges who were developing local drug court models. After visiting Guam I continued on to Australia, where I spent a week meeting with officials from every relevant organization and government entity, including the New South Wales prime minister and his cabinet. The following year I was asked to present to provincial officials in Western Australia.

The adoption of drug courts in Australia turned out to be our greatest international success. The Australians picked up on the idea quickly and implemented drug courts almost immediately. When I returned for further consultations and a conference in Western Australia the following year, I found a thriving drug court in Sydney working with the high-risk drug offenders, for whom drug courts were designed and for whom they work best (a drug court that many American courts have been so reluctant to establish). The Australians were so pleased with their drug court that others were already being implemented. Today, drug courts are present in the majority of Australian jurisdictions.

The Australians turned out to be well coordinated, more collaborative, and more appreciative of drug courts than many were in the U.S. They believed that drug courts would be most effective when working with those charged with more serious offenses (perhaps because of Australia's history as a one-time penal colony.) That was a position that NADCP supported at the time but without the scientific evidence that exists today for the Australian approach.[103]

From the founding of NADCP in 1994 to the creation of the International Association of Drug Court Professionals (IADCP) in 1999, I engaged the international community wherever and whenever I could. Through our National Conferences and other training events, individual consultations, discussions, and meetings were had both in the States and abroad.[104]

General Assembly was passed unanimously on a voice vote. And that is the sum of what I know about how U.N. resolutions are drafted.

103 "The research is clear that we can do harm when we target low risk offenders," write Edward J. Latessa and Angela K. Reitler in "What Works in Reducing Recidivism and How Does it Relate to Drug Courts?" They continue: "Drug courts should focus on higher risk offenders. By doing so, they will achieve the greatest effect on recidivism, and, just as importantly, they will not have increased the failure rates for lower risk offenders." For more on this topic see: https://law.onu.edu/sites/default/files/Latessa.pdf.

104 From 1997 on our national conferences had workshops and then whole tracks devoted to international drug courts. From 1997 through 1999 NADCP paid the hotel expenses of two official visitors per nation to encourage them to attend our national conferences and learn about drug courts.

The countries that had the most success were so-called modern, industrialized, Western nations with English-based judicial systems (in particular Australia, Canada, England, and Scotland). I was constantly on the lookout for ways to deal with drug abuse that did not require the financial or rehabilitative resources found in Western counties. I had embraced community-based drug courts early on in my career and was convinced that community was the key to a successful drug treatment court in other nations, as well as in the U.S.

I was skeptical of some of the claims for drug courts at home and abroad and painfully aware of the shortcomings of many of our courts. Drug courts that were ordering 30 days of jail time for a first positive marijuana drug test were not unusual.

There was a delicate juggling act being performed by drug courts, and it was the national organization's job to see that the field did not collapse into a more punitive system than which had existed before. An excellent example of this problem was taking drug courts international. While the concept can and was adopted successfully in Western countries, the idea that they could be easily adopted in third-world countries was somewhat problematic. Nations that didn't have drug treatment, drug testing, probation systems, or even clean drinking water would have a hard time replicating the Western drug court model.[105]

Everything changed on September 11, 2001. I was driving towards the Pentagon City Mall to purchase copies of the *Christian Science Monitor*, which contained my first (and last) major op-ed piece written as the director of the Center for Problem Solving Courts. Needless to say, I never made it to the mall, as traffic was streaming Virginia-bound after the attack on the Pentagon.

The next few months were brutal for everyone I knew. For me it had significant consequences: it marked the end of any real attempt to launch my nonprofit center. No one was talking about drug offenders, drug laws, or criminal justice issues; all were consumed with the 9/11 tragedy. I was depressed and

---

105 In 1999, at the fifth national conference in Miami, sufficient representatives were in attendance from nations with drug courts to form an international organization. Besides the U.S., countries that claimed existing drug courts included Australia, Barbados, Brazil, Canada, England, Ireland, and Jamaica. Approximately ten additional nations were represented at that initial 1999 Founders Meeting of the International Association of Drug court Professionals. Bylaws were adopted, officers elected: myself president, Judge Paul Bentley of Canada (Toronto's Drug Court judge) vice president, Andrew Wells (UNDCP representative) secretary, and Paul Hassett of Scotland (treatment professional) treasurer. The name of the organization has since been changed to the International Association of Drug Treatment Courts.

understood that I would not be moving ahead any time soon in my quest to establish myself in the problem-solving court field.

In November of 2001 I received a call from my friend and collaborator from the Oakland Drug Court, Frank Tapia, with a suggestion: "Why not leave Washington, D.C., and make a new start in the Bay Area?" The occupants of the cabin next to Frank's home had moved on and it could be rented for a very reasonable sum.

It made all the sense in the world to return to the bosom of the East Bay (Oakland, Berkeley, etc.). There wasn't much to do or learn while the capital remained in mourning. I had accomplished more than I had imagined possible in D.C. over the past seven years and over my decade as leader of the drug court field.

Karen-Freeman Wilson would turn out to be a generous and effective CEO whose leadership and management skills were fully displayed during her tenure at NADCP. Unfortunately, her tenure was cut short when illness and family responsibilities required her presence back in Gary; she tendered her resignation.

I anticipated West's ascension to CEO of NADCP. He had continued to serve as Karen's second-in-command, and everyone seemed to agree that he was effective in that role and that his turn would soon come. There didn't seem to be much I needed to do to promote his candidacy. A vote was taken by phone, and West was elected CEO unanimously.

I moved back home and slowly reintegrated myself into the Bay Area with the support of friends, in particular Frank, his wife Marna, and their son Nick, who would be my next-door neighbors for the next four years. At the time I didn't want to return to the bench or bar. I continued to play music daily, concentrating on my jazz chops and focusing on music as an occupation (though it was a fanciful aspiration at best).

NADCP was an institution now, accepted as such by almost everyone in the criminal justice field. There wasn't much I could contribute as a past president, but who knows, I might be able to do so in the future.

CHAPTER 20

COMING HOME

George wasn't very smart. He stood before me, an assigned judge, in the historic Mariposa County superior courthouse, as his attorney asked for mercy. George had been convicted by a jury of his peers of failure to register as a sex offender within five days of his birthday. The elected district attorney sat in the first row of benches, watching his deputy DA argue for a prison sentence of 25 years to life.[106]

George had never had a problem registering on time before, but in 2015 he'd hired a lawyer from L.A. who'd told him that he had "fixed everything" and that George didn't have to register anymore; and so he didn't. And the lawyer hadn't. If convicted, with his two prior felony convictions, California's "three strikes and you're out" clause would kick in, with its 25-years-to-life mandatory sentence.

It was a depressing trial. It was clear that George had a limited mental capacity. Sixteen years earlier he had served a six-year prison term for two felony priors: two sex offenses involving a single victim that didn't involve violence or its threat. He had led a blameless and apparently quiet life for the past ten years in his father's home, just down the street from the home of the deputy sheriff he was supposed to report to.

I didn't believe the DA would take the case to trial. I didn't believe that any jury would convict a fellow townsman of a felony under the facts presented. But all the above came to pass. I sat on the bench of that ancient courtroom and listened as both sides argued sentencing: the district attorney for prison

106 When a local judge decided to avoid the case and take a vacation, I was asked to preside over George's trial. The case was held in the Mariposa County Superior Court, home to the oldest continuously operating courtroom "west of the Mississippi River." Mariposa County is part of rural Northern California, just west of Yosemite Park, a pleasant assignment during summertime (I stayed at a bed and breakfast in the woods, with a stream running behind my cabin; one of the perks of being an assigned judge).

and the defense attorney for probation. I did my own research and wrote a judge's memorandum, as I found both attorneys' legal briefs wanting. This was one case where I wanted my reasoning to be irrefutable and unappealable.

The case itself had confounded me. It wouldn't have been filed in a county with a different demographic profile, such as Alameda County. But it was taken seriously by this DA and this community; they returned a conviction within hours. I was surprised. But upon further consideration I realized that the verdict did reflect the community's mores. It made me think again about how different communities feel about crime and those charged with criminal acts.

And then it was my time to rule. It was one of my more satisfying moments on the bench. I found that George's offense was technical in nature and minor in impact. I struck down the two prior felony convictions "in the interests of justice," placed George on probation, and ordered him released with a sentence of "credit for time served" for the months he had already spent in custody. I watched as the elected district attorney stood up, glared at me, and abruptly left the courtroom. I thought, *I won't be sitting on a case in this county again.*

Being a truly impartial judge can be a difficult job. In many, if not most counties, prosecutors have the expectation that you'll decide cases in their favor. Those who vote in judicial elections—often an older, white demographic—typically support law-and-order candidates. So an elected judge is justifiably concerned about the prospects of an electoral challenge. In a judicial election no judge wants to be accused by an ambitious, young assistant DA of being soft on crime.[107]

When I returned to the Bay Area in 2002 I thought about authoring a book about my experiences in the criminal justice system, but it was too big a project, and I felt no compelling reason to undertake it. Nor did I feel a need to put on the robe and return to the bench. I had the feeling that I had been there and done that.

Somehow, I reasoned that my experience as a drug court pioneer and criminal justice reform leader would point me towards a career in academia or perhaps the corporate world. Though I offered my services to the University of California at Berkeley and several other academic institutions, no one was

---

107 That was the last time I was asked to preside over a trial in which the local judge undoubtedly felt electorally vulnerable. I, as an assigned judge, made a decision contrary to the views of the local community but in accordance with my personal sense of justice. As an assigned judge from out of county, I couldn't be voted out of office. Nothing was between me and my next judicial assignment except the decision of the presiding judge to invite me back or not. Of course, the chief justice has the final decision as to whether to retire you from the program entirely. There would be no hearing or recourse of any kind from that decision.

quite sure what I would be teaching and why it would be relevant to the students of the day. My friend David—a classmate from Public School 209 in Brooklyn—who doubled as my accountant, brought me to my senses. He reminded me that I had no substantial assets and my pension, when it came on line, would be fixed at about 25% of what I would have received had I finished my career as a superior court judge.

I was faced with returning to the bench or a severe change in lifestyle; I chose to return to the bench. I met with the director of the California Administrative Office of the Courts, Bill Vickrey, who had been a longtime supporter.

Bill encouraged me to apply for a superior court judgeship. Frankly, this posed something of a dilemma. If I was to return to the bench it would be as a superior court judge in Alameda County, as California had eliminated municipal court positions in 1997. That might allow me to continue my career as a drug court or problem-solving court judge, which I of course wished to do. On a more personal note I'd have my pension reinstated and would continue to accrue benefits—which I would not as an assigned judge—as I moved towards retirement.

I thanked Bill for his offer but declined. I was a liberal, and perhaps worse, a judicial reformer as a judge. Governor Pete Wilson, a conservative, made judicial appointments and wouldn't take kindly to a judicial activist's application. More to the point, I had made a prodigious number of enemies in Alameda County (including the entire Oakland bench, whom I had successfully sued individually and collectively). I knew that, should I put my name up for a judgeship, they would do whatever they could to block it. I decided that I wouldn't give them that opportunity.[108]

As an alternative Bill suggested I consider applying for an assigned judge's position, called a "senior judge" in other states. It was actually closer to being a substitute teacher. Assigned judges fill in for judges who are sick, recently elevated, or simply on vacation.

I enjoyed my return to the bench in new and unexpected ways. Because I was moving from courtroom to courtroom and county to county, I began to develop a feel for what different localities sought in a judge and what justice meant in different communities. It turns out, not unexpectedly, that justice

---

108 A few years later I was assured by my former law partner, Luke Ellis, who was then chair of the Alameda County Bar Judicial Selection Committee, that my application for a judgeship to democratic governor Gray Davis would be granted, should I apply. With reservations, I did apply—only to have my nomination blocked by my former judicial colleagues.

is geographic and cultural and very much a reflection of each community's values.

I earned a newfound feeling of satisfaction from my experiences on the bench, as well as a certain confidence and comfort in working with staff and counsel. Drug court had left its mark on me, even a sense of humor about my work, which I imagine other drug court judges experienced when returning to regular duty.

I found sentencing to be an important opportunity to reach out to the offender and set the stage for later rehabilitation. It was the chance to speak, one human to another, to ask what effect the sentence would have on them, their family, and their children, and to find out whether they had any plans for their lives after incarceration. I know to some that approach may seem naïve, but I had many conversations with defendants at sentencing that seemed to resonate with them and others in the courtroom.

Judges don't have to leave their humanity at the courtroom door but can make the courtroom a friendlier, more humane place, without the dread often found there. I saw the small cadre of judge, staff, and counsel in a typical courtroom as a microcosm of what the drug court had been and what they could become. There was potential for using the drug court model and its collaborative, community-based approach in many criminal proceedings. Drug court judges were paving the way to a more human and humane criminal justice system.

INTERLUDE 8

THE TAUBER-BROWNING BAND

Photo by James Lareger.

I always wanted to play jazz. I loved the blues too. But jazz was where you went to play gorgeous ballads like "Misty," "My Romance," and "The Man I Love." I started playing jazz ballads almost as soon as I could play a blues scale.

Although I was for a short time a student of a great tenor sax player, Hal Stein, I never developed jazz chops. I took two semesters of music theory under the watchful eye of Mr. D'mante, music director at Laney Jr. College in Oakland, a wonderfully enthusiastic teacher. Mr. D'mante made you feel like you were on your way to being a pro. He never demeaned you for not understanding what for many of us was akin to rocket science. He began many a lecture with a reference to your average musician student, someone he called "Joe Ride-a-Bike," an endearing metaphor for the common man in music.

I was comfortable playing the blues, rock, and African highlife, but jazz always felt like a bridge too far. Part of the problem was a lack of technical knowledge and music-reading ability, but the other part was a lack of confidence. There is no safety net in jazz.

Returning from D.C. to the Bay Area gave me the opportunity I had been missing. I took my experience playing on the Alexandria Pier and transplanted it three thousand miles to Albany Beach and its own

pier. I especially liked the pier, though dilapidated, because it had an amazing view of the Bay and sometimes dozens of birds sat at its end, no more than twenty feet from me. I took some satisfaction from the fact that the birds didn't fly away when I started playing or, as I would later claim, they seemed to enjoy it.

That was in fact the name of a concert I performed a few years back—a one-man show, really. I called it "Playing to the Birds" and performed it at, of all places, Birdland. I played to a full house and the audience, like the birds on the pier, seemed to enjoy the evening.

Over the past three years I have played at local jazz venues with a wonderful Hammond organ player, Craig Browning. He covers the piano and bass parts with his hands and his feet, respectively. There is something about the Hammond organ and Leslie speakers that speaks to me of jazz played with a gospel sensibility and a blues voice. I'm still learning.

CHAPTER 21

AIN'T MISBEHAVIN'

Bleu stood before me, head bowed in resignation, and asked if I still wanted him to read his essay.

I had taken the bench that morning in early July of 2010, presiding over the San Francisco Parole Reentry Court (SFPRC). When I had called Bleu's name he had stepped forward, not ten feet from me. I lit into him, scolding him for his continuing use of methamphetamine and ordering him remanded into custody.

The defendant was a hard-working, middle-aged parolee, seemingly dedicated to his recovery. He had entered the SFPRC nearly eight months before. By most measures he'd done remarkably well: fully engaged in our court recovery community and encouraging others to succeed, he'd found work at a local non-profit (delivering meals to the elderly) and had created a monthly newsletter for our program.

About the only thing he *hadn't* done was stop using methamphetamine. He took drug tests regularly, but they were mostly positive for meth. After ten months in a program intended to reduce recidivism and help parolees rejoin mainstream society and stop using drugs, his urine tests were consistently coming up dirty.

It was not my finest hour. It was axiomatic to drug courts. You ordered incremental periods of custody to motivate participants when they failed to comply with court orders that one assumed they could comply with, typically to appear for court hearings, treatment appointments, and/or drug tests. On the other hand, you didn't punish those who continued to use drugs—an addiction over which they might have minimal control. Instead, you increased treatment conditions, such as treatment sessions, counseling, groups, and, only when necessary, detox and/or residential treatment.

I did have my reasons for blowing up at Bleu, though they didn't have much to do with him. I had just received notice from the presiding judge that the Parole Reentry Court, which was generally understood to be working better than any other rehabilitation program in the San Francisco court system and perhaps the state, now faced imminent closure.

I hadn't told staff about the scheduled closing yet, as I was hoping for a reprieve from the presiding judge. I was doing everything I could to convince the PJ to keep the program open. It wasn't an easy thing to do: programs were closing down across the state as Governor Brown—facing the "Great Recession"—slashed funding for the courts.

I'd had an unusually contentious pre-court meeting with staff that morning. Against the advice of the team, who wanted to give the popular Bleu one more chance, I had decided enough was enough: I would send him to an in-custody detox program and then a residential program. I just didn't believe the court should turn a blind eye to Bleu's continuing drug usage.

In my anger and frustration I had forgotten that a week earlier I had assigned Bleu to read an essay on his efforts to attain sobriety. I would have preferred to put Bleu in jail and move on, but it would have been difficult to ignore my previous court order, given the circumstances. I had a roomful of program participants and observers. So I told Bleu to read his essay.

He told us he was introduced to meth at the age of twelve by foster parents and had been addicted ever since. But that wasn't the point of his essay. He was down but not defeated. His work with the San Francisco Parole Reentry Court was a form of redemption, and by being a part of the court community he still hoped he could kick his habit and go on to have the writing career he'd always dreamed of.

When he finished you could've heard the proverbial pin drop. All eyes were on me. In that instant I knew that I couldn't apply the same standards to Bleu that I did to others.

As frustrated as I was with both my own and Bleu's inability to impact his addiction, I couldn't think of any reason why jail time would make a positive difference in his life. I withdrew my sentence and increased Bleu's rehab requirements and service to the community. I understood viscerally what I had always known, that one couldn't apply the same standards and solutions to very different people, even those with seemingly the same problem.[109]

---

109 Bleu's interview and his court appearance before the San Francisco Parole Reentry Court, four days before the program's closure, can be found at: https://youtu.be/3tesN8rnwZg.

I was sitting as the judge in the San Francisco Parole Reentry Court (SFPRC) because Presiding Judge Jim McBride and incoming Presiding Judge Katherine Feinstein were agreeable to my taking on the project.[110] It was my hope that the SFPRC would show how well a community-based court rehabilitation program could perform when serious offenders with different underlying problems and needs were dealt with within a single court framework; in effect, a "reentry court for all."

To be honest I approached the start of the SFPRC with trepidation. Though I had been a judge for over twenty years, I had little contact with parolees except for their initial sentencing to prison. I received the CDCR files of prospective program participants and blanched at what I saw: photographs of hardened criminals whose very countenance inspired fear. I steeled myself to the task. (Over the next year I was to learn how wrong I had been to pre-judge these men.)

The chances of my building an innovative reentry court within the San Francisco Court System, however, were not good. I was an assigned judge and served at the pleasure of the presiding judge. Though I got along well with San Francisco's judicial leadership, I had no political base.

I didn't know the San Francisco political playbook, and the city had the most entrenched political bureaucracy I had ever encountered. There was a Collaborative Courts unit within the court itself with perhaps ten employees (I never did get a fix on the number) whose purpose was never clear to me.

Katherine Feinstein, the incoming presiding judge, told me she wanted the reentry court to be free of the bureaucratic malaise that she believed infested the other collaborative courts in San Francisco. She assured me that I would have the authority to make changes necessary to move the project forward. And she was true to her word.

If there is a universal law of bureaucracy it is that if there are new resources available, you need to get your share. San Francisco was a wonderful example of that principle. Every agency within hailing distance wanted their piece of the action, but if I conceded that point, no resources would be available to provide rehabilitation services, which was ostensibly the purpose of the project.

---

110 The San Francisco Parole Reentry Court was a statutorily funded pilot project administered by both the California Administrative Office of the Courts and the California Department of Corrections and Rehabilitation (CDCR). The funding itself, some $1.5 million each to five counties, was provided by the federal government through the American Recovery and Reinvestment Act of 2009, also known as the "2009 Stimulus Package." Not surprisingly, its funding in California was the result of prodigious lobbying efforts before the California Legislature by Judge Steven Manley.

Several public meetings were held on how the reentry court could be staffed and structured with limited resources. Though the court would initially be in session only two half-days a week, representatives of the public defender and district attorney offices insisted they would needed full-time attorneys to staff the reentry court. Both agencies were willing to reject the grant entirely, as it didn't, in their view, provide sufficient funds to adequately and fully staff the program.

I did the research, talked to officials from parole and other state agencies, and came up with a structure that navigated around the district attorney's and public defender's concerns. By using state resources already available for dealing with state parolees, the SFPRC could do without county services.

While this was a correct interpretation of the law, it was bad San Francisco politics. For someone with no political clout in San Francisco I was putting myself in conflict with two of the county's most powerful entities.

To be truthful, much of the blowback was towards my plan to build a new court structure, rather than add to established county agencies. I knew from my experience over the past twenty years that building programs onto existing structures was often the equivalent of adding a second story onto a rickety wooden foundation. It will fail.

I insisted that the reentry court build its own structure from the foundation up, with new staff. And I would have the final say in staff selection. Apparently, no judge had done that in recent memory, and it was a precedent the agency bureaucrats were none too happy with. I knew that we could do the job with fewer resources and a fraction of the staff normally assigned to collaborative courts.

Allison West, our new program manager, was an extraordinary person and an inspiration to the entire team, someone with an infectious spirit who would go the extra mile for our program participants. She had begun volunteering at San Quentin prison a decade earlier. She had also created a non-profit, the California Reentry Program, staffed by volunteers who helped inmates in their transition to life on the outside. Most importantly, she had an enormous regard and affection for inmates.

It had not been an easy transition. We had been frozen out by the district attorney, public defender, and public health agencies. The financially responsible agency was attempting to take control of project staff. One rehab counselor threatened another physically and was terminated from the program during his probation period. There were complaints that our parole officer was abusive to program participants. That we survived, and worked through those problems and others, was something of a miracle.

We staggered across the starting line still setting up the program. Few on staff or in the courthouse gave us much chance of succeeding. And many if not most would have welcomed the program's demise and my banishment from San Francisco County.

But it didn't happen. Not by a long shot. The program was a wonder. Hostile staffers and others watching closely realized that there was something special going on the sixth floor of the civil court building. And they weren't the only ones. I, for one, was more than pleased that so many of our innovations were working for our participants.[111]

We set up the program so that participants felt comfortable and perhaps even at home in the courthouse. We were, to my knowledge, the only criminal courtroom in the building, so the atmosphere was actually refined and even calm compared to the criminal courts building downtown.

We served coffee (when available, fresh-brewed Guatemalan from Costco) and pastries or cookies every court session. We opened courtroom doors early and invited participants to meet with their counselors and each other in a positive social atmosphere. I would invite inspirational speakers to talk to us for a few minutes before sessions, and our program manager, Allison, would bring a cake to court once a month to celebrate our participants' birthdays. I stepped down from the bench and stood next to participants to present them with awards at the beginning of each court session.

We created an honor roll whose members were to meet for a pizza lunch once a month, during which we discussed how the program was working and honorees made recommendations as to how to run the court better. I invited participants to swap books with me or read poems or passages they had written. Bleu, whom I described at the beginning of this chapter, created an SFPRC newsletter that he was to distribute on a monthly basis to the court and participants.

And it all worked. We had amazed—and had amazing participants. We made it clear that the court and program staff were there to help them and not to catch them screwing up (although monitoring was still a major program responsibility).

I got to court early to prep for hearings. I would sit in my narrow, closet-like chambers and listen to the murmur of various rehab and counseling groups meeting in my courtroom. I never entered the courtroom during program sessions, often held before court and at lunchtime, although I wanted to.

---

111 Visit www.reentrycourtsolutions.com/the-participants/ for interviews with participants the week of the program's closure.

Their infectious laughter was inviting, for all of us a very different experience of a courtroom.

Those who had fought to stop us came to realize that we were doing rehabilitation better than any court in the county (if not in the state). When word got out about our success, we were visited by county and state officials from across California (and even the nation).

Though we had our problems I had never been part of a team that worked together so well. Along with Allison and staff, we handpicked a dedicated group of treatment professionals to staff SFPRC. The staff were willing to be there for the participants 24/7, if needed. The participants were eager for success in their rehabilitation and supported one another.

During my reentry court term I constantly pushed staff to come up with new ideas for incentives. We used everything, including awards, certificates, photos, monetary stipends, an honor roll, and a grab bag (for special achievements).

And every encounter had a sense of drama, as I often didn't know how exchanges would play out in real time. Cases were staffed starting at 8:00 AM (as court started at 10:00 AM), but that was only the beginning of the journey. The in-court dialogue was often based on information gleaned from our pre-court staffing, and I would riff off of that to connect with participants. Does that sound like jazz? It does to me too.

CHAPTER 22

I LEFT MY HEART
IN SAN FRANCISCO

Bill, a San Francisco parolee, stood next to his state public attorney, Alice. I asked him if he wished to enter the program.

Bill was in his thirties, short, slight of build, with dark hair plastered down across his forehead, covering a bald spot. Tattoos were showing on his arms and neck, and he wore ill-fitting clothes. He had watched the court session. Almost everyone called on the calendar had shown up. Some had failed to test clean and had been ordered to complete additional treatment sessions and/or community service hours. Most did well, according to our standards, and a few were given Gold or Silver Awards, reducing their term of parole, while participants who had shown substantial success in the program were given a small monetary reward.

It took over an hour to call all 25 or so parolee participants that morning. There had been the usual banter between myself and those in the jury box. Each, in turn, sat in a chair at a small table perhaps ten feet from the bench and about the same distance from a jury box full of parolees. Behind them, in the jury box and at the attorneys' tables, sat court staff, parole officers, and treatment staff.

Bill had discussed entry into the program with his attorney, and they had reviewed the program contract. Those who wanted to enter the program had to request admittance in open court. Bill would do so today after watching a progress report hearing. I asked him if he wished to enter the program. I then asked Alice whether Bill understood the program, its requirements, and the program contract.

All of this ceremony impressed upon the nominee the sanctity of his commitment and that of the judge and program staff to his rehabilitation and return to the community. I would then ask a final question: "What do you hope to achieve between now and the end of this program?"

Initially, the expected response was that the parolee would return to the community as a good citizen and stay away from drugs. Instead, what I mostly heard from parolees was heartfelt and deeply moving descriptions of loneliness, a wish to rejoin families, make new friends, and find something useful to do that would take the place of drugs. I would tell the new participant that everyone in the courtroom was dedicated to helping them and that they should rely on us and other participants to succeed.

In a breaking voice Bill told me that he was tired of sleeping in the streets and committing crimes; he hoped for a new life. Bill signed the written contract—which had little legal but great personal import—along with his attorney and had her present the contract to me for my signature. I then asked Bill to step forward, and I reached down from the bench and shook his hand, whispered a few words of encouragement, and handed him a small datebook for him to write court dates and appointments in.

Many of these admission ceremonies found staff fighting back tears. They were, after all, rituals of our reentry court community, welcoming a new member and marking their and our obligations and commitments. And they worked.

The New York Times published an article by Trey Bundy, "Parole and Probation Courts in San Francisco are Closing After Budget Cuts," on Sunday, October 8, 2011, days after the closing of the highly successful San Francisco Parole Reentry Court.

I then wrote on my website, "The SFPRC enjoyed the full support of the San Francisco court until this past summer, when drastic reductions in state funding caused many California courts to reassess their ability to provide rehabilitation services. San Francisco was one of the worst hit, with over $6 million of debt and prospects of closing down 25 of 63 courtrooms countywide."

The truth was somewhat different. I was told that the program might be shuttered about three months before its scheduled closing. I couldn't understand why that was the case, as all expenses were covered by a federal grant. I provided the new presiding judge with an analysis of the savings the program was delivering to the county and specifically to the county jail and other criminal justice agencies. I was told that she was only interested in its impact on the court. I was given one week's final notice before the court was to close.

I was distraught. I had been promised by the presiding judge—and I in turn promised staff and participants—that the program would complete its two-year grant period (seemingly guaranteed in a written agreement with the PJ). It seemed impossible to explain how a program as successful as this one could be closed down when federal funding covered all our expenses. The incredible explanation I was given was that high-end civil attorneys would be upset if a criminal court remained open at the civil court building when civil courtrooms were closing down.

I went to talk to former Presiding Judge James McBride, a tall, straight, politically savvy native San Franciscan with an Irish sensibility and sense of humor. I had always enjoyed our talks, but not this one. He had visited the court program recently and told me that he agreed with me, the court was working as promised. He then said something that caught my attention: while I could make the program work, he wasn't so sure it could be passed on to my successors. As I left his chambers I wondered why not.

The culprit in my mind was not Presiding Judge Feinstein, who I understood—while dealing with the court's serious financial crisis—delegated control over criminal matters to the assistant presiding judge.

I met with Assistant Presiding Judge Cynthia Ming-Mei Lee in her chambers at the Criminal Courts Building on Bryant Street days before the program was to close.

I asked her to delay the closing of the SFPRC.

She said that she wouldn't.

I reminded her that there was no cost to the county to continue the program.

She said that she didn't care.

I explained that the participants were doing better than any other San Francisco rehab program.

She told me she wouldn't change her mind.

I continued to argue the point.

She told me our conversation was over.

I accused her of being heartless and mean-spirited.

That was the end of our discussion, the SFPRC program, my four-year San Francisco court assignment, and any future court assignments in San Francisco.

The New York Times explored with Judge Lee her almost comical rationale for closing down the SFPRC, writing, "Ms. Lee said that despite the federal financing, the programs have cost the courts money for clerical work and other expenses, but that she did not know how much the closings would save."

To this day I believe that the program was shut down because San Francisco's judicial leadership was spooked. They feared that, as with many San Francisco programs—successful or not—the SFPRC would live on in perpetuity. They candidly admitted to me that they didn't want to take on any program not statutorily required with prospective financial costs, no matter their success.

It wasn't the first time, nor would it be the last time, a presiding judge (or assistant presiding judge, for that matter) tossed me from court and county.

The SFPRC's closing was painful. I had developed a great fondness for the participants and felt they had been betrayed when I told them that the program would be discontinued. It had been both the high and low point of my judicial career. I knew that it would be my last opportunity to demonstrate that community-based courts—specifically reentry court for all—could be extraordinarily successful.

Final CDCR data: San Francisco parolees had a nine-month return-to-prison rate of approximately 80% from December 2010 through August 2011. SFPRC had a return-to-prison rate of 12% for the same nine-month period. Equally important, our participants looked forward to coming to court (a rare thing indeed). The failure-to-appear rate for weekly court sessions was approximately 6% over that same nine-month period.[112] I would jokingly say that our attendance rate would compare positively with a Catholic school for girls.

And now my final project, acknowledged throughout the Greater San Francisco criminal justice community as being a phenomenal success, would end before the final data was in and would become, at best, a footnote to history.

---

112 Data compiled by Maria McKee, Policy and Program Analyst, San Francisco Collaborative Courts ("Parole Reentry Court 9 Month Update, December 2010–August 2011") and California Department of Corrections and Rehabilitation (San Francisco County Return to Prison Data, December 1, 2010, through August 31, 2011).

CONCLUSION

Community from the Beginning

Since the beginning, humans have lived together in "communities". Early communities provided the tools to support acceptable behavior, using affirmation, status, and other tangible and intangible rewards to encourage conformity to societal norms. The community also relied on what we would today call "alternative sanctions", to correct an individual's antisocial behaviors. This "traditional" sanctions" approach to misbehavior included admonitions, shaming, restitution (often the family's responsibility), corporal punishment, shunning and finally, if all else failed, banishment from the "community."

The group typically welcomed the reformed miscreant back into the community when the behavior was corrected. The "community" couldn't afford to waste an individual's productivity. Moreover, keeping the individual stigmatized created an unhealthy separation from others and prevented a healing within the community. It made far more sense, to return the outcast to the bosom of the community, the sooner the better.

To this day, Aboriginal communities use shunning and in extreme cases banning from the group, when persons refuse to follow community norms, resulting in destabilization in the community. It's interesting to note, that as in the drug court model, the Aboriginal community is more interested in the restoration of a peaceful community than the strict identification of the party at fault.

THE PAST

The view from 30,000 feet is indeed extraordinary. Beginning in 1974, when I became a public defender, and then over the next twenty years, I recall almost everyone from judges and prosecutors to the news media declaring that those who broke the drug laws needed to go to prison. At the time "Nothing Works" was the *slogan du jour* when it came to drug abusers.

Sometime after becoming a drug court judge I came across a book that spoke to a new generation of criminal justice professionals. Written by Professor Lawrence Friedman of Stanford University (mentioned earlier as the "dean" of American legal history) his book is titled *The Roots of Justice: Crime and Punishment in Alameda County, 1870–1910*.

What drew me to the book was its subject matter, a historical view of criminal law in my home county almost exactly 100 years before I became a public defender, commissioner, and judge there. I recognized that many of the issues described in that book persist to this day, although many have also grown exponentially in complexity and seriousness.

The book described how the courts as a rule would over-punish offenders who belonged to the working class or worse: vagrants and drifters, the unemployed, and social misfits. Friedman pointed out that those of the lower classes were considered to lack social and moral value as much as they did economic worth.

Before the dawn of the 20th century, the Irish were picked up for drunkenness, Chinese immigrants were arrested for gambling and opium addiction, and African-Americans (2% of all Oaklanders) were arrested—some would suggest for simply being black in the city of Oakland—at three times the rate of the general population. One fascinating insight I gleaned from Friedman's book was that "real crime"—violent or property crime—was decreasing at the end of the 19th century, while crimes against the social and moral order were increasingly being prosecuted. The emerging criminal justice professions, made up of white, middle-class males, were committed to protecting their own class privilege and sense of morality.

It is often thought of as a system that kept blacks and immigrants down. While that is all too real, it was part of a larger movement to control and punish immorality in the lower classes. More to the point, it would take a blind man to miss the history of injustice cloaked in the majesty of the law. Whether one looks abroad to the pogroms against the Jews in Russia, to the Nazi judges who sanctioned genocide, or to the South African judges who enforced apartheid, the history of the courts is too often the history of class, religious, and ethnic bias and injustice.

Certainly, the same arc of history can be seen in this country. From the Puritan Blue Laws of colonial times and the repeated abrogation of treaties with Native Americans, to the Chinese Exclusion Act and the Jim Crow laws, we cannot claim that justice necessarily prevails in our courts of law. In fact, it would be more honest to say that even the fairest of jurists could not operate in a system of laws that is inherently unjust and still reach just decisions. Though the law may be applied equally, institutional bias will prevent a just resolution for those in the lower classes.

I saw this firsthand in courts where I worked. While some may say that I was a part of it (and that I would not dispute), most jurists followed the law and were grateful to be a privileged part of that system, even if it meant keeping others down. That this was an issue of class is brought home by the fact that judges, prosecutors, and police who were black or brown applied the law with as much force and cynicism as their white colleagues (and in some cases considerably more so).

None of these revelations were new, exactly, when I became aware of Friedman's seminal work. At the time I had been a part of that criminal justice system for many years. I understood, sometimes at a gut level, the injustices of the criminal justice system. As a public defender and then a private defense attorney I saw too many poor and homeless citizens treated inhumanely. As a commissioner I saw traffic offenders (mostly poor defendants, both white and black) frozen out of the courts by huge fines, fees, and penalties. As a judge I watched as drug addicts (whose crime was to wave down customers for drug sellers in exchange for a tiny piece of the drug sold) were routinely sent to prison for a minimum of three years for selling drugs when the true extent of their criminality was being seriously drug dependent.

And I was the one doing the sentencing.

Dr. Michael Smith, a psychiatrist, was the director of the Lincoln Hospital's Recovery Center in the Bronx, New York. Dr. Smith was short, heavyset, somewhat disheveled, and typically wearing a crumpled suit. When he talked he often mumbled—but brilliantly—on concepts critical to the drug court field. Dr. Smith held important insights into why drug courts worked.[113] He was sort of the Pied Piper of the drug court movement and was widely acknowledged as influencing the structure of the Miami-Dade County Drug Court. Miami's signature acupuncture treatment protocol was also the creation of Dr. Smith.

As Miami espoused the importance of Dr. Smith's acupuncture protocol, I decided to visit Lincoln Hospital. A large room was set aside in the clinic for patients receiving acupuncture treatment. Reclining chairs reminiscent of those found in a hair salon were lined up along the walls. Perhaps a half-dozen patients had acupuncture needles sticking out of their ears. They appeared to be calm and relaxed, suggesting a meditative state.

Dr. Smith was a man of good intentions and great ability. He had developed his acupuncture drug treatment protocol based on the work of Dr. Hsiang-Lai Wen, a Hong Kong neurosurgeon. He believed in his protocol, as do thousands of patients and acupuncture practitioners around the world.[114]

I've have had the acupuncture protocol performed on me at several drug court conferences and thought it to have a positive, calming effect. Though accepted by many as an effective treatment for drug addiction, it is also opposed by many.

The point is, I am not an expert in the area of drug abuse. I cannot claim to know what is the best treatment. Even drug experts are at a loss as how to deal with drug abuse, whether through counselling, Narcotics Anonymous and/or Alcoholics Anonymous, short- or long-term residential or outpatient treatment programs, individualized or group treatment counselling, medically assisted treatment, acupuncture, or some combination of the above.

The example of Dr. Tom McClellan is illustrative. Dr. McClellan has had a long and illustrious career, with more than 35 years in addiction treatment research, and is considered one of the foremost academic experts on drug abuse. Yet, when his son became drug dependent, Dr. McClellan quite literally didn't know whom to turn to and had no idea as to which treatment

---

113 They included the primacy of measurements that could be objectively confirmed, such as drug tests, court attendance, and program compliance. He believed that continued drug usage should be met with an increase in treatment, not custody. He looked askance at programs that expected or required honesty from participants, believing we were asking too much from individuals who had so much to lose.

114 Dr. Smith was nominated for and received the NADCP Pioneer Award for his work in developing Miami-Dade County Drug Court's protocol, an award he richly deserved. The award was presented at the first NADCP Annual Conference in Las Vegas, January, 1995. Dr. Michael Smith died on December 24, 2017.

programs were effective. Tragically, his son died of a drug overdose before Dr. McClellan could place him in an appropriate drug treatment program.

During the Obama administration Dr. McClellan became deputy director of the Office of National Drug Control Policy. Among other accomplishments he established a hotline for people seeking information about the quality of drug treatment programs. But the reach of efforts like Dr. McClellan's are, unfortunately, limited and the ultimate efficacy of any one drug treatment modality questionable.

In this book's preface I described drug courts as the "crown jewel of the problem-solving court world." And so it is. All 50 state supreme court chief justices have resolved to "advance the application and methods of drug courts into ongoing court operations." Drug courts have given us a model to emulate and a path to follow in building a more humane criminal justice system.

With synthetic opioid deaths increasing sevenfold over the past five years, many desperately look to drug courts as the path forward for the criminal justice system. Those who believe that drug courts or any criminal justice program alone will be able to reverse the tide of drug overdoses are mistaken. The criminal justice system, and drug courts specifically, can at best be a partner to the treatment community, public health system, and local communities in staunching the catastrophe that is the opioid epidemic.

I sat on assignment in dozens of California drug and problem-solving courts over a fifteen-year period. I noted what makes them work. And what makes them fail. The difference is often determined by the quality of judicial and practitioner commitment and leadership, their adherence to drug court best practices, and the sufficiency of financial and human resources. But the critical factor, to my mind, remains the support received from the circles of fellow participants, dedicated practitioners, and the greater community that surrounds them.

Where the drug court model can be truly impactful is as a broader sentencing paradigm, providing a model to emulate and a path forward. Problem-solving courts, such as veterans and reentry courts, are prototypes for sentencing systems of the future, dedicated to providing effective alternative sentencing for all in need.

In April of 2011 I sat in my chambers reading progress reports for San Francisco Parole Reentry Court participants. Ben, our parole officer, knocked on the door. I glanced up and told him to come in. Ben was a burly man, balding, and wearing a light-blue jacket with the words "Parole Officer" in large letters on the back. He had a reputation for being tough and, according to some, abusive.

Ben was part of our team because he was the only African-American parole officer willing to take the job. I was trying hard to find staff that looked like our parole clientele, the majority of whom were black. We'd had a private conversation when he applied for the job, and he had acknowledged his reputation for being hard on parolees but expressed a heartfelt desire to help them avoid returning to prison. I was, in fact, pleased with his work up to that point.

Ben sat down across from me at my desk and told me his story. Peter, our Christmas poet, had contacted him by cell phone when Ben was off-duty, at home with his family. Peter was asking for help. Ben told him to check in with him at his next progress report session a few days later. In the interim, Peter had taken part in a home invasion.

Peter had been a model program participant just months earlier, and now he was being charged with a felony that would almost certainly result in his reimprisonment. Ben was devastated. His tough-guy exterior melted, and he appeared to be on the verge of tears.

I told Ben it wasn't his fault, that Peter had serious problems that drove him to commit the crime. I also had some idea of how this had happened. Peter had, early on, shined as one of our best participants. While still a convict in state prison he had volunteered to be a firefighter with the California Department of Forestry and Fire Protection.[115] He was attending classes at the local college, doing community work, and testing negative for drugs. But things began to change after several months. The team reported that he had become surly and uncommunicative and wasn't attending classes.

I asked Peter to join me in my chambers with his program counselor. He was a bit reluctant to speak up in court, and I thought he might be more communicative in chambers. We sat across from one another at a table. My chambers at the time were about the size of a medium-sized walk-in closet— not imposing and no doubt the smallest chambers I ever sat in. But it also conveyed an intimacy and a non-threatening atmosphere that many participants and staff appreciated. My desk was pushed up against the back wall, and I had moved a work table directly in front of it, with room for six staff members. A window to the left of the table looked out on Civic Center Plaza.

---

115 Several months into his participation in the SFPRC, I received a letter from his Department of Forestry and Fire Protection supervisor, Michael Ekindjian, praising Peter as "an exemplary employee… a dependable individual… who led the way for the rest of the fire crew during fire line construction."

I had searched for and found a perfect window seat for four to fit under that window.

I asked if something was bothering him and told him of the changes the team had noted. He wasn't angry, didn't deny the comments, and admitted that he'd had problems but couldn't discuss them.

I told him how important he had been as a role model for others in the program, that I believed in him, and that I cared about his recovery. I suggested that he work with the team and his counselor in particular on a plan to help him address his problems. I told him to keep in touch with the court through his program counselor. He agreed to do so, and the meeting ended.

When I discussed that meeting with the court team I learned that Peter was using drugs. There was reason to believe that a family member was providing him with said drugs. Then, about a week later, I learned that Peter had committed the home invasion.

I took the bench that morning with one thing on my mind. Peter was in custody awaiting trial, his parole revoked. He would be the first SFPRC participant to be sent back to prison. I didn't know what I would say but felt I should inform the participants in the project of Peter's fall from grace.

I told the assemblage I had terminated Peter's participation in the program, that he was someone they needed to mourn as a fallen comrade, and that if they took care of one another, such a fate might not befall anyone else. In closing I asked for a moment of silence to mark our loss.

And then we returned to our progress reports.

THE FUTURE

Judge Robert Russell had a long and storied career as a pioneering drug court judge, including two terms as chairman of the board at NADCP. But on a certain day in 2005 he sat on the bench in the Buffalo Mental Health Court looking down on Greg, wondering what he could do to get through to him.

Greg was African-American, as was the judge. Greg stood slumped over, belying his 6'3" height, with his head down, refusing to look the judge in the eye. Judge Russell complimented him on his program meetings attendance and tried prodding him into responding by recounting what his mental health court team had told him during their morning meeting.

"The team doesn't believe you're making progress in the program," Judge Russell said.

Greg grunted an unintelligible response.

Judge Russell was handling a caseload of 40 or more participants that morning. He was pressed for time and had every reason to pass on Greg's problems and continue with his work, but he tried again. He knew that Greg was an Iraq War veteran who'd been honorably discharged from the Army. He wondered if Program Manager Hank Pirowski and another county employee, Jack O'Connor, both Vietnam veterans, might be able to get through to him. He asked them to talk to Greg, passed the case for fifteen minutes, and moved on with his calendar.

Fifteen minutes later Greg stood tall before the judge at "parade rest," with his legs apart and his hands behind his back. When the judge asked him again about his poor performance, Greg's response was startling. In a clear, crisp voice he stated, "Judge, I'm going to try harder."

Judge Russell was surprised at his response and wondered what the two vets had done to change his demeanor. He called them into his chambers after the calendar and asked, "What the heck did you say to him?"

Hank Pirowski, a bear of a man who had briefly been on an NFL team, said that they talked about Vietnam and the Army. He also told Greg that not only did he care about him, but the judge and the court team did as well.

Veterans court is an outstanding example of how a community can take care of its own. When Judge Russell later met with veterans organizations to ask for their assistance in working with vets—half expecting to be turned away—he was welcomed with open arms and heartfelt promises to volunteer from individuals and organizations across the age, economic, and political spectrum.

It would take two years for the Buffalo Veterans Treatment Court to formally start up, but on that day in 2005 the idea for the veterans court was born out of one judge's concern and compassion for those who served and his court coordinator's empathy for a fellow vet. The Buffalo Mental Health Court's innovative offspring would be embraced across the nation as hundreds of veterans courts sprang up, following the Buffalo blueprint: vets volunteering to mentor vets in trouble.

The year 2019 marks the 25th anniversary of NADCP and the drug court movement. NADCP has acted as an anchor for the field, providing the education, training, and support to sustain and build a national movement.

But it has done much more.

From the beginning NADCP has been willing to push for real reform in the criminal justice system, by which I mean reform that's both doable and worth doing. Often bucking traditional court systems and their bureaucracies, it has become a beacon for those looking for a path to real criminal justice reform. NADCP has a history of calling out its own when courts cater to the dominant culture and ignore the needs of people of color, serve the middle and upper classes rather than the poor and disenfranchised, or treat those who don't need treatment, rather than those with severe disabilities.

It is what has kept me close to NADCP for so many years. Though it has strayed from time to time, it remains the most successful membership organization dedicated to healing the criminal justice system.

The current NADCP leadership, led by CEO Carson Fox, is an example of that dedication to a mission that has been so much a part of NADCP's history. He embarked on his long journey to CEO when he attended the seminal 1996 Drug Court Conference in Washington, D.C. As he describes it he was drawn by the "energy and passion of faculty and participants." As an assistant North Carolina state prosecutor in 1998 he helped start up the Mecklenburg County Drug Court. Soon after he was assisting in the training of drug court prosecutors at nationwide NADCP seminars. In 2001 he decided he wanted to be one of "the people building criminal justice reform in the U.S." and moved to D.C. to work full time at NADCP.

Today, with drug abuse recognized primarily as a public health crisis, some states are reducing drug offenses from felonies to misdemeanors, while others are dismissing most drug possession offenses (sometimes by way of a plea bargain), considering them at best minor crimes. Some predict the demise of drug courts as the result of the minimizing of criminal consequences for drug abuse.

Rather than passively accepting that doomsday prophecy, Carson sees changing circumstances as an opportunity for drug courts to do the work they are best suited for: providing alternative sentencing and rehabilitation for drug-dependent offenders charged with serious drug or non-drug related offenses. In other words, with the substantial majority of those in custody seriously drug dependent, drug courts are an important alternative to conventional sentencing for many offenders charged with serious and/or violent offenses.[116]

Like other drug court leaders, he has a history as a practitioner in the field, but more than that he has a missionary's zeal for the job. Carson, in casual conversation, describes the work as a "calling." That commitment to NADCP's mission appears to be infectious, something that is transmitted from one leader to the next and through them to the membership. Talking to Carson about his work schedule reminds me of my own during the first years of NADCP: overwhelming and only made bearable by the love of one's work and a wholehearted belief in reform that could heal lives.

My fifteen years sitting as an assigned judge in California courts—on drug and problem-solving courts in particular—gave me the opportunity to contemplate how courts could best deal with those convicted of both violent and non-violent crimes. I wrote about reentry courts as a systemic means for dealing with the massive numbers leaving our jails and prisons. Of course, the obvious also occurred to me: the best way to deal with prison overcrowding was to not put offenders in prison in the first place.

As my thinking evolved I found myself moving towards a new vision for the reentry court, one in which virtually all criminal courts are potentially reentry courts, where those who are sentenced to custody eventually return to their community and go through a period of transition. The longer the period of separation from the community, the greater the need for assistance

---

116 Carson cites a Columbia University study, discussed at www.centeronaddiction.org/newsroom/press-releases/2010-behind-bars-II, which shows that fully 65% of individuals in our jails and prisons, whether charged with a drug offense or not, are seriously drug dependent. Further, 78% of all violent crimes involve alcohol and other drugs.

in transitioning into society. Having one court seamlessly follow the offender from plea through sentencing to incarceration and then probation/parole— and finally graduation—makes the most sense to me. I believe it is an important vision of the future that judicial reformers should aspire to.[117]

The veterans treatment court pioneered by Judge Robert Russell and program manager Hank Pirowski in Buffalo was one of the first and best examples of a criminal court applying the "reentry court for all" concept. That the concept is a reality is something of a miracle. Of course, it was done with much humanity, because the court was dealing with a population whom society has great empathy and compassion for: the warrior who has defended his or her community and country. Veterans courts are a shining example of what can be achieved when a community supports a judge and team, dedicated to assisting all those before it in need of rehabilitation and/or treatment.

I have been schooled in the concept of restorative justice by my friend and colleague Judge Susan Finlay (ret.). Over the past ten years she has volunteered her time providing much needed assistance to a remote Massai tribe on the slopes of Mount Kilimanjaro. During that time she has become friends with village elders. She recounts how one day she asked if they used courts and lawyers to resolve conflicts. One elder responded that they did not have words for "court" or "lawyer" in their language. Disputes within the tribe were resolved by a tribunal of elders, both men and women, who had the respect and credibility to make decisions on behalf of their community. As I understand it that's very much the definition of restorative justice: the restoration of persons to their pre-conflict status through community mediation, restitution, and healing.

Judges, in a very real way, are village elders writ large, chosen for their wisdom, integrity, and credibility within the community. Perhaps the most profound effect the drug court movement has had upon the courts and criminal justice system is its impact on how judges themselves see their role. They are now more likely to see themselves and be seen as facilitators, intervenors, and community leaders engaged in resolving local problems.

Another friend and colleague, Judge Len Edwards (ret.)—an important judicial innovator in the juvenile court field—recently reminded me of how great an impact drug courts have had on us as judges. He posited that the

---

117 With the election of President Barack Obama I wrote a four-part policy paper focused on the need to divert offenders from incarceration into reentry courts, promising the possibility of reducing prison populations, costs, and recidivism ("Four Policy Papers: A Proposal for a National Reentry Court Initiative, Submitted to the Obama Campaign Transition Committee," NDCI, 2009).

advent of drug courts was one of the most important changes in the courts in a century. He likened it to the paradigm shift that took place when the juvenile court system emerged at the beginning of the 20th century: society began to treat children humanely, focusing on their rehabilitation and restoration to the community, rather than their punishment.

Len commented on how judges themselves have evolved since we were deputy public defenders in Santa Clara County, how drug courts have stripped away the layers of formality and separation that judges have traditionally displayed in court, creating a more open environment. In essence this has freed judges to share their common humanity with offenders and make a connection within the court-based community.

It was an experience I knew well: stepping down from the bench in the Oakland Drug Court or the San Francisco Parole Reentry Court, physically exhausted from engaging program participants over a long morning's court session and yet elated by the experience.

EPILOGUE

MERCY, MERCY, MERCY

To believe in the heroic makes heroes.
— Benjamin Disraeli

During my 1988 election campaign for the Oakland Municipal Court bench, I attended mass at the Greater St. John Missionary Baptist Church in West Oakland, a massive church by Oakland standards, with immense wooden doors, high walls, and colorful religious art. For a Jewish guy from Brooklyn it was not the most obvious of destinations, but I'd always been attracted to the gospel sung in African-American Baptist churches. I had been to this church on several occasions, as my court clerk Cindy was a devoted follower of the pastor. I especially enjoyed Christmas Mass and the pastor's gospel choir.

I had visited several churches that morning to be introduced by Assemblyman Elihu Harris's staffer, Patricia, as Elihu's choice for municipal court judge. Usually, the pastor would take a few minutes to say kind words about my candidacy, and I would make a brief pitch to the congregation and be gone in ten minutes.

However, I'd arrived at the Greater St. John Missionary Baptist Church alone that evening. The reverend, Dr. C. J. Anderson, stood at the altar, an icon to his community, pastor of his flock for 40 years, a man respected and revered by the entire Oakland community. The pastor was a large man with a powerful speaking voice that he unleashed with a passionate and rhythmic cadence. He called me to the altar and had me sit down in front, facing the congregation, then began.

He spoke of how the people of Oakland deserved a judge who would lead. He described how I as a judge was going to do great things for the people of

Oakland. He spoke for such a long time it seemed that I was the subject of his sermon that evening. I was embarrassed; I felt that I was somehow deceiving the pastor and his congregation. My campaign literature promised reforms to "stop the revolving prison door," but I had few ideas as to how to achieve them.

Thirty years have elapsed since the good pastor's sermon, and I still remember the power of his vision and the passion of his prose. I wonder from time to time if his sermon inspired a spark within me.

I spent much of my youth glued to one of the first TV sets found in Coney Island. My sense of morality derived from many sources but perhaps none more important than the TV Western. One movie in particular, "High Noon," a 1952 four-time-Academy-Award-winning motion picture, made an impact. If I were to give a personal drug court award to someone who inspired me in my career, it would be that movie's hero, played by actor Gary Cooper, the indomitable lawman facing overwhelming, almost insurmountable odds. The moral: sometimes you have the opportunity to rise above yourself, to reach heights that you might otherwise never achieve.

Some will argue that nothing happens unless—and until—the people have spoken. To that my reply is that while that may be true, without leaders willing to take risks and accept challenges and sacrifices, the people may never have that opportunity to speak. This, then, is not the work of a hero but of the child within the man, fulfilling a dream he thought he had left behind.

One thing needs to be said up front: there would be nothing to be accomplished, and no one to lead, without the initiative, involvement, engagement, heart, and energy of thousands upon thousands of drug court practitioners, bureaucrats, criminal justice practitioners, political leaders, and others who have embraced NADCP. I was fortunate to be in a place where I could tap into that energy and help focus it towards criminal justice reform.

I remained a board member and NADCP educator until 2014. I was actively organizing reentry court workshops and teaching reentry court skills at the national conference and other trainings. I believed in the importance of NADCP's leadership in promoting prison and parole reentry courts, as well as other problem-solving courts, across the nation.[118]

I decided that twenty years as founder, president, board member, and educator at NADCP was enough. I formally retired from active membership in

118 Reentry Court Solutions (www.reentrycourtsolutions.com) contains articles, essays, evaluations, monographs, and analyses relating to problem-solving courts and, more specifically, to court-based rehabilitation for those returning from prison.

NADCP at its twentieth anniversary and my twentieth consecutive NADCP conference, in Anaheim, California, in 2014.

Karen-Freeman Wilson, my successor at NADCP, was elected mayor of Gary, Indiana, in 2011, and continues to successfully serve in that capacity.

West Huddleston left his position as CEO of NADCP in 2015 for a job in the private sector. Looking back I see West's hard work, dedication, and commitment as critical to the success and extraordinary growth of NADCP. I salute him for all he did to build upon the initial success of NADCP.

Peter, our SFPRC Christmas poet, is presently serving a prison term at the Federal Detention Facility in Sheridan, Oregon, with a release date in 2022.

Bleu, the editor of the SFPRC newsletter, is presently serving a prison term at the United States Penitentiary in Lompoc, California, with a release date in 2021.

In February of 2017 I turned 70. With Social Security about to kick in, I planned to back away from my assigned judge's role and move towards a full-time musician's calling. I had been playing in a jazz band two or three times a month for over a year, and I was finally playing lead on jazz tunes.

While I have been a capable attorney and trial judge, what came more easily to me was being a drug court judge, the founder and leader of NADCP and the drug and problem-solving court movements, and finally a reentry court judge. Much of the time I felt like a fish swimming downstream. Without prior experience I found myself lobbying Congress, writing legislation, speaking at the White House and before dignitaries at home and abroad, leading focus groups and trainings, writing an almost constant stream of manuals, monographs, articles, and newsletters, planning and presiding over NADCP conferences, and developing educational curriculum and training methodologies.

I understood on a visceral level what needed to be done and when. From relying on a bottom-up or grassroots approach to building a practitioner-based national organization and to the creation of a web of interlacing, regionally based mentor court sites; from the creation of an annual NADCP conference to the development of the respected, science-based National Drug Court Institute; from the formation of the nationwide Congress of State Drug Court Associations to successfully advocating for the institutionalization of the drug court model before the Conference of Chief Justices—all of it came together as the foundation of a national criminal justice reform movement.

In April 2017, upon returning from a friend's wedding and a brief vacation in Hawaii, I found a letter from the Office of the Chief Justice (both Chief Justice Ron George and AOC Director Bill Vickery having retired). It informed me that the California courts no longer had need of my services as an assigned judge and wished me well in my retirement.

It was a surprising letter, as I had received no criticism from the chief justice's office during my fifteen-year tenure as an assigned judge. It also informed me of the reason for my retirement: my reviews from presiding judges were not favorable. (In retrospect I wondered how I had survived fifteen years of presiding judge reviews.) The most recent complaint from a presiding judge alleged that I had problems with "collegiality." In other words, I didn't get along with my peers. So my career began and ended on the same note, with yet another "Unsatisfactory" in the "Works and Plays Well with Others" category.

And this I hope may be my legacy: when my time came I understood what needed to be done and did it, ultimately influencing the criminal justice system just enough so all could see the humanity of the offender, worthy of returning to society, not as a pariah but as a healed member of their community.

At the 14th Annual NADCP Training Conference in St. Louis, NADCP bestowed upon me the singular honor of "President Emeritus of NADCP for Life." The plaque reads:

> *For Creating the Spark That Revolutionized the Justice System.*

As the old adage goes, he who laughs last, laughs best.[119]

---

119 In the interest of full disclosure, I remain NADCP president emeritus for life and a friend of CEO Carson Fox, NADCP's Public Relations Coordinator Chris Deutsch, and many of its directors, staff, and members. However, this is not an NADCP publication, nor has it been authorized by NADCP. It is solely the work of its author, and he alone is responsible for its contents.

ACKNOWLEDGMENTS

This book comes together for the twenty-fifth anniversary of the National Association of Drug Court Professionals (NADCP). To put on paper what I consider to be my life's work has taken over five years. The truth be known, I would never have been able to complete it without the assis¬tance, support, and encouragement of many friends and colleagues.

I start by thanking my friends who have volunteered to be readers and fact-checkers; I owe them a debt of gratitude for reading segments and in many cases the entire book manuscript: West Huddleston, Dr. Robert Jones, Janet McCuller, Eddie Pasternak, Marc Pearce, Susan Rosenblum Ravens, Richard Ravens, among others.

I would also like to thank the members of the California judicial com¬-munity who have read my work and provided critical feedback; Judges Len Edward (ret.) and Susan Finlay (ret.), in particular, have been helped me under¬stand the historical context of this work. I'd also like to thank Bill Vickrey, former Director of the California Administrative Office of the Courts, who has contributed to this book and done so much to further judi-cial reform in California.

Malaga Smith of Malaga Smith Corp., had been an incredible resource and partner to me during the preparation of this book. She started out pro¬viding technical assistance and being a savvy web expert. Over the years she has morphed into a reader, advisor, and sometime editor for my website; reen¬trycourtsolutions.com. Believing in my vision of a community-based criminal justice system, she has read countless versions of this book.

Frank Tapia has been a major actor in this story. He has also served as a reader, commentator, and photo editor during the writing process. While he was a probation officer in the Oakland drug court when I first met him, he has for a number of years been one of the top commercial photog¬raphers in the Bay Area. Two of his fine photographs are found in this book. Frank and his wife Marna and son Nick have become close friends over the years.

I could not have published my book without the assistance of a wonderful editor, Christopher Ryan. I have spent many an early morning in a Skype conversation with him from somewhere in Finland. He has provided me with meticulous editing, but more importantly, he has been an advisor and confidant.

And a more recent acquaintance, David Kudler of Stillpoint Publications, who has done fine job in assisting me in the book's publication.

I wish to thank my dear friend Vivian Vosu who has read my manuscript untold times and who has survived this descent into darkness, with the mantra, " I am consciously non-codependent".

In particular, I wish to thank CEO Carson Fox and NADCP's Public Relations Coordinator, Chris Deutsch, both of whom have read my book, and provided archival information, commentary, and assistance in getting this book out to the drug court field and the greater community.

About the Author

JEFFREY TAUBER has been a defense attorney and a criminal court judge. He is also a world traveler, with a sociologist's eye; and a saxman who frequents the blues and jazz clubs of Oakland California. Judge Tauber was the founding president of the National Association of Drug Court Professionals (NADCP) and is currently its president emeritus. He has been a pioneer in the development of court-based rehabilitation systems, spearheading the devel-op¬ment and growth of drug courts and other problem-solving courts across the United States.

Judge Jeffrey Tauber (ret) is currently the Director/Editor of Reentry Court Solutions (www.reentrycourtsolutions.com), an educational initiative that provides nationwide support, technical assistance, training, and advisory services to the field.

Jeffrey Tauber is available for select reading and lectures. To inquire about his appearance, please make contact through jtauber@reentrycourtsolutions.com, or (510)847-2374.